# The Long Journey Home

## A True Story of Years Lost and Love Found

BETH & JIM AUBREY

ISBN: 978-1-7374638-0-1

# Disclaimer

This work depicts actual events in the lives of the co-authors as truthfully as recollection permits. Characters and events are actual, but names and identifying details have been changed to respect privacy of individuals and anonymity of organizations. Any similarities in names or organizations are unintentional. Due to the span of years this work covers, much of the dialogue has been recreated to bring the reader into the actual scenes to relive and experience those same moments as the authors felt them.

Those who may recognize these events, either people or organizations, may have differing opinions of the details and we challenge them to write their own memoirs. We are keeping our story true in the hope that what we have laboriously written serves to inspire and give hope. Lack of integrity and the failure to value others comes with high tangible and intangible costs. Some never recognize that until it is too late. Our journeys weren't easy, but hang on for the ride. Our destinations were worth it.

*The Long Flight Home* is based on the true story of a fifteen-year-old girl from a small coal mining town in southeastern Kentucky who wrote a letter in 1967 to a pirate radio station near the Isle of Man, requesting a pen pal. A reply came from a sixteen-year-old boy living at a large fishing port in the northwest of England.

They became great friends, corresponding through letters for almost two years. After an unexpected turn of events, the girl was forced to abandon their friendship. They lost touch, never knowing what happened to each other. Forty-two years later and now grown, he came across the bookmark she sent him in a Christmas card when they were teenagers, prompting him to conduct an Internet search. This is the amazing story of their journeys.

# Dedication

To my children "Sara" & "Sawyer" who have both given my life purpose and reasons to laugh. Ecclesiastes 4:12 says "Though one may be overpowered, two can defend themselves. A cord of three strands is not quickly broken." Even in the womb, a child is bonded to the mother with a cord of three strands, the umbilical cord, consisting of two arteries and a vein. With our strong bond as a family, we stood firm and defied the odds of adversity.

To my friend Angie, who recognized that Jim was in love with me when I was too blind to see it for myself.

To Jim, whose journey merged with mine. Without you, this book would never have been written.

To our Heavenly Father who continues to work all things together for our good.

B.B. Aubrey


To our family, friends and beta readers: without your constant encouragement, our story would not have been written. Special thanks to my wife B.B. who helped make this journey possible.

J.D. Aubrey

# About This Book

For the adventurous young dreamer longing to see the world beyond their immediate circumstances

For the person disappointed in love, feeling rejected, betrayed and alone

For the struggling single parent

For the disadvantaged facing the hurdles of adversity

For those searching for humor beyond the pain

For those puzzled by coincidences that weren't really coincidences

For those struggling to believe there is a purpose and plan for their life

For those determined to get up just one more time than they fall down

Our story is about hope

BB & JD Aubrey

# Introduction

## B.B.

My dad, born in 1912 in Pike County, Kentucky, was next to the youngest of ten children. After losing his mother at age eleven, he was raised by his older sisters in their family home. For generations, their family's livelihood came from farming. As coal mining gained prominence in the region in the early 1900s, my father's older brothers abandoned farming and ventured out to obtain jobs working in the coal mines. Men were judged then by their work ethic, not their educational accomplishments. Times were hard, and when he was nearly sixteen, my father lied about his age so he could get a job working in an underground coal mine.

When my mother was only three, her mother and father divorced. Regardless of the reason for the split, a divorced woman in that era was considered a harlot. The reason for that divorce was never discussed. While doing genealogical research, I found the record of their divorce at the county courthouse. In 1921, there was no such thing as a no-fault divorce, and the filer was forced to tell all. Some stories remain untold for a reason.

My grandmother found work as a cook in a logging camp. Since this was no place to raise a three-year-old, my grandfather and his new bride raised my mother. Together, they had ten additional children. When farming alone couldn't sustain their family, my grandfather went to work in a coal mine and eventually became a section boss. To further supplement their income, he was known to make and sell a little moonshine on the side.

In 1928, my dad began working for Diversified Coal. He married my mother in 1936 when he was twenty-four and she was eighteen. My mother had completed her sophomore year of high school and was the more educated of the pair. She was the one who usually managed the household business. Together, they rented a double coal camp house on the outskirts of Jenkins. The rent was thirteen dollars per month, which was automatically deducted from his payroll account.

Diversified Coal Company, or "Diversified" as it was best known, actually built the entire town of Jenkins, Kentucky, starting in 1912. Typically, houses were two-story, wood framed and painted white. Each had nearly identical architecture, except for the double houses and those built for the company elite. Most had separate outhouses and no indoor plumbing for bathing.

The wages at the mines were pathetically low. A miner could manually load coal cars all day using a shovel and not be paid a dime if his coal car contained too much rock. There were no sophisticated coal preparation plants to clean the coal and remove the rock. The sorting of rock from coal was done by the miner himself.

Prior to the organization of coal mining unions such as the United Coal Workers Union (UCWU), miners had to pay for their own powder to blast the coal by conventional mining methods. Dad was paid so little, he had nothing to lose and everything to gain when he signed a union card and agreed to join a picket line at the very first UCWU contract strike. He was an organizing member of the United Coal Worker Union in Kentucky in the 1930s and was a faithful dues-paying member for over sixty years, until his death at age eighty-five.

Diversified Coal Company was purchased by Nazareth Steel Corporation and eventually became Nazareth-Elkhorn Corporation around 1956. In total, Dad worked over forty-two years underground, before retiring disabled at age fifty-nine due to uncontrolled seizures. Throughout the course of his working years, he had been knocked unconscious many times, fractured a finger, and had once been trapped in a major collapse of the mine roof.

I remember well the evening he didn't come home from work on time. Later, my dad recounted these details. He and his buddy Reuben were in a section of the mine where Dad was bolting the roof. They heard a loud thump from the mine roof high over their heads, indicative of a huge break of the mine strata beyond the length of the roof bolts. Both started to run to safety, but Reuben was already far in front of Dad. When Dad realized he wouldn't be able to make it through the dangerous intersection in time, instinctively, he turned around and ran back toward the active working face. This was where the mine roof had the largest undisturbed pillar of support. When the roof collapsed, it fell almost right up to the face of the coal where Dad was, trapping him for several hours.

Finally, over the top of the fallen rock and coal, Dad saw the cap lights of fellow coal miners coming to rescue him. The electrical cable leading from his roof bolting machine was covered by the fall. This was an indicator to his rescuers that the roof bolter himself might be under the fall. The miners called out to Dad, and he answered. The rescue team shouted out, asking Dad if Reuben was with him. It was then that Dad realized his buddy didn't make it out to safety. Dad told them where Reuben was running when he decided to turn back and run toward the mine face. Based on the information he gave them, they were able to locate Dad's buddy, sadly crushed beneath the roof fall.

For months after that, Dad never let us venture far from his sight. He had trouble sleeping, haunted by those memories of Reuben and no doubt experiencing survivor's guilt. Dad never fully recovered from the trauma of that experience. Even in his mid-eighties, when this story would come up in conversation, Dad's eyes filled with tears as he relived the painful memories of that tragedy.

This close call with death was a major reason Dad never wanted his own son to work in a coal mine. He stressed the importance of getting an education instead. Traditional mountain culture was to educate the son and marry off the daughter.

I grew up in a neighborhood of mostly rambunctious boys who were several years older. We spent summer days exploring the hills, creeks, and streams around my small hometown. Whether it was collecting odd wheels from wrecked tricycles or scavenging for lumber to build a crude racer, the boys were always into something interesting, and I was always trying to tag along. By definition, I suppose that made me a tomboy. I remember riding one of those crude gravity racers downhill, pulling back on a short piece of 2" x 4" used as a makeshift brake while guiding the front wheels with a piece of rope. There were no tragedies, but plenty of scolding by adults as they attempted to drive on a one-lane road in our uphill neighborhood.

Winter fun usually involved lots of snowball fights, snowman building, and sledding downhill on a 1200" x 24" inflated inner tube typically used for coal truck tires. The more cautious among us built a snow berm as a safety stop to keep us from slamming into a hillside at the bottom of the hill. The more daring sometimes ended up wearing casts their witnesses got to autograph.

Televisions, all black and white, were not turned on until evening, once it was dark outside, and the evening meal had finished. Signal reception utilized two single-strand, uninsulated wires that were separated by spacers strung uphill above our home, then connected to an antenna from the top of a tree or the highest point with no foliage interference. The absence of a signal resulted in a crackling sound and a distorted "snowy" screen. Signal loss could be attributed to rainy weather, wind knocking down the antenna, or another person commandeering our television wire or antenna for their own reception.

There were only a few girls in my neighborhood who were close to my age. I was not at all interested in the boring role-play of changing clothes on a doll or pretending to feed it. I'd much rather be damming up a natural spring to go wading on a hot summer day or wild berry picking with my brother. I remember one humid summer day when all the boys pulled off their shirts while they were out playing. I was an innocent age ten at the time, thought it was a great idea, and decided to follow their example. Since I was chubby, I wasn't exactly flat chested as were my male counterparts. When I ran, this only accentuated my obvious differences. After my mother heard the news, that was my last public moment of topless freedom. Amazingly, it was never mentioned again, and my playmates never teased me about it.

When I reached my early teens, I spent summer afternoons at our local swimming pool. I marvelled at the girls lying beside the pool in their swimsuits, lathered up with suntanning oil and iodine, squealing when they got splashed with water, and never dipping their toes in the pool the entire afternoon. I didn't see the point until I was much older. The endless flirtation between coy females and their would-be male suitors showing off with daring stunts in the pool filled the afternoon. Predictably, those stunts evoked the shrill whistles and cautious scolding of the lifeguard. I learned vicariously as a silent observer, concluding that this courtship routine was a waste of valuable pool time. Even now, I remember and smile inwardly.

But this teenaged girl felt as though she was living in a showbox and had a curiosity for the world beyond. She wanted more, so she reached out beyond the mountains of her eastern Kentucky home with a single letter.

# Chapter One

## B.B.

*"Reading was her escape from the world, and within the pages she could become anyone she wanted to be. Sometimes she was a beautiful princess, and sometimes she was a brave heroine."*

—Carla Reighard, *The Web of Loki*

Encircled by the hilly ridges of the Appalachians and tucked away in a small Kentucky coal camp, I was a dream-struck thirteen-year-old girl. Lying across my bed, I gazed out my window, focusing on three lone pine trees on a distant hillside. I daydreamed about the world beyond those mountains and spent countless hours exploring the world vicariously through books from our local library. Each time I visited the library, I checked out the maximum number of books the librarian would allow and I could easily carry. Isolated and protected by those mountains, I gave flight to many dreams, if only through the pages of a book. I visited distant lands, falling asleep at night with a book in my hands.

Each time I heard a coal train whistle blowing in the distance, I fantasized about where those trains came from, and what their final destination would be. *Whoo-whoo* came the haunting sounds of a whistle, while the train was well hidden by the mountaintops. Who was on that train? Was it someone I knew? Where did they live? What was their life like?

"All men dream, but not equally. For the Dreamers of the Night awaken to find that it was merely their vanity. But the Dreamers of the Day are the dangerous ones for they dream with their eyes open and they make things happen." —Lawrence of Arabia, *Seven Pillars of Wisdom.*

In spring 1967, I overheard some of my classmates talking about having pen pals from England. They had discovered the address of a radio station, Radio Avaline, in a teen magazine. Radio Avaline was a pirate radio station off the coast of the Isle of Man in international waters, out of the jurisdiction of the British government and the British Broadcasting Corporation (BBC). Of course, I didn't know any of this. As far as I knew, it was no different from any other radio station. I obtained the station address and wrote them a letter, telling them I wanted a pen pal.

The day Radio Avaline finally read my name out over the airwaves, a sixteen-year-old boy named Jim was listening from Thornton, England. I was fifteen at the time. His first letter came about two weeks after.

The day I came home from school and found an envelope addressed to me, postmarked from England, I was giddy with excitement. I read and reread that letter, then sat down to pen my reply. Through our exchange of letters, Jim and I developed a real friendship. We talked about and compared our lives in our respective countries. We talked about our families and school. Since the school systems in England and America are set up differently, classes were difficult to compare.

Often, we talked about music and which groups were popular at the time, including the Kinks, the Beatles, and Otis Redding. I had never heard of some of the groups that were popular in England. I wrote to Jim as my confidant, my letters much like entries in a diary. We exchanged information regarding how our cultures differed. We discussed our parents, siblings, friends, and extracurricular activities such as band and rugby. I had never heard of rugby and knew nothing about how the game was played. Jim had a passion for the sport and was always eager to explain. From time to time, we even shared corny jokes. I saved all of Jim's letters, rereading them over and over.

Through Jim, I developed an interest in stamp collecting, and we often exchanged stamps. I talked about playing clarinet in my high school band, and Jim talked about being in the Marine Cadets. We talked about customs and apparel such as bell-bottomed pants and hairstyles. Eventually, some good-natured ribbing took place about that little "difference of opinions" our countries had in the late 1770s.

"Does your voice sound like the Beatles?" I once asked him.

Jim replied, "No. The Beatles are from Liverpool, and their accents are unique to that city. Would you like to exchange a tape recording of our voices?"

I quickly declined. "My voice sounds too country, and I have a twang." I didn't think Jim would find my voice to be charming, even though I was positively certain I would love to hear his voice. All I had was a huge, old-fashioned reel-to-reel tape recorder with tubes rather than circuits. I had asked for a tape recorder, and my grandmother had obliged me with a used one bought from an old radio station. I should have specified compact and portable. Postage for a letter was expensive enough, and I didn't know whether Jim had a device that would play a reel recording that large anyway. This was my excuse for not sending him a recording of my voice.

Jim and I wrote back and forth for almost two years. As soon as I got a letter from him, I immediately stopped whatever I was doing to respond. My letters were written on thin, lightweight, onionskin paper to save postage costs. I scented my envelopes with my favorite perfume, the scent of blooming lilacs in early spring. I wondered whether the scent would remain by the time he received them, despite all those miles and delivery routes. At best, we were only able to exchange an average of two letters each per month. We were completely authentic in all our communication. There was no point in pretending: we were too far apart to feel the need. We had little hope of ever seeing each other face-to-face. We shared our dreams. In the process, we developed a strong bond of friendship. We exchanged photos as well. One Christmas, we sent each other small token gifts that would fit in an envelope and not be too expensive to mail. That was the Christmas I sent Jim a bookmark with the Irish blessing:

"Wind At Your Back"
May the road rise up to meet you
And the wind be always at your back.
May the sun shine warm upon your face
And rains fall soft upon your field.
And until we meet again
May the Lord hold you in the hollow of his hand.

Jim was always in my thoughts, even though we were thousands of miles apart. His letters always put a smile on my face. He was the secret best friend that few knew about. That same Christmas, our mothers even got in on the fun and exchanged letters.

## ROLE MODEL

There was no finer model of grit and determination than my maternal grandmother. When her husband refused to share his retirement pension with her, my grandmother realized she did not have sufficient income to support herself. At the age of fifty-four, she left our family behind and moved to Covington to work as a nursing assistant in a nursing home. I was only three years old when she boarded a passenger bus to make that journey. She earned just twenty-two dollars a week, and her boarding costs were included as an employee of a nursing home in northern Kentucky.

Of that meager wage, she saved twenty dollars and lived on the other two dollars. She bought all her clothing and other necessities from local thrift shops. When she had finally saved up enough for a down payment, she bought a historic three-story brick townhome, built in the late 1800s, and took in boarders. Boarders provided the income she needed to meet her modest expenses and pay for her home.

She lived on the only remaining brick-paved street in the city of Covington, Kentucky. Every room had an ornate mantelpiece and fireplace. The winding staircase from the first to the third floor was solid mahogany. Each room had chandelier lighting and transoms over the doors. It was a lovely old house, filled with character. In a tiny backyard garden, she grew the most beautiful flowers and even maintained a small vegetable garden. She managed to grow corn so tall it was visible from the street and towered high above her head. It was so impressive that it caught the attention of a reporter for a Cincinnati newspaper who came to photograph her standing in front of her corn.

That abandoned woman who had been unable to provide for her three-year-old in the 1920s had certainly developed survival skills. She wasted nothing and was as frugal as they come. It would take a lot for me to fill those size seven shoes of hers.

## ASK GRANDMA

As a teen, I had nothing but a transistor radio to listen to music as I stretched across my bed and gazed out the window. Most of the music played in my region was country and bluegrass, both totally unappealing to me. The best station for the rock music of the '60s was located over four hundred miles away in Fort Wayne, Indiana, with a signal that faded in and out throughout the day.

A stereo system topped my Christmas wish list that year, but Christmas came and went, and my parents couldn't afford to buy one for me. I was accustomed to hearing the word "no." I had located a cheap, basic record player in a local hardware store in Jenkins with a thirty-four-dollar price tag. I pleaded my case, but the answer was still "no." When you can't get what you want from your parents, what do you do? You ask Grandma.

Several months later, my grandmother (who we lovingly called "Granny") had one of her boarders drive her to our home in Jenkins for a visit. She surprised me with a huge tabletop-sized portable stereo with dual speakers that she had picked up from a local pawn shop in Covington. I was thrilled. It was far better than anything I ever dreamed of asking for.

After that, I hardly came out of my room. Over and over, I listened to LPs of the Beatles, whose albums *Meet the Beatles* and *Hard Day's Night* were released in 1964. I was a huge fan, like most crazed teenagers of that era. As I penned letters to my British pen pal, I was inspired by the music from the stereo my grandmother bought for me.

# Chapter Two
## J.D.

### THE BEGINNING, 1967

It was just another dismal January day. The Christmas holidays were over, and I was back at school. I had just returned home, and Dad had just come back from his parents' house. He was a very slight man, and his build belied the fact that he worked as a coalman. All day, he would carry hundredweight (112lb) sacks on his back from the lorry parked in the roadway and take them to where they would be needed outside the customer's house. His thin face was grim as he bent his back to take the weight. He carried this slight stoop as he walked for most of his life. His pale blue eyes were sunken and dark around the edges from strain and lack of sleep.

Dad broke the news to us that Grandma had just passed away quietly in her sleep a few hours earlier; she had suffered a long illness. Mum took in a quick gasp of air. She, too, was of slight build, and a little taller than Dad. His stoop made her look even taller. Her grey hair was styled in tight, permed curls. She was dressed in a plain skirt and a nylon blouse with the top two buttons left unfastened. She immediately crushed her cigarette in the ashtray as she rushed to turn off the television set, then continued into the front room to draw the curtains. I got up to put the television back on and promptly got a clout over the head from my father. "Have a bit of respect for your grandma!"

The television stayed off, and all the curtains in the house were kept drawn for about a week afterward. This was the custom in those days. I can recall walking past a house whose curtains were drawn and hearing my mum say, "Ooooh! Somebody's died in that family." Now it was our turn. I was sixteen years old at the time.

I reflected on the last time I saw Grandma. She was in the front room of their home, lying peacefully in bed. Various members of the family and neighbours sat round chatting and drinking endless cups of tea. The whole house had an air of foreboding. Conversation was stilted and whispered.

Grandad was sitting in his chair by the fire, as always, chewing something or smoking a hand-rolled cigarette.

The memories began to flood back. I hardly knew Grandma, apart from the forced trips with Mum to visit her and Grandad. We visited fairly regularly, but I rarely wanted to go. For me, it was a case of sitting on the settee and keeping quiet whilst the grown-ups spoke. The house had a small garden at the front and a large garden at the back. These gardens, kept immaculate and weed-free, provided a sense of pride for the occupants. From spring to autumn, the long rear lawn was perfectly mown, showing straight light and dark lines with the edges clipped clear.

When we arrived, there was a cup on the sash window, an indication to neighbours that the kettle was on for those who wanted a cup of tea. We entered the house through the back door. The front door was only for special visitors or strangers. My place was in the middle of the settee between Mum and an aunty. Nothing had changed. I can still see Grandma seated opposite Grandad by the fire. Grandad had a very slim build and thin face and was bald on the top of his head. He would be dressed in a dark suit and white shirt. He always wore a jacket. The suit was not pressed or cleaned as this was for indoors wearing only. By his chair, on his right, was a small table with a small glass, cup, ashtray, and tobacco tin; he rolled his own cigarettes.

Grandma was a large woman, in sharp contrast to Grandad. Her hair was grey and tied in a bun at the back. She always wore a Paisley-patterned pinny over a thin, coloured cardigan and a long, flowered skirt. The fireplace was to her left as she faced the window so she could see who was visiting. On the Formica table to her right stood her workbox on the plastic table cover. She would be sitting there, busy crocheting intricate designs of swans and the like, yet able to keep up with the gossip. She did not follow a pattern; she knew what she was making and how each stitch would be.

Soon, it was the day of the funeral. The house was very quiet, and conversation was in whispers. Grandad was still sitting by the fire, smoking, chewing something, and spitting bits of tobacco into the fire. Without Grandma sitting opposite Grandad, the room seemed empty. We were ushered into the front room; it was full of women in black, already sipping tea. On a trestle in front of the window was the open coffin. I could just glimpse the protruding features of Grandma's face.

"Go on, son, give your grandma one last kiss." The women turned around and looked at me. I recognised a lot of them as Grandma's friends and neighbours and some aunties. I hesitated. I didn't want to be there. I preferred to remember her alive.

"Go on. She won't bite you," one of them said. I couldn't. Instead, I turned and walked away. How could anyone expect a sixteen-year-old boy to do that? I saw Grandad look over at me. He gave a slight nod. I'm sure he understood.

I can't remember much about the funeral, except that it was cold and damp. The church was full of people dressed in the same morbid black. Some were crying. Grandad was in the front row, solemn and quiet. This was one of the few times I ever saw him when he wasn't smoking or chewing.

After the service, we all paraded out after the coffin, Grandad first, then my uncle and aunts. It was all done to order, choreographed. The procession took us to the graveside. A eulogy was given, and a couple of my female cousins started crying, almost uncontrollably. They knew her far better than I, as they once lived with Grandma and Grandad. A box of dry soil was passed around. Each of us took a small handful and gently cast it on the coffin in the grave.

Afterward, we slowly made our way to the car park and then to the catered wake. Immediate family members expressed thanks to those who came to show their support. Finally, we headed back home.

Dad was late returning home, but when he did, he hit us with a bombshell. "We're moving in with Grandad." Stunned, Mum asked what the hell was going on. Dad said Grandad could not look after himself. Since he wouldn't leave his home, someone would have to move in and look after him. A lot of arguing had taken place, but none of the other relatives would move and leave their own homes. They gave their excuses, but in the end, Dad said, "We'll bloody well move in, then!" So that was that.

I had worked years to develop a good paper route and was finally earning decent money, so I would have to give that up. I'd also be leaving all my friends behind; probably I'd be changing schools at a critical time. I was due to take my General Certificate of Education (GCE) exams in a few months. There would be new teachers and a new environment. I didn't know how far ahead or behind I would be compared with others in the new class. I'd be a new boy, open to all sorts of investigation by my classmates.

When I mentioned this to Dad, he was obviously already in a bad mood. He said he had more important things to talk about. I was told to shut up and keep out of what didn't concern me. The main concern was that we owned our house, but Grandad's was a rented house. I knew Mum always liked those large houses and gardens where Grandad lived and would be in favour of the move.

Many thoughts went through my mind. If I was to stay at school, I'd have to catch the bus every day. I'd be a "bus boy." That seemed alright as I could leave class earlier to catch the bus. Maybe things weren't too bad after all. I'd miss all my friends. I didn't know anyone my age around Grandad's. They were all retired or older people. Apart from my cousins, I didn't know anyone else. I attended Marine Cadets twice a week. I'd have to bus it there and back as well. All this busing around was going to be expensive. I didn't know how my family could afford it.

Mum and Dad came in later to tell my brother and me we were moving, and that the decision was final. My older brother, who was getting married in a couple of months or so, could buy the house so he'd have a place to start up. This worked out well for him. He and Natalie, his fiancée, had been saving to buy a house, so this became immediately affordable to them. It was also decided my school wouldn't change. Mum said she'd speak to Mr. Dunstan, my headmaster, about it, so there wouldn't be any problems there.

The day eventually came for the move. Mum had the removal people come to the back gate, as she didn't want any nosy parkers seeing what we were doing or surveying our personal possessions. As our home was cleared of our furnishings, I took one last look at my empty bedroom, then went downstairs to board the waiting removal van cab.

It didn't take us long to move into Grandad's house. A few of the uncles turned up to help. Aunts came to be nosy and took mental inventory of the items we brought with us. This proved to be their routine for the next few years until Grandad died.

I went up to what would be my bedroom. I would share it with my elder brother. It was big, but not with two beds in it. Later, there would be a third bed in the same room for an uncle. At least it was a front bedroom with views across the playground, tennis courts, and a farm. Maybe the move wasn't quite so bad.

Downstairs, I could hear the clink of teacups and talking. The house was full of people. It soon became Mum's duty to provide all the tea and biscuits for visitors. When I went downstairs, I found that the back kitchen, which was basically used as the main living room, was full of women. Grandad sat in his chair, as usual. The men were in the front room, talking and drinking tea. The uncles were all patting Dad on the back, saying,

"You're a good'un, Ted, lad." My dad just said flatly, "Aye." I could see the look on his face that told me how disappointed he was with them all. They had all made their excuses as to why they and their families couldn't move in with Grandad. Their reasons seemed to be petty but were important to them. The only uncle who wasn't there at the time was Uncle Ken. He worked in Liverpool. I was soon to know him much better, as he was later to occupy that third bed in my bedroom. He was to become my favorite uncle.

The weekend finished, and I was catching my first bus to school. I could have ridden my bike, but it was just too far, and the weather was bleak. It wasn't long before the word spread that our family had moved, and all my friends and classmates wanted to know the details. I told them what I knew, which was very little, but omitted the fact that my dad felt he had been tricked into moving in with Grandad due to the lack of space, yet an aunt had lived in that house with a larger family without any problems. Besides, that was family business, not theirs.

The rest of the day went well; classes finished, and there was plenty of homework and studying to be done for the next day. After I got home and ate my evening meal, I took my books out to do homework. The television was on, and Mum and Grandad were talking. I got up and made my way to the front room, where I could concentrate in a quieter environment.

"Where are you going?" snapped Grandad.

"Into the front room to do my homework and studies, Grandad," I replied.

"No, you don't!" he retorted. "That's for special occasions only."

"But I've got homework to do, and it's too noisy in here," I pleaded.

"Then get up to your room and do it," Grandad commanded.

"It's cold up there," I protested.

"Don't argue with me, lad! This is *my* house, and you'll do as I say!"

I looked at Mum for help. None came. She couldn't argue with him because this was his house.

I went upstairs and put on a few more jumpers to keep warm. There was no central heating in those days, not even a coal fire in the bedroom. This was how it was going to be, writing essays on my tiny bedroom cabinet and shivering with cold while trying to study for my examinations.

A few months later, at Easter, my brother was married, and I finally had the bedroom all to myself. One day, I was in my bedroom, listening to Radio

Avaline as usual. Radio Avaline was what was called in those days a pirate radio station. It was a ship anchored outside the three-mile limit, and it broadcast pop music as it was not subject to government rules and regulations of broadcasting.

Whilst I was listening to the radio, the disc jockey announced that after the next record, he had a couple of girls from America who would like to have English pen pals. Some of my classmates had pen pals, and I didn't want to miss this opportunity. I searched for a pen and paper, but could only find a pencil just in time to hear the end of the record and get the names and addresses of the girls. They were both from somewhere called Jenkins in Kentucky. As I couldn't find any paper in time, I peeled back some of the wallpaper from underneath the window and wrote the names and addresses on the exposed plaster. I later went out and bought an airmail pad and envelopes. I could feel my hands trembling as I began writing. "Dear Beth…" Then the other one, "Dear Carol." I copied the same letter to both girls. I wrote about myself: height, eye/hair colour, what interests I had (Marine Cadets, playing chess, collecting postage stamps), my school and subjects I was studying, where I lived, and my family.

Once I'd finished, I read through the letters and hoped they could read my handwriting. I folded and placed the letters in envelopes. I nervously sealed them and put them in a drawer of my bedroom cabinet. After school on Monday, I would go to the post office and send them.

Classes that day seemed eternal. Finally, I was on the bus home with the two important letters in my briefcase. I felt like a courier for a spy network. The bus finally arrived at my stop. I got off, crossed the road, and headed straight to the post office. I walked up to the window grill and pulled out the letters from my case.

"I'd like to send these, please."

"Put them on the scales one at a time" came the postmaster's response. When he told me the price, I was astonished. My stammer, a problem I had lived with for all my life, got worse as I was told how much the postage would be. "H-h-h-how m-m-much?" I stammered. He told me again. I reached into my pocket and counted out the change. I just had enough with a few pence to spare. I handed the money over. He put the stamps on and placed them in a sack.

A couple of weeks passed. One day, when I arrived home from school, my mum told me, in her childish singsong voice, that I had a letter from a girl in America named Beth. I asked her how she knew. "I opened it, of course!" she replied, very matter of fact. I was angry. "That was private and addressed to me!" I shouted.

"Don't shout at your mother. She had every right to open the letter," said Grandad.

"No, she didn't!" I replied. "It's my letter, not hers!"

Grandad began to get up from his chair and reach for his walking stick. "You talk to me like that again, and you'll get this across your back!" he said as he brandished his walking stick in my direction.

I snatched the letter from the mantelpiece and went upstairs.

"Aye! And you can bloody well stay there n'all!" shouted Mum.

I didn't care. I had a letter from America. One of the girls had replied to me. I removed the pages from the torn-open envelope, unfolding them carefully. As I began to read her letter, I noticed that Beth's handwriting was much better than my own. Mine had been described as a drunken spider crawling across the paper. Hers was distinct and easy to read. I thought she sounded like a nice girl. She had written about her hometown, parents (her father was a coal miner, which I found interesting as my dad delivered coal, so we had at least something sort of in common), school, and how she played a clarinet in her school band. It was just a pity Mum had read it first.

After reading the letter numerous times, I got out my airmail pad and began writing a reply. If Beth answered my letter, then we could become real pen pals. It was something to tell my classmates tomorrow.

It didn't take long for me to get my revenge on my mum for opening Beth's letter. The next Saturday, I saw the postman arrive with the post. One envelope was addressed to Grandad, the other to my mum. I handed Grandad's letter to him and opened Mum's letter. As she came in, I handed her the letter. "Mum, this is for you." She took the opened letter and noticed it had been opened. "Who opened this? You?" she demanded.

"Yes. You opened mine, so I'll open yours. That's fair, isn't it?" Well! You'd think World War Three had broken out! Grandad was all set to get his walking stick, and Mum was looking for the fire poker. I slipped on my shoes, grabbed my bike, and made a hasty exit.

Dad was always fair with me. When I eventually returned, he asked why I had opened Mum's letter. He went on to tell me that because I was still under twenty-one, he and Mum were responsible for me. I asked if this applied to my privacy. He said in some respects, yes, but that Mum would not open my personal letters again. Mum had been put in her place. Grandad just snorted and mumbled about him being too soft on me, and that a damned good thrashing was what I needed. Dad responded by reminding Grandad that I was his son, and this was his decision.

As a compromise, I was made to promise I wouldn't open any more of Mum's letters. I agreed, as long as she didn't open mine. Mum just sniffed, and nothing more was said about it. My father then asked about this American girl. I told him, so it was all out in the open. I had a pen pal, nothing more.

The letters to and from Beth kept crossing, and I felt we were really getting to know each other well. I never heard from the other girl, but at least it kept the postal costs down.

I told her what had happened to me at school and the Marine Cadets. We wrote about the music we liked, including the Beatles, who were also popular in America. She told me she played clarinet in her school band. I remember telling her I used to play a recorder. I once sang in the church and school choirs, but not anymore. Our correspondence was just the usual chat between friends, except we exchanged letters instead of talking.

Beth told me her father was a coal miner; I told her my dad was a coalman. He didn't have his own business but worked to deliver coal for a small family business. I was really interested in her heritage and discovered she had Cherokee and Irish ancestry. I told Beth my mum was Welsh.

I looked forward to receiving her letters. I counted the days between each letter. This way, I had a rough idea of when I'd receive the next one. Every day when I returned home from school, I checked the mantlepiece, hoping to receive another of those thin blue envelopes. When I saw one, my heart leapt for joy. I'd head straight to my room to read it. I read Beth's letters over and over because I found them so interesting.

I had no idea what her hometown looked like, although I did find it on a map in an atlas and marked it in blue ink. She often told me how she and her family sometimes drove to Virginia to do some shopping, as she lived only a mile from the Virginia state border. We never had a car; we just couldn't afford one. Besides, neither my dad nor mum could drive. We didn't have a telephone either. The only TV we had was Grandad's small, old black-and-white rental in a polished wood case. I kept all of Beth's letters in the drawer of my bedside cabinet. I hid them under some clothes and gently rearranged them, marking the edge of one, just to see if Mum had been snooping in my room. I knew she was capable of that. Sometimes, I hid them elsewhere. If Mum was going to read them, she'd have to hunt for them first!

As I began writing, I put on the radio that was always tuned to Radio Avaline. They played all the good music of the time. I listened to groups such as the Mamas and the Papas, the Kinks, the Who, the Beatles, the Rolling Stones, and Jimi Hendrix. Sometimes, we would write about our music preferences. Some of the groups Beth mentioned, I had never heard of.

It was nearing the summer of 1967. The GCE exams were just a few short months away. My English teacher, Mr. Hartman (whom everybody called "Old Heartless" because of his unforgiving, vindictive, and bullying character) made it known that he wasn't enrolling me for English Language or English Literature, yet he still expected me to do my homework. He was so vicious, he should never have been allowed near children, much less to teach them. He was also the deputy headmaster, and he reveled in the power that came with the post. Old Heartless was a heavyset man who had a squarish head, topped with combed-back dark and grey hair. His thick eyebrows characteristically poked over his heavy, dark-rimmed spectacles. These eyebrows tried to meet when he was angry, which was his usual mood. A thin, perfectly trimmed, straight mustache lined his upper lip but never went past the crease of his mouth. Like all teachers of his generation, he always wore a suit, a white shirt, and a tie. There were always a few pens in his top pocket that he used to mark our work. The few times he smiled, it was a sinister and unaffectionate smile that matched his character. To most of us, he was evil.

Throughout my five years there, teachers at the school made it abundantly clear they had no real time for me. In fact, most of the teachers only seemed interested in the pupils who performed well in their respective subjects. Those who struggled and probably needed a bit more attention were ignored by them. These pupils were told they were "useless," or admonished to "stop trying to waste my time." That was the culture of that school. A long time before this, I lost all interest in school.

In terms of extracurricular activities, I decided to join the Chess and Stamp Clubs, eventually becoming the Stamp Club secretary. This was run by the music teacher, Mr. Leadbetter. He was an oasis of calm in the school, a very gentle man who I only saw cane a boy once, and that wasn't very hard. He was the school choir and orchestra master. He helped everybody who needed it. I recall one day, I wrote a piece of music and gave it to him for his opinion. It wasn't a long piece. He took it, sat down at the piano, and actually played it in front of me. When he had finished, he congratulated me on the piece. Even though it only lasted a few seconds, it meant a great deal to me that he took the time to play it.

Soon, it was time for a careers evening at school. We all had to attend, so I entered the school hall looking hopefully for a Nautical College or Merchant Navy display. I could easily see ones for the Army and Royal Navy, but most of the others were more discreet. I was surprised that the person behind the Merchant Navy desk was casually dressed and not in uniform. I took a seat and began to share my dream of going to sea. I had wanted to be a navigation officer and later a captain of my own ship in the Merchant Navy since I was about thirteen. He asked a number of questions regarding why I thought this career was right for me. He wanted to know whether I had ever been to sea and whether I'd considered other career options. I told him this was the only career I'd ever wanted to do and had ever considered. I told him I had spent two weeks on a trawler. He smiled at this. I asked about entry qualifications. I would need to pass a medical with a Doctor's Certificate of Health and a Board of Trade Eyesight Test Certificate, and pass the college entrance exam. Depending upon the results and the numbers who passed the entry requirements, I could be accepted. He allayed any doubts I had regarding acceptance. Most shipping companies required a minimum educational standard. The college would teach to GCE standards in mathematics, English, and physics as well as various nautical studies. I thanked him and left with the college prospectus in my hand.

I was about to leave the hall when Old Heartless stopped me.

"Where do you think you're going?" he demanded. I noted his forehead furrowing and his eyebrows trying to meet. I waited, anticipating the upcoming anger that would be aimed in my direction.

"Home, sir," I replied.

"But you've only just arrived, sonny."

"I have all I need, sir," I said, showing him the prospectus.

He looked at it and laughed. His eyebrows nearly met. "Better get back in there and take up something more realistic!" he bellowed.

"This is all I need, sir."

"I said get back in there and look at other options, boy!" he snapped.

"These people have given up their valuable time to help ingrates like you, so get back in there and make them feel it's been worth their while!"

I grudgingly returned to the hall to have a wander at other prospects: the local major engineering works, kitchen cabinet makers, Army, Navy, Royal Air Force, police, fire brigade, trawler companies, and a few other assorted employers. Nothing suited me or could compare with what I really wanted to do. I looked round, and since Heartless wasn't in sight, I quickly left the hall and made my way to the bus stop. I tossed the few other brochures I acquired due to the interference of Heartless into the litter bin by the bus stop. The bus arrived, and I headed for home. On the bus, I avidly read through the pages of the prospectus, looking at the photographs of cadets. I remember thinking, "In a few months, that will be me."

I arrived home and excitedly showed Mum and Dad the prospectus. Grandad just sniffed and shook his head. Dad asked if I knew this was really what I wanted to do. I replied that I was certain. He asked what was required and seemed happy with the information I gave to him.

I believed it was all settled, as long as I passed all the requirements.

Eventually, the time came for me to see our family doctor for my medical examination. Once the examination was over, he pronounced me "fit for sea duty," and duly gave me the signed certificate. I handed over the required fee and left, elated. I had passed the first requirement.

Next, I had to arrange the Board of Trade vision test. My mum wrote a letter to my school, requesting I be allowed to take time off to attend the test, and it was approved by Mr. Dunstan. When it was time for me to leave the maths class I was in, I explained to the teacher, Mr. Carter, why I was leaving early. He nodded at me when it was time to go and wished me "good luck." He was well known as a strict disciplinarian. However, he never played favourites and treated every boy equally. He was another of the few better ones in the school.

Once I arrived at the Board of Trade building, an examiner took me into a darkened room and directed me to a seat. I was then told to wait until my eyes had adjusted to the darkness. The tests started about fifteen minutes later. First was the form vision, just like the standard optician's test. Then the colour test, or in this case a lantern test where I had to name the coloured circles as they appeared on the screen. At the conclusion, he congratulated me, and I was issued a certificate. Now all I had to do was pass the entrance exam. Once I took the certificates to the college, they would schedule me for the date, time, and location of the exam.

One day at school, our class was given a free period due to a teacher's absence. We were told to go to the technical drawing classroom. As we entered the classroom, we sat and began talking.

"Quiet!" It was the teacher in the stockroom.

Mr. Watson came out, not looking too happy. We had taken up his free period by being here. He stood tall and menacing, as he always had. He told us that there wasn't anything he could teach us during this lesson. Instead, he asked about our futures after school. He seemed quite calm, and receptive to our careers. When he came to me, I told him I was going to the Nautical College to be a navigation officer in the Merchant Navy. When I had finished, he looked at me and just burst out laughing. Not just an ordinary laugh, but a loud belly laugh! As though that weren't enough humiliation, he encouraged the rest of the class to laugh at me as well. "Ha-ha-ha-ha! You'll never get that! Ha-ha-ha-ha!" I just looked at him and thought to myself, "I will! If only to spite you." I had already passed two of the three requirements. I just remained quiet. After this period was over, a few taunted me, but I just ignored them. They were most likely going to work in a factory, but I was going to the sea, where I would see the world.

# Chapter Three

## B.B.

### THE PROM

In the US, the junior-senior prom is a traditional formal dance, considered a highlight of the high school years. For one enchanted evening, students typically aged fifteen to eighteen and their dates make a one-night transformation to princes and princesses. Girls are given corsages by their dates; boys receive boutonnieres from the girls.

Beginning about a week prior to the prom, the chosen location (in our case, the school gymnasium) is transformed by the junior class into a themed fairy tale. It is exhausting work, but it becomes an amazing backdrop for lifelong memories. That year, 1968, our prom theme was "Fantasy of the Sea." Prom was a couples-only event. No teenager went to his or her junior-senior prom without a date in our small town, and it was unthinkable to miss it.

Spring 1968 came, and I was a junior in high school. The prom was coming in May. I had not been invited to the prom by one of my junior-senior classmates. One very undesirable classmate gave some hints, which I quickly discouraged. He was not a good student and was well known for being obnoxious. It was better not to attend than to be seen with the wrong person. I could barely tolerate this boy's sarcasm and behavior in class, much less have him ruin an important evening of my life.

In need of a potential date for the prom, I agreed to attend a Saturday night dance at the local American Legion Post with a friend. There would be teens from various schools throughout Letcher County there, so it was a great opportunity to meet other teens and socialize. Two close friends of my mother were chaperons for these dances and promised to keep a watchful eye on me, so this became acceptable recreation on Saturday nights. I was grateful my mother consented, but she was rigid with an 11 p.m. curfew. My instructions were to be standing outside on the front porch of the American Legion promptly at 11 p.m., where she and my friend's mother would be waiting in the parking lot for us. The consequences for not complying were made clear. If I wasn't on that front porch waiting at the designated time, she promised to make a huge scene by coming in after me. My social life would be ruined forever. Needless to say, I was always early out on the porch.

It was at one of these dances that I met Steve. He was about 6'1" tall, aged nineteen, and slim. His hair was curly but short, his shoulders broad, and his two front teeth slightly protruding. His accent was thick, even more so than my own. I was raised in a town, whereas he was raised in a rural country hollow. Even in the hills of eastern Kentucky, the difference in dialect is noticeable.

Two things caught my attention right away. First, he wasn't bad looking, and second, he was an amusing sight on the dance floor. He appeared to be all arms and legs when he was dancing. Whatever dance he thought he was doing, I had never seen that variation. He came over and asked me to dance.

For a sixteen-year-old girl who had never been on a date and certainly had never been kissed, the fact that he showed an interest made me feel special. We met at the dance every weekend after that. I had only known Steve for about a month when it was time to seriously think about a date for the May prom. The harsh reality was that Jim wasn't coming over from England to escort me. I briefly daydreamed about what it might be like to have Jim as my prom escort, but it was a fantasy I entertained only for a fleeting moment. I never imagined we would ever be more than long-distance pen pals. Consequently, I invited Steve, and he eagerly accepted. He had dropped out of high school following the death of his mother and had never been to a prom.

Like all protective mothers, my mom did her usual background checks and quickly found out where Steve lived and who his dad was. According to the "mom grapevine," he was clean, so she didn't raise objections.

I had been unable to find a prom gown I liked locally, so my grandmother, age sixty-eight, went shopping in Cincinnati and selected and mailed one to me. I had no input whatsoever. It was yellow (not my favorite color), sleeveless, with a lacy overlay at the bodice, and accentuated with white, teardrop simulated pearls. The body of the gown was lined with yellow taffeta with a sheer yellow overlay. Elbow-length white gloves completed the ensemble. It was hot and uncomfortable to dance in, but still I was gracious and grateful. My grandmother cared enough to be part of something she never got to do for my mother.

I had a good time with my friends that night, but later learned from my best friend that Steve was flirting with her. He had asked her to dance, then asked her out while they were dancing. She was a good friend, so of course, she declined. I wish I had been mature enough to understand the future implications in terms of integrity and trust.

# Chapter Four

## J.D.

It was soon time to take the entrance exam for Nautical College. After getting off the bus, I headed towards the college. This was a new construction, just about a year old. I can remember it being built. The external walls were bright white and the windows dark in comparison. I walked through the main doors for the first time, feeling very nervous. My stomach was churning as I was directed towards the gym, where there were rows upon rows of desks. They were the standard wooden school desks with a wooden chair behind each one. The floor was highly varnished wood with various markings on it for the different sports played there.

Numerous candidates were already seated. Many were engaged in conversation. I found a place at an empty desk and sat down. I looked around at the gym and saw the usual climbing frames, ropes, and folded trampoline. It looked very much like the gym equipment at school. I then turned my attention to the other candidates. Somehow, they looked like any other sixteen-year-olds. Some were dressed more smartly than I was, probably grammar school kids. These were who I was competing against for a place. My self-doubts began to creep in. I could hear Mr. Watson's laughter and taunting go through my mind. Eventually, the testing procedure was explained, and an exam paper was placed in front of us. We were told the exam would last three hours, and to answer as many questions as possible in the allotted time.

The questions looked complicated and difficult. There were maths, English language, and physics questions. I read through them about three times before actually putting pen to paper. After the rereading, it seemed the questions began to make more sense. Once I started to answer them, the information seemed to spew out of me. I finished in plenty of time, so I went back to the beginning to check my answers before handing in my completed paper. Some candidates had already gone, but many were still working. As I walked out, I felt reasonably confident I had done well. I just hoped it was enough to get me into the college.

It wasn't long afterwards that my last day at school arrived. I couldn't wait for the bell so I could leave there for good. Before that, we had to assemble in the Hall for Mr. Dunstan's farewell speech. The Hall contained fifth-year boys and a few sixth-form, some of whom would be going to university. The rest were the fourth-year boys who would be leaving school at the age of fifteen, with no qualifications whatsoever. They were from the lower streams, and they didn't take any exams in their classes. They would be unskilled and semiskilled labourers when they found work.

Eventually, Mr. Dunstan entered the hall. He was dressed in his graduation gown as he always was for morning assembly, the tails flowing behind him. He was tall and slender with a balding head. His face was thin, but with a purposeful look. He walked up to the dais and to the podium. He stopped and looked down and across at us. He began his speech about how we were a credit to the school, how well we had done, and how we would be shaping our workplaces in the finest traditions of the school. His speech went on a bit. All I wanted to do was to tell him to shut up so I could get out of that place. He wished us all well on our futures and then turned and walked down from the dais. He was then replaced by Heartless, who just glared at us.

There was no ceremony, just a few quick words; then we were dismissed. To him, we were factory fodder, nothing worth wasting good air on. I felt like a prisoner who had served the required sentence. As I walked out of the hall, I felt elated. I passed my old classrooms, remembering the canings my classmates and I had endured for such pettiness as bad handwriting, misspelling, being late because of a conversation with another teacher, or just because a certain teacher was in a foul mood. As I walked past my old English classroom, I could almost hear the swish of the cane as it traveled through the air, making a thwack as it made contact with skin, flesh, and bone. I was also remembering hearing the cries of "rubbish" or "bad grammar" as an exercise book was thrown across the room, or pages torn out and thrown in the bin. I remembered the time I was awarded two house points for giving a perfect answer on a Religious Knowledge exam. When Heartless saw Mr. Dunstan's initials by those points, he accused me of forgery. "Don't lie to me, boy! Mr. Dunstan rarely gives house points, and certainly not *two*!" I remembered seeing him reach into the drawer of his desk to get out his cane.

One of the boys in my class spoke up in my defence. "It's true, sir. We all heard Mr. Dunstan congratulate him when he awarded him those house points." Others in the class agreed. With that, Heartless got up and angrily stormed out of the classroom, snatching the house point book to take with him. "Wait here, and don't move!"

A short time later, he returned with the house point book. His face was a purply crimson. Before he sat down, he just threw the book back in my direction without even looking at me. Of course, there was no apology.

"Sit down!" he commanded angrily. As I sat, the bell for the end of the lesson rang. As I walked past him, I pitied his next class.

All I wanted to do now was get out as quickly as possible. Eventually, I walked out, past the heavy external dark blue wooden doors, down the worn stone steps, and past the iron railing playground, and exited those school gates for the very last time. As I walked out of the gate onto the pavement, I felt as if a huge weight had been lifted from me. That moment was one of the happiest in my life. They couldn't hurt me physically or mentally anymore. I was free from all the bullying, taunts, and mistreatment of five long, dark years. I never once looked back.

It wasn't long before the bus passed the Nautical College, its white walls gleaming and enticing in the sunshine. Some of the cadets were walking towards the tram stop. They looked so smart in their brass-buttoned uniforms and bright white caps. I smiled as I thought, "In a few months, I'll be wearing that uniform." With that, all thoughts of the school vanished. I sat thinking of what lay ahead. I was now waiting to hear the results of my entrance exam. I did not care about my GCE results. That was school, and therefore history now. I didn't need them.

All the while, I continued to receive letters from Beth. By this time, I had learned a great deal about her and hoped one day we might actually meet. When we first started exchanging letters, we also exchanged photographs. She sent me a photo of herself in her band uniform, holding her clarinet. As I recall, the uniform was a dark green, and the hat was tall and flat on top. She wrote about going shopping with her family in Virginia and described the shops and what they had bought. For her, it may have been very ordinary, but to me, it was exciting.

One morning when the postman came, I dashed down to find a letter addressed to me from the Lancashire Education Committee. I instinctively knew it had to be the results of my college entrance exam. Mum was there, and so were Dad and Grandad. "Well, don't just stand there looking gormless! Open it!" Mum said.

As I was reading the words in the letter, Mum asked, "Well? What does it say?"

"It looks like I'll be going to sea," I replied.

"Awwwww, love!" Mum said, pleased.

Dad was happy, and Grandad just grunted and spat a piece of tobacco towards the fireplace, as usual.

I was accepted to the next Navigation Cadet training course in September! Despite all the reservations and mockery of those teachers at school, I'd done it! I was elated.

I remember waiting with anticipation for the next letter from Beth, eager to tell her the good news. I went up to my bedroom and began daydreaming about my future life in the Merchant Navy as a navigation officer. Maybe, just maybe, if I docked in an eastern American port, I could get enough shore leave time to visit Beth. That would be great.

My brother had put me right on that idea, and any notions I had of a romantic life at sea. He had spent three years in the Merchant Navy as a seaman and told me a number of stories about the real life at sea. He said it was hard and grueling work. Most of the time, especially in the North Atlantic in winter, I'd be cold and wet, and probably hungry too. I had wanted to join a tanker company, but my brother soon put me off sailing in tankers. He'd sailed in an oil tanker. He told me a lot that the glossy brochures I'd received didn't tell me. Very little time ashore, berthed miles from anywhere, usually out at the end of a jetty. In the end, I was under no illusions whatsoever of the life that I had chosen. I was ready for it.

# Chapter Five
## J.D.

### NAUTICAL COLLEGE DAYS, 1967-1968

While I was happy to be going to the Nautical College, I could see the concern on my parents' faces because of the expense. In the acceptance letter, there was a list detailing the uniform, equipment, and books. My father's wages barely kept us clothed and fed with very little left over. Fortunately, I was friends with the son of the college secretary, Mrs. Parker. She was kind enough to come and visit us, crossing certain items off the list and leaving only a list of what was absolutely necessary for the course. This helped ease the financial burden. She was able to get a second hand uniform for me, saving the greatest expense. She also helped sort out a grant for me, which amounted to a very small percentage of the overall cost.

The day came when Mum and I went into Blackpool to Rawcliffe's Outfitters to get the rest of my uniform requirements. Somehow, she was able to pay for it all with cash. How and from where she had got the money, I do not know, but I swore I would somehow pay it all back once I was earning. The required textbooks would be on sale on the first day at college.

During this time, the letters from Beth kept coming. She shared the things she was doing plus subjects of general interest. In return, I wrote much the same, sharing my excitement about going to college and then joining the Merchant Navy. I hoped my enthusiasm hadn't bored her, but she kept writing back.

The summer holiday of 1967 was magical for me. It was the end of a phase in my life, and the beginning of another. It was the Summer of Love. The music being played on Radio Avaline was fantastic: Scott McKenzie, the Beatles, the Move, the Mamas and the Papas, the Young Rascals, Cream, Small Faces. It was a great time to be alive and listening to great music.

The summer holiday finished, and my first day at college arrived. I bounded downstairs with excitement that first morning, smartly dressed in my uniform. I felt really good. At last, my dream was being realised!

Grandad looked towards me, shaking his head. I remember how he had preferred I got a trade and gone out earning money. "Book learning," he had said, then raised his hands. "These are where you earn your money. Get a trade behind you."

My brother had soon put him right. "He is getting something better than a trade. He is getting a profession." I shall always be grateful to my brother for supporting me that way.

After breakfast on my first day, I picked up my near-empty briefcase, which would soon be filled to capacity with new books. Upright and proud, I walked to the bus stop, my brass buttons, gold braid of the cap badge, and lapel tabs gleaming in the late summer morning sunshine.

Whilst waiting for the bus, I saw another cadet heading towards me. We greeted each other and introduced ourselves. His name was Scott Matthews. It was his first day too. I noticed early on he was also sporting lapel tabs, so he was going to be in the same course of study.

Recollections of my first day are still fairly clear. My uniform was clean and well pressed, and my shoes were gleaming. The white of my cap cover was brilliantly new. The ring in my cap was still present, making it obvious I was new. As I got off the bus, I saw others in uniform heading towards the college. As I entered the building, I noticed a smell of fresh polish and cleanliness. The wooden floor was gleaming. The cleaners had been busy over the summer break.

I followed others to a flight of stairs to my left. They led the way towards a large room identified as the Common Room. As I entered, there was a smoky haze inside. I could see a number of tables and chairs around the side of the room. Groups of cadets were sitting, smoking, and talking. It was all so strange and bewildering to me. The lad I had met at the bus stop recognised somebody and brought me over to meet him. He, too, was wearing the same lapel flashes on his jacket. Scott introduced us: "Charlie, this is Jim Aubrey. This is Charlie Henderson." We said our hellos and shook hands. We found some vacant chairs, sat, and told each other a bit about ourselves. Meanwhile, a radio was playing songs like "Ode to Billy Joe" and "Excerpt from a Teenage Opera." Both records now take me back to those first days at college.

A short time later, some of the cadets began to walk out of the common room and head downstairs. One looked at us and told us it was time for the assembly in the gym. We got up and followed. A tall lecturer entered and headed towards the front of the assembled cadets. He began speaking to welcome the previous year's cadets and the new cadets. A prayer was given, followed by some notices. We were then called to attention, and he began to inspect us. This inspection would be carried out every Monday morning in the future.

After the assembly, we were escorted to the various classrooms where we would be taught navigation, seamanship theory, practical seamanship, boatbuilding, chartwork, physics, and maths. After the tour, we were taken to a classroom that resembled a bookstore. The front desks were piled high with books about nautical tables, navigation, seamanship, almanacs, and ship construction. We took one of each, paid, and chose a desk to sit. Our main lecturer, Mr. Ormrod, began explaining what we would be learning and how it would fit in with our future life at sea. He made it all sound so simple, yet I could still hear my brother's words, "Life at sea is not romantic."

At the end of the day, I was totally befuddled! I had so much to learn! I returned home with my briefcase full of books. After tea, I began looking through them and wondering how I would learn all that was contained inside them.

A few weeks after we had begun our course, we were taken out sailing for the very first time. Mr. Ormrod took us out in pairs in a dinghy, a GP14. As we glided through the water, I felt the cool, exhilarating spray hit my face and immediately loved it. I couldn't wait to take command myself.

Letters continued to arrive from Beth. When Beth responded to my letters, she shared genuine stories from her life. Our letters were unscripted, and we took the opportunity to teach each other things unique to our respective cultures. She continued writing about her school and performing in the high school band and how she used to freeze on the benches (she called them 'bleachers") as she waited for their turn to perform. I wrote, telling her about what I had been taught in my classes: sailing, navigation, seamanship, signals, and canvas work. I read each of her letters over and over, not wanting to miss a single detail. We were more than pen pals.

The first term at college flew by, and soon, it came time to prepare for Christmas and the first college test. Close to Christmas, I received a small package from Beth containing a letter, a card, and two presents. Beth sent me a beautiful tie tack of jade mounted in a gold-coloured surround. I had never owned a tie tac. The other was an Irish linen bookmark with the Irish Prayer on it. Now I needed to find her a corresponding gift, but I had little money. Eventually, I bought Beth a small gift and sent it with a Christmas card and letter, thanking her for the lovely presents. To be honest, I cannot recall what my present to her was, but I know it could not have matched her presents to me.

Soon, it was back to college to await the results of the Christmas test. Summed up in one word: disaster! I had come in twenty-first out of the class of twenty-eight. I could almost hear Mr. Watson laughing and taunting me again, "Ha-ha-ha! You'll never get that!" My poor result in class was a wake-up call for me. I needed to do much better if I wanted to pursue my chosen career. I vowed to devote myself to studying, allowing myself only one night out on Saturdays.

I received another letter from Beth. The envelope was filled with American Christmas stamps she removed from the envelopes of Christmas cards her family had received. I had written telling her I was in the school Stamp Club, so she sent stamps for my collection. There were too many for me, so I decided to return to my old school and give them to Mr. Leadbetter, the teacher who led the Stamp Club. I didn't especially want to go back into that school, but this wasn't about me. I was doing a favour for the teacher who had shown me kindness. This time, I entered by the main door of the school, as I had said I would never walk through the school gates again.

The school secretary directed me to Mr. Leadbetter's classroom. As I turned to walk up a long, familiar corridor, dressed in full Nautical College uniform, I saw Mr. Watson walking in the opposite direction. Just as we were about to pass each other, I looked at him straight in the eye and said, "I made it then, sir." He walked straight past me, with no acknowledgement or recognition of any kind. I never looked back. I just kept walking and laughed to myself. "Who's having the last laugh now?"

When I entered Mr. Leadbetter's classroom, his eyes lit up like a beacon, and his face broke into a broad smile that nearly touched his ears. We shook hands, and he congratulated me on getting into the college. We talked for a while; then I presented him with an envelope containing some of the stamps Beth sent me. He was grateful to accept them and to share the stamps with the club. We talked until I needed to leave to devote myself to my homework. This time, as I walked along the corridors, I felt nothing. The classrooms were empty, and they held no emotion for me. This would be the last time I ever entered that school. It was also the very last time I would see Mr. Leadbetter. He had been an oasis of calm in that place, and I would be forever grateful to him.

Part of our college course was hiking and orientation. This was mainly done in the Lake District. On the last day of our final hike, it rained heavily. We broke camp and headed out. Soaked with the cold rain, our group ascended just over 2,600 feet to the summit of Old Man of Coniston Mountain, which was totally immersed in clouds.

Once we finally descended to our base camp, we recognized our college van and were greeted by the two lecturers who were assisting us. They had a large pan of stew cooking on a stove. After we changed out of our wet clothes and warmed ourselves, we waited for the rest of our teams to arrive. Only then were we able to devour the stew. We had no idea what the ingredients were, as each group contributed to the contents from their unused food. However, it was the hottest, most filling, and most delicious meal we had had in days.

I received more letters from Beth. As I read each letter, I grew to like her more and more. She had become a major part of my life. The time between her letters seemed greater and greater as I eagerly waited for the next to arrive.

Whenever Uncle Ken came home from Liverpool, he always brought me back a plastic kit of a ship. "This is for you, Sneaky Beak," he said with a smile. He always called me Sneaky Beak. He never told me why. I would joyfully build up the ship and paint it, then show him on his return home next time.

I found I was having a bit of a hard time remembering the flags of the International Code of Signals, so I cut up an old cereal box into the shape of the flags and used the model paints to colour the pieces of card to represent the flags. On the other side, I wrote the corresponding letter and meaning. I would then use these as flash cards to help me. I asked Grandad if he would help me. He agreed, and he would hold them up, and I would tell him the letter and meaning. If he thought I wasn't quick enough, he'd tell me to relearn it. In the end, I could recognise and recite the flag meanings very quickly. I was always deeply grateful for his help with this.

One of the most memorable pieces of advice I ever received at college came from our Seamanship class lecturer, Mr. Ormrod. One day, he stopped his lecture, turned to the class, and imparted words of wisdom. He had passed down many titbits of useful information. On this occasion, he put his hands down towards the cuff of his sleeve.

"In a few years, you will get a gold ring on the bottom of your sleeve. That gold ring does not give you the respect of the crew. That has to be earned. You respect the crew, and the crew will respect you." This is a philosophy I have kept with me throughout my whole life.

After several months at college, it came time to apply for a cadet apprenticeship with a shipping company. I looked at various company information booklets and prospectuses; I seriously considered a company that comprised ore and bulk carriers, finally deciding on a company based in Newcastle upon Tyne. I applied and was called for an interview. They were a shipping management company and maintained a number of smaller companies with a very wide range of ships, including ore/bulk carriers, general cargo, refrigeration, and tankers. My range of experience would be greater than with a general cargo shipping company. After the interview, I left excited and confident that I had done well. A few days later, I received a letter from the company stating they would accept me, provided I had exam passes in a minimum of three subjects that must include mathematics and English language.

Next month, it was time to take the GCE examinations. The first examination was navigation. I felt very nervous as I knew my whole future depended upon the results of these examinations. The first three questions were chartwork. We were handed a chart as part of the examination. Answering the first question, I had completed the calculations when I realised I had plotted my position in the middle of an island! I rechecked my calculations, found my mistake, and made corrections to the position. I attempted to erase my previous lines on the chart but found they could not be erased! The writer of the question knew he was laying a trap for unsuspecting cadets. I swore under my breath. My heart was pounding. I had lost a lot of confidence, which really threw me off for the rest of the examination. Every answered question afterward left me filled with doubt. I made another error by misreading a question. I went back to recheck the question and realised what I was writing had no bearing on the original question at all. My confidence was destroyed for the rest of the exam. Even calculations I had done hundreds of times before filled me with doubt. When I left the exam room, I felt deflated. I could envisage my future being swept away.

By then it was lunchtime, so I decided to go for a walk to clear my head before the next set of exams. The other exams went without too many problems, except physics. I did the math calculations without any trouble but had a difficult time remembering the theory and definitions. I found explaining experiments and how the experiment proved somebody's theory or law to be very challenging.

During this period, the seamanship examination was seemingly endless. The exam covered theory, signals, Morse code, the International Code of Signals, semaphore, ropework, sailing, rowing, power boat command, regulations, lights, symbols, and buoys.

Once the GCE examinations were completed, next came the general college final exams. These were much the same as the GCE Exams, but not as essential to get taken on with a shipping company. Once all the examinations were completed, we spent our time honing skills using the sextant, taking bearings, plenty of sailing in the estuary of the River Wyre, signaling, and boat work.

At one point, the college was presented part of an old ship's mast and a large number of blocks and tackles. These were put in the boat building room (located underneath the college, like a basement). It became our job to clean and paint the blocks and tackles with red lead. During this cleaning and painting period, one of my classmates complained about getting rust all over his shirt and trousers. Mr. Ormerod overheard him and told him, "You'd better get used to this. You'll be doing a lot of this when you get to sea."

After a couple of weeks, our college exam results were announced. My intense study regime paid off. I moved up from twenty-first to fourth place in my class ranking. I was extremely pleased with that result.

On our final day, we had an assembly where, after a brief talk by the college principal, our names were called in turn to receive our Sea Remission Certificates. This allowed us six months off our cadet apprenticeship sea service prior to taking our Second Mates' Course. There was a prize given for the top three cadets. I missed an award but was told afterwards that if they had a prize for the most improved cadet, I would have won it. That was my last day at college. I went home with my briefcase once again full of books and proudly holding my certificate.

That summer of 1968 was full of anticipation for me. I waited patiently for the day the GCE results would come out. Meanwhile, I looked forward to letters from Beth. By this time, I felt I was getting very, very close to her.

Obviously, we had never met, but by the way she wrote, I felt she was a very kind and loving person who had a sense of humour. For example, when I was writing to her about going canoeing in the Marine Cadets, she asked, "What canoe do?" It made me groan, but I found it very funny. Also, she looked so beautiful in the photo of herself in her band uniform. Her smile was like a beacon. Strange as it may seem, I felt I was in love with her, even though it was unlikely we would ever meet.

# Chapter Six
## B.B.

## TURNING POINT 1968

One evening, my brother Ret, now attending a university, broke the news to our parents that his girlfriend was pregnant. Still reeling from the impact of what this meant for my brother's future, my parents became ever more watchful of me. A short time after this announcement, he and his girlfriend June were married. My brother managed to finish college, eventually moving into married student housing with his new bride. Upon the arrival of their new little bundle, we grew to love that sweet little brown-eyed, red-head, Mikala.

Meanwhile, my mother had emotionally taken Steve in, knowing he had recently lost his own mother. Steve essentially had no home life since his mother passed and his dad was seldom home. He had been coming every weekend to see me, spending way too much time at our house. He reluctantly returned home to a cold, empty house with little to eat. My mother, a kind, compassionate sort, stepped in to nurture this motherless young man. She set no parental boundaries for when he could come and how long he could stay. He was treated like a son.

One night after Steve left, I overheard my parents talking. My dad, obviously upset, didn't trust me. His blunt, crude words to my mother hit me like a fist. He "didn't want me bringing home a b_ _t_ _d."

Without ever having a conversation with me, and without my ever asking their permission, they both went to the county courthouse and signed consent for me to marry Steve. Steve bought two plain, unmatched yellow gold wedding bands without ever officially asking me to marry him. The decision had already been made for me. It wouldn't be until well after my mother's death that I learned she was pregnant when she and my dad married. In eastern Kentucky culture in the late 1960s, by the time a young woman finished high school, she had one of two courses of action already chosen, her college or her husband. The nearest college was a two-hour daily commute. I had made no such plans. My parents, already wearing threadbare clothing, could barely afford to send my brother. The elbows were worn out of my dad's shirts, and my mother's simple, homemade cotton print dresses were paper thin from wear. I was already wearing some of the shirts my brother cast aside as blouses. Sending my brother to a university was a tremendous sacrifice for them.

In August 1968, I married Steve in a simple church ceremony with no fanfare. My dad had been laid off from his job in the coal mine just two months before our wedding. Since my mother never worked outside the home, there was no money to fund even a meager wedding. While working on a summer youth program at my school, earning about $1.25 per hour, I managed to make enough money to buy my own wedding dress—a short white dress—from a mail order catalog. The veil was borrowed. A friend of my mother's baked our small two-layer cake as a gift.

I thought choosing my dad's birthday as our wedding date would pay respect to him. The irony is that, after giving his consent, Dad chose to show his disapproval by boycotting the wedding. Steve's dad didn't attend either. There was no music and only a few artificial flowers. Nobody gave me away, there was no walk down the aisle, and there was nothing memorable. I wonder if many girls actually cry on their wedding day because they don't want to get married. I did.

Steve, who still didn't own a car, had borrowed his dad's car for the weekend of our wedding. The honeymoon is a lackluster, painful memory. We were a few miles over the Kentucky border into Virginia, about twenty-three minutes away from my home, when Steve pulled into the first motel he could find.

I was sixteen, and he was nineteen. There was no candlelight dinner, no flowers, no music, no romance. There were no soft kisses, no tenderness. There are no memories of a gentle, loving husband making love to his bride, her very first time. There are, however, memories of the scarring words he spoke to me. "You sure look better with your clothes on than you do with them off." My face burned with humiliation, and I can remember nothing else he said to me after that. My body could not compare with the airbrushed magazine images of nude women he had spent his time fantasizing about.

I was a virgin until our wedding day. Staring at my left hand at the plain, unmatched yellow gold band, I tried to reassure myself that this was really okay. At least for me, it felt totally wrong, like I had been thrown away as a matter of convenience.

## THE BREAK

I resigned myself to making the best of my new life. When the next letter arrived from Jim, I received it with dread. I knew I couldn't continue to have a pen pal relationship with Jim. Steve most definitely wouldn't understand. I struggled to compose a final letter to Jim. How could I explain something I couldn't understand myself? I was riddled with feelings of guilt and remorse. Saying goodbye was awkward, uncomfortable, and very emotional. Jim was my very best friend and confidant, yet I couldn't tell him how this had happened. I ended our pen pal relationship by simply telling him I was married now and wouldn't be writing to him again. For lack of details, Jim was left only to imagine that maybe I was pregnant and was somehow forced to get married. I was definitely not pregnant.

I no longer had health insurance under my dad's plan, and Steve had no coverage either. Shortly after we were married, I got strep throat. My throat felt like somebody was stabbing it with a knife, and I could barely swallow. I went to a doctor for medication, and he prescribed penicillin. I had taken that drug over and over throughout my childhood, usually by injection. Each time, the surrounding area had a worse reaction. Our family doctor, Dr. Petry (who delivered me at home), predicted, "One of these days, penicillin is really going to knock you for a loop." This time, penicillin was given as an oral medication. I had a severe, near-anaphylactic reaction to it. There was a thick, raised rash from the top of my head to the soles of my feet and between my fingers and toes. I was miserable with incessant itching. My whole body was swollen, my face grossly distorted.

Dr. Petry would have hospitalized me, but I had no health insurance. Instead, I was given 50 mg. capsules of oral diphenhydramine. I began to take them, and all I wanted to do afterward was sleep. This happened so shortly after the wedding that people jokingly asked whether I was allergic to Steve. It took longer to recover from the adverse drug reaction than the strep infection.

This ordeal was a wake-up call for my mother, if not for me. Without my knowledge, she made a trip to see Dr. Petry, then came home with oral contraceptives (OCPs) for me. OCPs had just been approved by the Food and Drug Administration (FDA) in 1960. She handed me a round package full of pills, told me that they were birth control pills, and explained how I was to use them. Dr. Petry was out of the milder 1 milligram strength, so these were 3 milligrams. She also obtained an abundant supply of condoms and handed them to me in a brown paper bag. "I got you these from Dr. Petry. The last thing in the world you need is to get pregnant without health insurance or a good job."

My face went crimson. I was sixteen years old and completely humiliated. I don't even remember what I said in response.

These blunt words were coming from the same woman who wouldn't even have a face-to-face conversation with me about the changes in a girl's body during puberty. I reflected on the number of times my mother had sent me from the room when I was younger as she and Marie, our next-door neighbor, were "talking women's talk." I once asked what the word "pregnant" meant, and it was her face that became crimson.

I dutifully began to take those pills, and each day I took them, I got more and more nauseated. They made me so sick that I had to stop them completely. By that time, Dr. Petry had gotten the lower dose back in stock (he also dispensed pills like a pharmacy), and she got some of those for me, all without being seen or examined by a doctor.

Steve was still staying with his dad and working two to three days a week at best. I was still at home and working to complete my last year of high school, despite all the pressure from Steve and his dad to drop out. Education was not important to either of them. The expectations were that Steve would work in a coal mine doing manual labor, and I would assume a traditional female role. I should cook, clean the house, do laundry, and have babies. They thought I should be performing that role as soon as we were married, even if I had to move in with him and his dad to "play house" in a house that was not my home. I chose instead to finish high school and continue to live with my parents until Steve got a stable job.

Hormonal changes brought about by oral contraceptives caused so much nausea I couldn't attend high school classes the last semester of my senior year. Lacking only two credits to complete requirements for graduation, I enrolled in correspondence courses through a university in Richmond, Kentucky. It took a tremendous amount of self-discipline to complete the coursework on my own. At completion, I was proctored for the final exams at my high school principal's office and graduated with my high school class.

During the week, my days were filled with the chores of helping my mother do the cooking, canning, and preservation of food from Dad's garden. I also did the housecleaning. Apart from television and reading, there was not much to do for recreation. I didn't hunt, fish, or hike the way boys do. I didn't have a car, but when my mother wanted to go somewhere, usually a short trip over to the Neon district of Norfolk, Virginia, or Whitesburg, Kentucky, I drove her there. My world was small and my life mundane.

I missed senior prom. The idea of attending a prom had lost all its glamour for me. Being married and completing my last semester of school through correspondence courses ruined it, and I couldn't afford the formal attire anyway. I no longer felt a part of my senior class and was referred to as "the married woman." The way they said it made me feel dirty. There was, of course, speculation among those who knew me that this was a marriage to hide an illegitimate pregnancy. As nine months came and went and there was no baby, those notions were proven to be false.

I rarely saw my classmates because I was home with my mother while they were in school. On weekends, they were doing their fun extracurricular activities, and I was at my parents' house, with a husband living fifteen miles away.

Steve earned less than fifty dollars a week, working limited hours in a small family-owned coal mine. He had no transportation of his own and could barely feed himself. At the age of only sixteen, I was far better off with my own parents. He had applied for a more dependable job with health benefits for the same coal company where my dad worked, and we were hopeful he would soon have a better job.

I saw my classmates the day we walked across the stage at graduation in early June 1969. After that, they slowly disappeared from our hometown. Many of my classmates moved away to attend colleges, while many others were drafted into the military and fought in Vietnam. The first Selective Service Lottery since 1942 has just been implemented in December 1969. Steve had received notice to report for a pre-draft physical exam before we met, but received a deferment for medical reasons.

# Chapter Seven
## J.D.

### HEARTBREAK

A couple of weeks after college, I received a letter from Beth, in that familiar, pale blue airmail envelope Beth always used. I hurriedly took it upstairs to my room. Once alone, I quickly opened her letter. I read the first few words, and I couldn't believe the devastating news. Beth had written to tell me she had got married and would no longer be writing to me. I was heartbroken. I had never felt this way before. I had girlfriends before, but none like Beth. The pain ate through my insides.

I reread the letter over and over. Each time, the pain seemed worse. I began crying. I would never hear from Beth again. My plans of possibly docking in an American port and getting leave to visit her were now gone forever. My world now seemed empty.

I went downstairs with tears still in my eyes, ignoring Mum and Grandad. I went downstairs and wheeled my bike out of the verandah. "Where are you going?" Mum asked.

"Just out for a ride." I wheeled the bike down the garden path, opened the wood spindle gate, got on my bike, and just rode. I had no idea where I was going. I just wanted to go…somewhere.

Eventually, the tears stopped, and I arrived at my brother's house. When Natalie greeted me at the door, she immediately saw that I was upset. Fighting back the tears, I told her that Beth had written to say she was now married and wouldn't be writing anymore. She sympathised with me, but it was little consolation. After a while, I left and rode home.

A few weeks later, the GCE results came out. I went back to the college and met up with others from my course. We had a good chat with each other until the secretary opened the office window, called our names one by one, and handed each of us an envelope containing our exam results. I received my envelope and ripped it open. I looked at the enclosed printed list.

Navigation—Fail. This was disappointing but expected.

English language—B. A pass.

Physics—Fail. Again, expected. Now I really needed the next results to be a pass. If I didn't pass, I would need to either change my shipping company or stay on for an extra term to gain additional time to take their exams again in re-sits. My heart was beating rapidly. I felt my hand shaking as I read the next line.

Seamanship, signals, and rules of the road—B. A pass.

Mathematics—C. A pass. I had done it! I was ecstatic. I had achieved the results I needed for acceptance by my choice of shipping company. My entry into the Merchant Navy.

Sadly, some of my classmates had not achieved the results they required. I felt sorry for them. Some were already talking to Mrs. Parker regarding a place on the next course to take their re-sits.

I cannot recall riding back home as I was imagining myself at sea. I must have been beaming from ear to ear when I got home. I was so happy and bursting to tell everyone the news. Mum looked happy, but I could sense she was a bit concerned about the cost of kitting me out for sea. The next job was to write to my shipping company informing them of my exam results.

A couple of days later, a letter arrived for me from the company. I had been accepted as a deck apprentice. They included details instructing me to report to the Shipping Federation in Liverpool to obtain my seaman's documents and registration. I would finally be realising my dream of a seagoing career. I just wished that I had been able to write to Beth and tell her of my good news.

The morning came to make the journey to Liverpool. I finished breakfast, picked up my letter of appointment, and made my way to the railway station. I was in uniform with trousers perfectly creased and shoes shining. It was a small railway station, roughly a five-minute walk from home. I bought my return ticket for Liverpool, knowing I would be home in a matter of hours with all my seaman's documents.

Arriving at the Shipping Federation, I waited for what seemed an age until my name was called. I was escorted upstairs and told where to wait. It looked like a doctor's surgery. I wondered why I was told to wait there since I already had a medical certificate from my family doctor.

When my name was called, I walked in tentatively. I was directed to sit in a chair by a man in a doctor's white coat who wasn't even looking at me.

He said, "I appreciate you have passed medical and vision test examinations, but this is a requirement for your documentation." I was given a piece of card and instructed to place it over my left eye, ensuring it also covered the bridge of my nose, and to begin reading down the chart.

I did as I was instructed but began to shake my head. The letters below the sixth or seventh lines were blurred. I could not read them clearly. He asked what my problem was, then exclaimed, "Didn't you have a Board of Trade vision test before?"

I acknowledged that I had a vision test the previous year and had passed.

He crouched down in front of me and examined my eye. Then he took a cloth and wiped my eye. "Right. Try it again." The result was the same. My stomach began to churn. Something was going horribly wrong. He tried a few other things and asked me to read the chart again. The result was the same.

"Right," he said solemnly. "Your sight is below the minimum standard required for deck service. I cannot medically pass you fit on those grounds. I have no option but to inform your shipping company that you are "unfit for deck service!" No shipping company will take you."

Those words cut right through me. My insides felt as though they had been torn out of me. I felt hollow. My mind could not fully grasp what was happening to me. My career at sea was finished before it had even started. I had never felt so empty and low in my whole life.

I was told to go and have lunch and return later. I walked out of the building a sad, broken, and empty shell. I was living a nightmare instead of my dream. I walked and walked the streets of Liverpool that day, with no idea where I was going. I can't remember if I even ate.

Eventually, I returned to the Shipping Federation. The receptionist told me to sit and wait for someone to see me. After a long wait, I eventually made myself known again. Someone finally came and apologised. They had forgotten I was there. I was now deemed unimportant.

I was escorted into another office, where I was asked to consider an engineering apprenticeship. I declined. I knew nothing about engines and had been thrown out of the metalwork class at school. I was then asked whether I would consider being a ship's writer. This was basically a ship's secretary under the purser. I considered that but was told there was a long waiting list with no telling how long it would take before I could get a ship. I asked to have my name added to the waiting list.

The journey home on the train that day was the saddest of my life. Only a few hours ago, I was ready to begin the career I had always wanted. Now I had nothing. I saw my reflection in the grey, grimy, water-streaked carriage window. I saw my clean white shirt, black tie, and shining lapel tabs. My eyes focused on the tabs, and I reflected on how this was the last time I would wear them.

This should have been a joyful journey. Instead, I was completely empty inside, without a future. Looking out of the window, watching the world going past, I hoped the train would crash and leave me physically as dead as I already felt inside.

Eventually, my train arrived at my station, and I walked that seemingly long walk back home. A little boy ran up to me and asked whether I was a captain. I looked down and smiled. "No, son, not yet," I replied. The words had a very hollow ring. I would *never* be a captain.

When I arrived home, Mum asked, "Well? How did you get on?"

"Failed the vision test, and I'm unfit for deck service. I won't be going to sea at all." My voice was flat. Unemotional. A dead voice. The long-awaited tears nearly broke through.

"What now?" she asked without any emotion. Mum was very much a matter-of-fact person. There again, I was too engrossed in my own feelings to have noticed anyway.

"First thing is to get these off," I said, gesturing to my lapel tabs.

"I'll do that for you, son."

"No! That's *my* job." I took a pair of scissors and went up to my room, looked in the mirror at the navigation cadet that was not to be. I slowly turned away from the mirror, having seen myself for the last time in uniform. I removed my jacket and sat on the bed, holding it. I looked at the tabs proudly stitched onto the lapels. I thought of all the places I could have gone with those. Now the journey was over before it began.

I took one of the lapels and snipped the stitching slowly and with sad purpose. Each snip seemed to tear out another piece inside of me. It was then the tears flowed uncontrollably.

When I finished, I held both lapel tabs in my hands. They seemed like amputated limbs, an integral part of me cut away and made useless. I looked at my uniform jacket, now bare without the tabs attached. I looked down at the tabs in my hands, tears dropping onto them. I fell face down onto my pillows, holding my tabs against my face, and continued crying until I could cry no more.

The past month had been a roller coaster ride. I hadn't been prepared for the sharp plummets. First Beth marrying and leaving my life, then passing the exams I needed, getting accepted by the shipping company, and going for my registration, then the final twist of failing the vision exam. "Unfit for deck service!" The words echoed in my brain over and over. I asked the same question over and over. Why? Why? *Why?*

The next day, I went back to college. There was nothing they could do, but I suppose I just needed someone to talk to. Maybe they knew a shipping company that would take on a cadet with poor eyesight. My maths and physics lecturer, Mr. Law, saw me and was quite surprised when I told him my news. He empathised with me, then took me to see a couple of other lecturers, Mr. Ormrod and one of the radio lecturers.

After a discussion, the radio lecturer asked if I had considered transferring to the radio officer side. I thought about it for a while. I knew Morse code. I enjoyed doing electricity and magnetism in physics, so why not?

I was told it would be an eighteen-month course, but if I applied before my next birthday, I would not have any need to pay tuition fees, only for the books I would need. However, I was advised very strongly to talk to my parents first, and if they were prepared to let me do the course, to ask them to come to the college for further information.

Suddenly, I began to feel a bit happier. Maybe I would be going to sea after all!

# Chapter Eight

## B.B.

I felt as though I had been thrown away and forced into marriage simply because my parents were concerned that I would disgrace them with an illegitimate pregnancy. I got no further response from Jim. It was over between us. I reluctantly discarded his old letters, but I held on to the two photographs Jim sent me. One was a black-and-white Polaroid of Jim standing in the front doorway of his home, looking uniquely British. He had a strong, handsome face with straight dark hair combed to the side. The sun was shining directly in his face, causing him to squint. He wasn't smiling. Off to the right side was the silhouette of the photographer, his uncle. He was wearing long-sleeved clothing with a turtleneck sweater. The second was a group photo with his class of Marine Cadets, all in smart, military-style uniforms. Unfortunately, the images were too small to recognize body or facial features. I kept both photos safely tucked away in boxes of my treasured family photographs.

## LEFT BEHIND

Only one of Steve's brothers had continued his education beyond high school, completing a two-year associate degree at a junior college. Several siblings had not completed high school. By contrast, my parents had always stressed the importance of an education, especially for my brother. Steve had no skills other than coal mining, so he worked in a non-union truck mine where shortcuts were taken with both safety and compliance with mining regulations. He earned a stingy thirteen dollars a day, paid in cash in an envelope at the end of every week. No deductions were taken out and he received no benefits. If he was lucky, he got to work two to three days a week, hardly enough money to support either of us or even put a roof over our heads. For this reason, he lived at home with his dad, and I still lived at home with my parents.

After high school graduation in May, 1969, I attended a year of vocational school to acquire business and office skills. My mother's dream vocation for me was to become somebody's secretary. My dream was to be a nurse. I had abandoned that idea because of stories I heard about the practical skills portion of nursing education, my own modesty and the reputation of the strict, military-like nursing instructors. I wasn't mature enough for the intensity of that kind of training.

As if by mass exodus, I watched my former classmates disappear from our small town. Some, including my best friend, Ann, left for colleges or universities. Some got married while others joined the military, took jobs in the coal mines or moved away. I felt as though the whole world had suddenly moved on and abandoned me while I was still trapped there. Most of those who left would never again return to their mountain homes.

## THE STRUGGLE

Steve still couldn't afford a vehicle of his own and usually asked a friend to drop him off on Friday evenings. We drove him back to his dad's home on Sunday night. Steve was nineteen and next to the youngest in his dad's second brood of children. He always seemed to be the black sheep of his family. When the family was together, a couple of his three older brothers consistently crossed the line between what I perceived as good-natured teasing to belittlement. This style of family dynamics was totally foreign to me, but Steve always pretended not to notice.

Steve didn't get invited on most of the hunting and fishing trips with his older brother, even though he loved to do these things just as much. I struggled to understand why he never expressed his feelings to those who excluded him. I was the one who saw the impact later when he withdrew and sulked in silence. To insert myself into that situation and address that exclusion would cast me in a parent-like role. He was an adult and it wasn't my role to be his personal defender. That battle was his to face.

There was a sharp contrast in our upbringings. Steve's dad was in his late fifties and had been widowed twice. He was lonely, but he wanted more than companionship. He wanted a much younger woman of childbearing age so he could have more children and raise a third family. Even with seven grown children by two different women, I found it quizzical that a man who was already a grandfather would want to start over again, raising a third family he would likely never live to see grown.

48

Of the blood relatives, I liked his oldest sister, Connie, and his youngest sister, Anna, best. Connie was funny, extroverted, and always welcoming. Anna was genuine, with a kind, loving heart. She was also close to my age and still living at home.

One week, I went over to stay a couple of days with Anna while Steve was at work. She wanted to go into Whitesburg to have her hair done but couldn't drive a car and didn't have a driver's license. I was sixteen and had a driver's license but had never driven a vehicle with a manual transmission. Anna came up with a plan. I would drive her dad's red 1968 Chevrolet Chevelle Malibu. When the gears needed to be changed, she would tell me when to press down on the clutch with my foot; then she would shift the stick in the console to the proper gear.

I have no idea how we made it up that steep Sandlick Mountain from Colson to Whitesburg. I have no idea how the clutch survived the abuse and how we made it back to Colson. All I remember is the jolting of that Chevy jumping railroad tracks, largely because we were going way too fast in an effort to keep the vehicle from dying. If the engine died, we'd have to go through the ordeal of shifting the gears again. I can't remember the number of times I peeled out, laying a trail of rubber on the asphalt behind us. We were a comical pair as I tried to coordinate pressing my foot on the clutch and gas pedals while Anna used the stick shift to search for the right gears. Each time, we laughed until the tears were rolling down our cheeks. This is one of my best memories of Steve's family.

What my own dad lacked in education, he always compensated for in motivation and hard work. Steve was nothing like my dad. As long as he had food to eat and clothes on his back, he was satisfied. Men with the same education as Steve were motivated to learn how to operate a variety of underground mining equipment or become certified as coal mine foremen. In the event of a layoff, these men with diverse skills would be first to be recalled. I tried to explain this rationale to Steve, but he wasn't interested. He wasn't a born leader and had no desire to become one. He was an introvert and would rather sit quietly on the sidelines than take on additional responsibility. I tried to encourage him, but eventually gave up the exhausting effort of trying to motivate him.

I credit my dad for approaching every person with influence in the hiring process to speak on Steve's behalf and get him hired at a union mine. Steve wouldn't speak for himself, so my dad put aside his fear and spoke for him. He did that for me. My dad's longevity with the company, attendance record, and strong work ethic made him a positive reference. Eventually, Steve got a job at a union mine for the same company where my dad worked. He was finally earning a fairly decent wage and working in a safer mine, with employee benefits.

In 1970, we rented a five-room coal camp house just up the hill from my parents' home for twenty-five dollars a month. Steve didn't want to commit to living in Jenkins, so when the house we were renting came up for sale, he refused to sign with me to buy it. I was just nineteen when my parents cosigned the loan so I could buy that house for $1,695. Our payments were just over twenty-eight dollars a month.

Our home furnishings were sparse, bought from the previous owner as she was leaving. She had lost the house to foreclosure, and since we were living in the house at the time, we were given the first opportunity to buy before it was auctioned.

In the kitchen, we had an ancient monstrosity of a refrigerator and a small, cheaply made, Formica-topped kitchen table with spindly legs and four vinyl, print-covered padded chairs. In the living room, we had a tan vinyl sofa and chair, accentuated by several melted areas from mislaid cigarettes. Two cheap glass lamps, a simple composite wood-look coffee table with two matching step-up style end tables supported by toothpick-like legs, and plastic curtains completed the décor.

Our first purchases were a nineteen-inch black-and-white portable TV on a flimsy metal stand, a full-sized box spring and mattress, a simple metal bed frame with no headboard, and a Warm Morning coal-burning stove to heat our home in the winter. We didn't have a forced air furnace with ductwork to circulate the heat like my family home had. The quickly and cheaply built camp house had no insulation whatsoever in the walls or attic. In the winter, it was so cold that ice froze on the insides of the windowpanes, and the wind howled through gaps in the window frames. When the wind blew hard outside, it was so drafty we could see our curtains flutter.

There was no air conditioning in the summer, only screens on the windows that kept out some of the mosquitoes. Sometimes, it was too hot to sleep. We had a choice. We could either cover up with a sheet, drenched in perspiration, or sleep uncovered and become a mosquito smorgasbord. It would be around 3 a.m. before the house finally cooled enough to allow us to fall asleep. We bought an electric window fan to exhaust the hot, humid air from an upstairs window.

The empty cardboard box that once contained our window fan became my makeshift dresser. I disguised it as best I could under a scrap of orchid-colored cloth. Although the coal camp house I was born in had been built in the same time period as the house I now lived in, there was a huge difference in how those two houses had been cared for.

Despite how hard he worked underground in the mines and raising a garden in his spare time, Dad was still meticulous in terms of home maintenance. Small repairs weren't neglected. There were no squeaky hinges, doors that stuck, or leaks that went uncorrected. In the fall, he made certain there was fresh glazing around windowpanes and caulk around window trim. He took pride in our home and invested sweat equity in its upkeep.

Our lawn was kept meticulously mowed and edged. My dad never knew the word "vacation" because time away from work meant more time to work in the garden or do needed repairs on our home. My dad's philosophy was "if you take care of what you have, it will last." Our home furnishings had been basic but well-made and sturdy. As was common then, our curtains were made from fiberglass fabric, an itchy nightmare to sew. I know, because I had to help make some of those curtains.

The house I bought had not been treated so kindly. The focus of the previous owner had not been on maintaining the home. She bought furniture cheaply and replaced it often, never taking care of what she had. Repairs had been neglected. Steve did not grow up with the same priorities of home maintenance as I did; consequently, he showed no interest and was not industrious like my dad. If there were windows that needed to be replaced, glazed, or caulked, Dad would show me how, and I would do my best. After Steve left, there were many things I couldn't do, and I didn't have the money to hire someone to do them. There are degrees of poverty just as there are degrees of wealth. The difference is that if you are willing to roll up your sleeves and work when disadvantaged, you can come out of poverty. My dad modeled wealth in industry.

# Chapter Nine
## B.B.

**M**y life didn't change much as a newlywed. I stayed with my parents and finished high school, seeing Steve only on weekends. During the day, my mother babysat for my new niece. Invariably, she would get fussy at the very time my mom's favorite TV show came on. Since Mom didn't feel well, I would do my best to entertain her. I knew very little about babies, but at least I could entertain her and give my mother a break. Sometimes, I took her out in the backyard swing. Sometimes, I would put her on a blanket on the floor and drag the blanket through the house. She would squeal and giggle and eventually settle down.

After high school graduation, I enrolled in a business and office course in vocational school. When classes ended for the summer, I got a part-time job in a small hardware store. The job didn't pay much, but at least I was earning something. It was a seasonal job, mainly to help out doing inventory. Counting nails, screws, and bolts was probably the dullest, most mundane task ever. The diversion of sweeping the floor and waiting on customers was a welcome relief. Once Steve got a reliable job with benefits, I was happy to quit.

## BEGINNING A FAMILY

In June 1970, at age eighteen, I got pregnant with our first child. It was a planned pregnancy, but I was young, self-conscious, and reluctant to subject myself to the embarrassment of a gynecological exam. In November, late in my second trimester of pregnancy, my mother forced the issue and scheduled a medical appointment for me.

In October, prior to my doctor's appointment, my mother became very ill. She had completely lost her appetite and started losing weight. Since she was considered morbidly obese, when she complained about loss of appetite to her doctor, he remarked "Good! You need to lose weight anyway." He never bothered to order diag nostic tests to determine why she had lost her appetite.

Despite her own failing health, my mother was looking forward to having a second grandchild. While we were out shopping one day, she bought two crib blankets and two adorable outfits, both for a girl. This was long before ultrasounds were done, so you never knew the gender of the baby until the birth. I tucked those gifts safely away in a special cedar chest, my baby hope chest. Still, I found it hard to be a happy expectant mother as I watched my mother's health steadily decline without explanation.

## LOSING MY MOTHER

As I reached my sixth month of pregnancy, my mother's health continued to decline. It was late December 1970, and I was getting dressed to return for a prenatal check. I was attempting the simple task of fastening my above-the-knee nylon stockings to the garter belt I was wearing. Every time I bent over to fasten the backs of my stockings, then stood erect, they popped off. What began as an annoyance quickly turned to frustration by my third attempt at fastening. I felt the blood rush to my face, then began jerking them off, flinging them on the floor. My magnified reaction to such a simple thing made me realize something was wrong. I had battled blood pressure issues throughout my pregnancy, but this tantrum told me something was different.

When I arrived at my doctor's office, I learned I had gained ten pounds in one month, and my blood pressure was a critically high 226/114. My doctor was surprised I hadn't developed seizures. I was hospitalized for several days with severe preeclampsia, and Steve was the only one allowed to visit. Later, I learned that severe preeclampsia can interrupt blood flow to the placenta, cutting off oxygen, blood, and nutrients to an unborn child. I could have lost my baby as a result.

Shortly after I returned home, my mother, now rapidly losing weight, had developed symptoms of nausea and vomiting. She was admitted to our small-town hospital, and a series of diagnostic tests was done. The backs of her hands and inner elbows were black and blue with contusions from a multitude of needle sticks for infusion of intravenous fluids and drawing lab work.

Pill after pill was prescribed, but still my mother's health did not improve. There were so many pills, it was no wonder she couldn't eat! Even more frightening was when she told us she had lost her eyesight. Barium enemas and eventually a bone marrow biopsy was done in an effort to make an accurate diagnosis. Finally, her doctor referred her to a urologist in Pikeville, who admitted her to the hospital. She was promptly taken off all the medications she was on so he could determine her true symptoms. Her eyesight returned.

The hospital was two hours away; therefore, visitation was a challenge. There were too many commitments in managing both households for me to spend an entire day with her. I couldn't get detailed information about my mother's progress from her nurses, so one day I arranged a phone call with her urologist. The news was ominous. She had been diagnosed with a hereditary birth defect known as polycystic kidney disease. Most people with this disease didn't live much beyond the age of fifty, and my mother was fifty-two. She could not survive without either a kidney transplant or dialysis. She was not a candidate for either. Nothing else could be done for her. The news came like a sucker punch in the gut.

I was only nineteen years old, in the late second trimester of pregnancy, with the dual responsibility of cooking for and getting both my dad and my husband off to work on different shifts. Dad was on the day shift whereas Steve was on the night shift.

Day by day, my mother's health steadily declined. One day, when I went to the hospital for a visit, she pleaded with me to bring her home. Her words were haunting: "I've been poked and prodded at until I don't feel like my body is my own anymore. I just want to come home!"

The next day, she was released, not because she was better, but because there was nothing more they could do for her. I had spoken with her doctor only by phone because I could never predict when he would make rounds and was unable to stay at her bedside. He made it clear that her condition was hereditary and encouraged me and my brother to be tested for the same disease.

Apparently, children born to a mother who has polycystic kidney disease have a fifty-fifty chance of inheriting the same disease. Her urologist told me she might have good days and bad days, but the good days would be short-lived. Since she was not a candidate for dialysis or a kidney transplant, she was deemed terminal.

I was allowed to ride in the ambulance with Mom the day she came home from the hospital. As we made our journey home along winding roads, in an attempt to cheer her, I told her if our baby was a girl, she would be named in her honor. She was lethargic but responded with a weak smile.

My grandmother Martha, now in her seventies, arranged to leave her home in Covington and her only remaining boarder to come help take care of my mom. She realized that my mother's condition was rapidly declining and that I was wholly untrained and unprepared to deliver the kind of care she would need at home.

I was awakened early one morning by a conversation between my dad and grandmother. My grandmother had been up and down all night as my mother had grown increasingly restless and had started having hallucinations. Later, I learned this was a symptom of uremic poisoning from nonfunctioning kidneys. It was clear they had given up hope for my mother's recovery. I just couldn't let her go.

Upon hearing their conversation, I got up out of bed, stormed into the kitchen, and scolded them for their lack of faith. "As long as there is breath in her body, there is hope!" Then, as though on cue, the three of us went directly to the bedroom where my mother lay, finding her already with eyes fixed. She was gone. No words can express how broken I was, just three days before my due date.

## THE CIRCLE OF LIFE

Mom was laid to rest on March 29. I was physically exhausted, emotionally numb, and feeling hopeless. At 4 a.m. the next morning, I was awakened with the severe cramps of labor. I had hardly slept, my grief so overwhelming that my mind kept replaying the painful details.

While Steve lay sleeping beside me, I got up, bathed, got dressed, and calmly called my brother and sister-in-law to inform them I was in labor. Within an hour, they came, then awakened Steve. The four of us made the journey to the hospital together. Sara was born at 10:20 a.m. that morning. The circle of life continued, but my joy was crushed by grief.

# Chapter Ten

## J.D.

### RADIO CADET DAYS, 1968 TO 1970

After I talked to my parents about my discussion at college, they were supportive. I knew this wasn't the career I had anticipated, but I just wanted to go to sea. A couple of days later, my parents and I returned to the college to discuss whether I could return to study on the radio course. The costs would be minimal as I already had the uniform and equipment. I would just need the additional books plus items such as headphones and meals. My college record had already proven my determination and diligence to study. The lecturers told my parents of my strong desire for a career at sea and said the college was happy to have me return. The course was explained to them, and so were the requirements expected of me. I found the details quite daunting, but then I recalled how daunted I felt on my first look through all my navigation and seamanship books a year previously. After a brief discussion, my parents agreed to allow me to attend the course. I was not quite as happy as I had been a year ago, but still pleased to get a second chance.

On my first day back, I went straight into the familiar common room and met a couple of my previous navigation course mates who had to return to take re-sits of exams they needed. They were surprised to see me, especially without my "nav tabs." I told them what happened. They, too, were stunned at the news. I told them I was starting a radio course. We were still chatting when it was time for assembly.

Out of habit, I walked down to the gym for assembly with them and prepared to stand with them. Mr. Law directed me away from my old classmates and towards my new class. It was at this point I realised this was no longer where I belonged. I found my new class, their uniforms all new and shiny, as mine had been on my first day last year.

As I joined my new class, one or two looked at me, noticing my bent and worn cap. The outline of my nav tabs were still clearly visible on my lapels, indicative of one who has been dishonoured and stripped of rank.

My new course included electronics theory, Morse code, and radio theory. All quite easy at first. None of these subjects really stretched me. I soon made friends and was eventually asked how most of the lecturers knew me at the beginning. My classmates inquired about what happened to the lapels of my jacket, and I told them the painful truth. They were sympathetic, but nothing more. After that, we just got on with our studies.

In time, I increased my speed at sending and receiving Morse code, and some of the electronics theory was making sense. The equipment side with actual real circuits was still a bit of a puzzle, but I was coping.

I studied hard, but eventually, the parts of the course that were not initially challenging became far more intense. Others in the course already had a good working knowledge of electronics and radios. I found I was lagging no matter how hard I studied. I did alright on the tests, but not as well as I wanted to, or as well as I had done on my navigation course. I kept going because I didn't want to disappoint or betray my parents or lose the confidence and trust of the lecturers. This time, the college just didn't seem to be the same. Now it was simply just a building. The spark of being a part of it and what it stood for had gone.

In September 1969, the second year of the college radio course began. In a few months, we would be taking the PMG (Postmaster General) Certificate of Competency Second Class examination. It would be a two-part exam covering basic electronics theory and radio theory. We were warned it would be tough. There were just three grades, A, B, and C. Grade A was a pass, while B and C were fails. Candidates had to attain As in both papers to proceed to the practical exam side of the course, which tested more in-depth knowledge of the equipment, Morse code, Q codes, accounting, regulations, etc. Our class spent time in the radio cabin, learning to operate all the equipment, diagnose faults, and do repairs. This was real hands-on experience, not just book learning and memorisation.

When it came time for the PMG, I entered the exam room with trepidation. I answered all the questions I could, but the level of knowledge required was very deep. I did not feel at all confident of passing. On the contrary, the exam highlighted just how much I did not know. Eventually, the results came, and I attained two Bs. Those who passed with two As were very few. These were the ones who already had a good working knowledge of electronics to begin with. Most of our class had to retake the exam.

The exam retakes were looming. The more I studied, the more knowledge seemed to evade me. Failing the previous exams was a real blow to my confidence, and I felt that my dream of going to sea would never happen. My interest began to wane. I was depressed, disheartened, and burned out. I restarted college after Christmas, more discouraged than I had ever been. Seeing others complete the course while I remained behind in classes took away any remaining enthusiasm. I was simply going through the motions, not really caring. I studied, but I just seemed to be reading words, not absorbing the information. Nothing made sense anymore.

Dad sensed this, even without my telling him. One evening, he called me aside for a frank discussion. He told me if I failed these next exams, he and Mum couldn't afford to support me anymore. If I passed, they would continue to support me as best they could. Otherwise, I would have to leave and get a job. I told him I understood, and I would do my best. He replied, "That is all I can ask of you."

The exam results were announced. Again, I had attained two Bs. My heart sank. This meant I wouldn't be going to sea at all now. My prospect of a future in the Merchant Navy was now gone forever. That evening, when I got home, I had to break the news to my parents that I had failed again. My mum tried to comfort me, but it was useless. Later, I talked things over with my dad. He asked what my plans were. I had none. I only knew that tomorrow would be my last day at college.

# Chapter Eleven
## J.D.

### LEAVING COLLEGE, 1970

D ad and I had a lengthy talk about jobs. I told him there was nothing in the area I really wanted to do. He nodded. He wanted more for me than he had for himself. He suggested I join the Forces. I rejected the idea of the Army or the Royal Navy. He wondered why I wasn't interested in the Navy. He pointed out it would mean the possibility of being at sea. I told him I couldn't bear to look up at the bridge and see people navigating, knowing that was what I should have been doing. He understood. He suggested the Royal Air Force. I thought about it for a while before deciding, "Why not?" This decision changed my life.

With that, my dream of a career at sea ended, and my new career in the Royal Air Force was to begin. Browsing through Mum's daily newspaper, I noticed a coupon for the Royal Air Force. I listed my name and address, then posted it to request more information. A few days later, a large envelope containing a few brochures and other information arrived. I looked through the brochures and information sheets. Naturally, the men looked happy in the brochure photos.

I put on my shoes, got my bike out, and began to ride. In the distance, I could see the Nautical College, gleaming white in the sunlight. As I approached, I could see the various classrooms and knew who would be in each room and what they were studying. I cycled past, knowing I would never walk through those doors again. I continued past the tram tracks and the cricket club, then onward toward the beach. I passed my old school with its imposing railings and tall windows.

I arrived at the beach, got off my bike, and sat on the bench in the same place I had sat whilst taking a break between the radio coursework and the evening typing lessons. I looked down and gazed at my shirt. During those breaks, I had worn a dark jacket with brass buttons and had my cap resting on my lap. Suddenly, I remembered a popular Otis Redding song, "(Sittin' on) the Dock of the Bay," and my eyes filled with tears. I have no idea how long I sat there, watching the waves roll in and out as memories washed over me, just like the lyrics of the song. I rose from the bench and walked towards the sea. I may have considered keeping on walking; I can't remember. These few minutes are forgotten to me now. I do remember picking up some pebbles and continuing to walk towards the sea. I stopped a foot or so from the water. Looking out towards the horizon, I called out, "Eleven Plus exam. *Failure!*" With that, I threw one of the pebbles as far as I could. I reached back and threw another pebble. "Sight test. *Failure!*" I watched the plume of water rise above the surface as I reached for another pebble and threw that. "Radio officer. *Failure!*" I then threw a further three pebbles into the sea in rapid succession. "Failure! Failure! *Failure!*"

Watching the ripples disperse, I once again focused on the horizon and imagined what might have been, had I achieved my goal of becoming captain of my own ship. It had been all I had ever wanted since I was thirteen years old. I had been laughed at and taunted because of it, but I had never wavered from my dream. As I watched the tide ebb away, I was reminded that my dream wasn't just ebbing away, it was gone forever.

At that moment, I felt like a complete failure. Anger welled up inside me as the tears rolled down my cheek. With the word "failure" still ringing in my head, I returned to the bench, got on my bike, and headed home past the workshops and the factories, hoping there would be something to keep me here, then realising there was no future for me in my hometown. There was nothing to keep me here.

Upon arriving home, I went directly to my room and completed the RAF application form, placed it in the prepaid envelope, and then walked to the post office and sent it.

A week or so passed before I received a letter scheduling me for an interview at the recruiting office in Preston. My new journey had now begun, and I met it with a feeling of uncertainty.

Eventually, I received a letter asking me to return to the recruiting office for the tests and a medical exam. When I read the word "medical," my heart skipped a beat. Surely this wasn't going to be a repeat of the last medical exam I had where I failed the vision test!

The day came for my test and medical exam. Upon arrival, I was ushered into a room with a number of other applicants for attestation. The first test paper asked the usual intelligence questions: which shape will follow the sequence, which is the odd shape out, and so on. A second test covered a whole range of subjects, including English, maths, science, electronics, electrical, engine, metalwork, and woodwork. The questions were very basic, and each question was followed by a selection of four answers. Only one would be correct.

When my results came in, I met with the warrant officer. "You have done extremely well," he began. "From these results, the Royal Air Force can offer you a number of trades. The number is most unusual."

"Thank you," I replied.

"We can offer any ground or air radar or communications mechanic, navigation instruments mechanic, and marine craft. The choice is yours."

Marine craft! I had seen those sweeping past when I was holidaying in Holyhead with my family. My heart skipped a beat, then started pounding with excitement. I quickly held back my initial excitement at the prospect of going into marine craft as I envisioned another medical exam that would probably include a vision test. I couldn't bear the possibility of another failure. I considered the options and chose ground radar, as I felt I needed a fresh start and a different direction.

"Good choice, my man!"

I signed a few forms, then was directed to the medical centre for an examination. There was no drama and no surprises. These tests were all done in a matter of about fifteen minutes. The sight test was not the horror I had been dreading. I had passed the medical but was strongly advised to wear glasses. I was then dismissed to wait for a letter with the results of the medical and a date for my swearing-in ceremony.

My joining date was Thursday, 25 June 1970; I was nineteen. I was up early that morning, suitcase packed and ready to go. I felt no real joy or enthusiasm. It was just something I had to do. The taxi came, and I set off as Mum and Dad waved their goodbyes. I was now a member of the Royal Air Force, not going to sea, and with no idea what to expect.

My mood on this journey was far different than when I went to my interview with the shipping company in Newcastle. This was a cold and empty journey. I had no real sense this was what I wanted to do with my life. I just wanted a job that would give me practical experience to back up my paper qualifications. Hopefully, I would have opportunities to travel in the RAF.

I needed to change trains a number of times before arriving at

Grantham. When I finally arrived, a corporal was waiting on the platform. He was holding a clipboard in one hand and a pen in the other. His uniform was well pressed, with razor-sharp creases in his trousers. These were the creases I had learnt to do whilst I was in the Marine Cadets.

"Royal Air Force Swinderby?" he called out. I and the others who had got off the train with me acknowledged his call. He then ushered us into a rickety old blue-grey bus for our ride to RAF Swinderby.

The bus squealed to a halt outside what looked like our accommodation. We were to be Number 3 flight and on the ground floor. We passed other rooms: washrooms, toilets, an ironing room, plus rooms containing beds and lockers. Most of these rooms were already occupied. As we entered my room, I saw others sitting on metal-framed beds with a bare mattress on each. By the side was a small cupboard and a tall cupboard. The room also contained two long tables with six chairs around each one. There were eight beds on each side of the room. At the end of the room were two bunk beds with three tall cupboards separating them. By the end of the day, each bed was occupied. The floor was brown lino, and I noticed how dirty it was; the walls were also dirty. The distinct smell of polish seemed to belie the state of the room. I could not understand why. Dark blue curtains hung on the metal-framed windows. I thought the blue was significant to the RAF. By each bed was a small blue or green mat, about 3 feet by 2 feet.

This was our introduction to the Royal Air Force. It was fairly quiet and without fanfare. Our time here would be for six weeks. It was what you'd expect from basic training. There were endless drills, inspections, rifle drills, lectures, marching, and lots of shouting from the drill corporal and sergeant. Next came the inoculations. We were marched to a building and up a flight of stairs, where we were told to wait in line by an open door. We were called in one by one in fairly rapid succession. As I waited for my turn, I saw my predecessors come out. Some appeared okay, some a bit groggy, but some walked a few paces and collapsed in a heap. "Oh God!" I thought. "What the hell is going on in there?"

As I entered, I saw the tables were arranged in a U-shape, similar to those found at a wedding reception, but definitely minus the celebration. Men administering the inoculations were standing behind the tables, and we were ordered to stand on the other side with both sleeves rolled up.

As soon as I entered, I was asked for my service number, full name, and date of birth. Another called me over. "Left arm." Jab! "Next!" I moved over.

"Right arm." Jab. "Here! C'mon! We don't have all day!" Jab! Left arm, jab. Right arm, jab. Both arms, jab, jab, something on the tongue. Right arm, jab, both arms, jab, jab. Left arm, jab and so on until I had done "the circuit." So far, I didn't feel too bad. Others were receiving assistance from medics after collapsing. We were then ordered back to the block and told to rest.

"At the NAAFI" (Navy, Army, Air Force Institute, club and shop for "other ranks"), "the bar is out of bounds to you all tonight! If any of you are caught drinking tonight, you will be charged and severely punished!" ordered Corporal Jacobs, our drill corporal. He was a slim person, about 5 feet 8 inches tall, and his voice was normally quite low. Low that is until he was on the parade ground, where his voice boomed at us. He was always immaculately turned out. He had a sense of humour that helped us get through some rough parts of our training. When a recruit turned left instead of right, he would call out, "The *other right*!"

When I returned to my room, I noticed that some had already collapsed on their beds. Some were sitting crouched over and holding their heads in their hands. I still felt okay, so I went with some others to the mess for tea. I felt fine until I was in the queue for my meal. Suddenly, I began to feel a bit woozy. I turned around, went back to my room, and collapsed on my bed, where I lay for the rest of the night.

The next morning, after a small breakfast, we were called to line up outside our barrack block. Our arms were stiff and aching after all the injections we had the previous day. Corporal Jacobs marched us off, straight to the armoury for arms drill. "This is the best way to loosen up all those aching arms, lads!" called out Corporal Jacobs, with a sly, knowing grin.

## MOCK REQUIEM

On the evening of our second payday, a lad from my room got extremely drunk. It took five of us to get him back to the room, where he passed out on another lad's bed.

We decided to teach him a lesson about excessive drinking. We got the broom cupboard (spare locker without any shelves), emptied it, and placed it on one of the tables in the middle of the room. The interior of the locker was padded with his blankets, and his sheets were draped over it. We laid his pillows at one end, then gently picked him up and laid him in the locker and crossed his arms. We took turns watching for signs of him waking up.

Eventually, he roused, and we immediately sprang into action. Each of us took a sheet and draped it over our heads. We stood around the locker box, each of us holding a lit candle in front of us. The candles were used to "burn in" the polish on our boots to give them a high-gloss shine. We began a slow chant, like monks. When he opened his eyes and saw these ghost-like figures holding lit candles and chanting over him, he must have thought he was dead. He had a look of complete horror on his face as he frantically struggled to climb out of that box. We never saw him get that drunk again during the time we were there.

Six weeks of basic training went by quickly. Our passing out parade was punctuated by a fly-past by a Nimrod Maritime Patrol Anti-Submarine Search aircraft. Corporal Jacobs congratulated us on a smart turnout and on our hard work. At the conclusion, he ordered us to return to our barracks and stand by our beds, where he proceeded to hold a final inspection of each room.

When he completed his inspection of our room, he announced, "Disgusting! This room is far too clean! Do you want the next entry to benefit from all your hard work?"

"No, Corporal!" we responded in unison.

"Then trash the place! Make it as filthy as you found it. You have fifteen minutes. Now, move!"

We didn't hesitate. We smeared shoe polish over the floors, and we took dustpans outside to collect dirt and dust, which we then scattered and ground into the polished floor. We had a great time. Now we knew why the place was so filthy when we moved in.

Once we completed the sabotage work and Corporal Jacobs was happy with the filthiness of the room, we were dismissed to go on a week's leave. We each shook his hand and thanked him for what he taught us. He was a good guy, fair, and nowhere near as bad as he could have been.

My trade training for ground radar mechanic was at RAF Locking in Somerset. I was to travel by train to Weston-Super-Mare. At Bristol, I met up with a couple of other lads also going to Locking whilst waiting for the train to Weston-Super-Mare. On arrival, we caught a taxi and were dropped off at the RAF Locking Guard Room. We tentatively walked to the window, and as the sergeant opened the window, we snapped quickly to attention and told him who we were. He asked for our ID cards and checked them on a sheet of paper on the ubiquitous clipboard. He told us where our accommodations would be and where to pick up our bedding. Just before we left, he told us that we were now in the *real* Air Force, so there was no need to stand at attention when speaking to him. We thanked him and headed towards our accommodation.

The accommodation used to be an unused apprentice block. The rooms were larger than at Swinderby. Each room held twenty beds with the same large and small wooden lockers on one side of the bed. The floor was highly polished blue lino. Most of the beds had people lying on them, some reading, others sleeping. I couldn't believe my eyes! This was a Wednesday afternoon, and people were just lying around doing nothing. We chose our places, picked up our bedding, and made our beds. One of the new lads I traveled there with asked why everybody was just lying around. "It's Wednesday. Sports afternoon," one replied casually. "If you don't play sports, you just hang around. You'll get used to it." This was unbelievable to me. I was beginning to like this place!

As my course wasn't due to begin for another two months, I and three others were allocated into the Pool Flight whilst waiting for our radar mechanics course to begin. Pool Flight was a designated group of people who were awaiting a course. In this section, they were allocated various nontechnical jobs that were required around the station. At times when there were no jobs allocated, we just sat and read, or played cards or darts. During these times, we would take home leave for a few days to break up the monotony.

Eventually, I began the sixteen-week course. The basic electronics theory and maths I found easy, compared to my time at college. The radar theory was a bit more stretching, but nothing I couldn't cope with. Soldering and metal work were my biggest struggles. Overall, I found the course easy. My test results were always high, and I was given a grade that would put me in line for the next available Fitters' course once I had passed my Senior Aircraftman examination.

A few weeks before completion of the mechanics course, our postings were announced. After an error with a couple of us, I found myself and two others heading by train to our posting at RAF Henlow in Bedfordshire. Each of us had brand-new leading aircraftman (LAC) badges on our sleeves with a fist and sparks badge (badge denoting personnel of the communications/ electronics trade. It shows a clenched fist holding six lightning bolts) stitched beneath the rank badge on the right sleeve.

A minibus eventually came to pick us up at Hitchin Railway Station, and we headed towards RAF Henlow.

After arriving at the guard room, we were assigned accommodation on a temporary basis until our sections had been allocated to us. The driver took us and pointed out the mess and NAAFI. He headed towards four buildings that seemed a long, long way away. Each of the four blocks looked identical. Each had a flat roof, metal-framed windows, and a board with faded, peeling paint indicating the block number and squadron. On the opposite side stood a couple of black, rust-streaked old metal buildings called Bellman Hangars. The windows of one block (Block 569) were filthy, with drooped, sagging, dirty nylon curtains barely held up due to missing hooks. This block looked the worst of the four. This was where I was headed.

My expectations of life in the Royal Air Force had just taken a nosedive. I began to question my decision to join, in total disbelief at the squalor this building exuded. Once inside, I was directed to a room with an empty bed and a filthy, heavily stained mattress. I received my bedding from the bedding store (upstairs in the same block) and prepared to make my bed, looking again at the filthy mattress in complete disgust.

One of the men in the room, who introduced himself as Dan, observed my reaction and said, "Don't worry, it'll not be the last time you'll sleep on somebody else's piss stain." Another of the men, Jock, showed me his mattress. It was in much the same condition.

I gazed around the rest of the room, observing the plain brown lino flooring. A scruffy piece of mat lay at each bedside. The walls were painted pale yellow, scuffed and marked. A wooden table with four chairs sat in front of the only radiator. On the exterior wall of the room were two once-white steel-framed windows, now scratched and nicotine-stained. "Welcome to the Ground Radio Installation Squadron, known as GRIS!" said Paul, another of my new roommates, without looking up from his girly magazine. Paul was chubby with dark hair and a moustache.

"GRIS?" I asked.

"Yes, this is the GRIS block." Paul pointed towards his left. "The one next door is the MT Section. The next one is EES, known as the Factory." MT stood for Mechanical Transport and EES for Electronic Engineering Squadron.

"You want to keep out of there if you can. It's a hellhole," continued Paul. "Yes. The one behind that is for the shineys." The term "shineys," I soon learned, was a derisory name for the clerks. It came from the belief that they spent so much time sitting down, the rear of their trousers shined.

"Do you reckon I've been posted to GRIS?" I asked.

"Not yet, but you can ask when you arrive at Engineering Wing Headquarters tomorrow," said Dan. "You don't want the Factory if you can help it."

Soon, a beeping outside was heard.

"Polly's here!"

"She drives the NAAFI wagon. Sells drinks, buns, pies, sweets, et cetera," said Jock.

"Usually better than the crap the mess serves up!" said Paul, still reading his magazine.

Soon, it was time to go for tea. I was invited to go with them. Fortunately, Paul had a car, a Vauxhall Victor Estate, so we piled in with another friend of theirs. We passed a number of others walking along the road, all headed toward the mess.

The mess was an old rickety wooden building that Paul said was one of the original buildings of the station. "Food's crap, but better than nothing," he told us.

We entered, and directly in front of us was a small fountain, no doubt to give the mess a touch of class. It failed miserably. The servery was ahead of us. Each of us took a plate, and I looked at what was on offer. A pie, a stew of some sort, some scrawny-looking chicken legs, and what looked like dried-up pork chops, baked beans, and chips. That was it.

Jock was behind me and said, "Dinnae tek the pie. Ye dinnah know what's in it!"

I took his advice and opted for the stew.

"Thah's jess'as bad," said Jock.

I helped myself to some beans and chips. I took a couple of slices of bread and followed Dan to a table. I put my plate down and headed to get some tea. As soon as I put my fork into the stew, the nameless friend made a shrieking cat sound! With that, we all burst out laughing. I tasted the stew, and surprisingly, it was quite good. I looked at the friend and said, "Mmmm! Best moggy stew I've had in a long time!"

Paul was having a drink of tea at the time, and most of it suddenly burst out of his mouth. He looked at me and said, "Thanks a lot, bastard!" to which we all laughed. Then Dan introduced me to this friend, Dave. As we shook hands, Dave nodded and said, "He'll do!"

During the meal, I found out that Dan, Paul, and Dave were communications (radio) mechanics and were members of an ongoing circuit of installations to replace the voice recorders for all the RAF stations. Jock was an aerial erector, and they erected or pulled down antennae and towers. They were all senior aircraftmen.

The next morning, I met up with the others from my course in the mess. After breakfast, we headed for Station Headquarters (SHQ). We told the clerk in the general office who we were and that we had just arrived. He took our ID cards, then came back with a number of blue cards.

"Go to Engineering Headquarters first to get you allocated to a section, then just go round to all the others that haven't been crossed off." We had no idea where we were going, but eventually we found Engineering Headquarters.

Once we arrived, a flight sergeant looked us up and down as we handed him our blue cards. One by one, he began adding names into "Radar Flight (EES)" on a large wall chart behind him. Just before he added my name, I asked, "Can I go into GRIS, please, Flight?"

The flight sergeant stopped in his tracks. He looked at me, then at his chart. "Why do you want to go into GRIS?" he asked.

"I've heard what they do, and I believe that type of work would really suit me."

The flight sergeant grunted. The others looked quizzically at me. He consulted his chart again. Picked up an inevitable clipboard and rifled through the attached papers. I wondered how the Air Force would manage without clipboards. He then picked up the phone. He spoke to somebody and explained the request. "That's fine by me." With that, he put the phone down and wrote my name in the "GRIS" column.

It was as quick as that. We left the building, and the others jostled me and called me a few choice names. I was glad I had the nerve to speak up.

We had arrived together, but we soon split as they went towards EES, and I went to GRIS.

As I entered the GRIS building via a small door, I was confronted by a long corridor with a highly polished brown lino floor. On the wall were two large whiteboards. One was labeled "DETACHMENTS" and the other "PWRs" (Preliminary Warning Roster, showing future postings). Each board had lists of names and RAF stations. I would soon recognize the need to check these boards daily for my name.

There were a few doors on either side. These had wood plaques indicating their purpose. Further up, there was an office with a large glass window. I headed in that direction and knocked on the window. A corporal slid the window open and asked what I wanted. I handed him my blue card and told him who I was. He walked away and into another office. Next, a warrant officer came out, smoking a thick, slightly curved wooden pipe.

"So, you're the one who wants to join us, then?" he asked. Before I could answer, he puffed on his pipe and walked out of the office. He puffed on his pipe again as he looked me over. "Hmm. Follow me."

I followed him back down the corridor, until he walked to another door. It was one of the first ones I had noticed when I first entered the building. The door had a varnished wooden sign which read "Public Address Section." We walked through the door and into the room. It was fitted out with work benches, test equipment, and electronic units in various states of assembly or disassembly. The warrant officer took me over to another office where he spoke to the flight sergeant, who was sitting behind a desk.

"This is LAC Aubrey. Just arrived. First timer. He's yours if you can use him." The warrant officer left, continuing to puff on his pipe as he walked away.

The flight sergeant rose from his chair and walked towards me. "Aubrey, eh? What do you know about public address systems?"

"Absolutely nothing, Flight," I answered honestly. I had a feeling that my time on GRIS was going to be short-lived.

"Good! No preconceptions. We'll show you. Keith!" A young-looking corporal stood up. "Take Aubrey here and show him around and explain everything to him." He turned to go back to his office.

"Walker! Where's my bloody coffee?" he called out.

"Coming, Flight," a voice replied.

The flight sergeant mumbled something as he grabbed his coffee from some SAC's hand.

Keith introduced himself to me and the rest of the section.

"We are the PA Section, and we go round the air shows, displays, and events and set up the public address equipment. That includes microphones, speakers, cables, and amplifiers. We travel all over the country, and all the gear has to be working perfectly; if not, we're in deep shit! That is why we're always stripping the equipment down, cleaning it, and replacing anything and everything that is a bit iffy. OK?"

"OK" was all I could say.

"How much more arriving have you got to do?"

I showed him my card.

"You're nearly done. GDT (Ground Defence Training) is the worst. These 'rocks' (RAF derisory term for the RAF Regiment) will have you on one of their training courses and out on the shouting range. I'd avoid that if you can. It's not fun."

I was then introduced to the rest of the section.

A few days later, I was told to report to the Ground Defence Training Section. This happened with every new arrival. At the end of the training session, the warrant officer teaching the course said, "Next week, you'll all be going to the range. I'll inform your sections and when you'll be required to be there."

When we got the word to go to the range, the flight sergeant declined us, saying we were too busy. I and another never did get on the rifle range. We were glad, because we could hear the instructors bawling and shouting as we walked past, a good two hundred yards away.

One evening after work, I was lying on my bed reading and having a smoke, when Dan and his mates asked, "What are you doing tonight?"

"Probably the usual. Read, couple of beers, then back here," I replied.

"No, you're not. We're going out to Bedford in fifteen minutes. Be ready."

Finally, I was accepted as part of their group. It wasn't really that I felt rejected before, but I found they were a very close-knit group who went out on short time installation jobs together. I felt I was alone most of the time. The lads I was in the same course with had their own friends in EES and in a different block. I had made one good friend, Cliff, who was an old hand, having been posted in from Singapore shortly before me. He was also in the Public Address Section, and we got on really well. Cliff told me that before joining the RAF, he had worked in London. We often spent weekends in London with Cliff showing me around. It didn't take me long to get to know my way round the main parts of Central London.

Most of the time, Dan, Paul, and Dave were away from Monday until Friday, and Jock would be away for longer periods. I was alone in the room. It was nice having the peace and quiet, but a bit lonely. I was eager to accept any offer of company. I soon learnt there was a bowling alley about 100 yards away that had a bar. It was where the vast majority of GRIS personnel hung out. The bar itself was usually lined with aerial erectors (or as we referred to them, "riggers"). Most were rough and ready, with strong features, and had little time for small talk. They were down-to-earth, and so was their language. Their job was hard, moving tons of metal girders around and bolting them together a few hundred feet in the air. They stood no nonsense. Somehow, I sort of became one of them. Maybe it was because of my attitude towards them. I laughed and joked with them and gave back as good as they gave me. They welcomed such two-way banter. Whatever the reason, they respected me and looked upon me as a mate.

I only did one job in the PA Section. The job was for an Officer Cadets Passing Out Parade across the road at the Officer Cadet Training Unit. Eventually, I was moved off the PA Section.

A couple of weeks later, my name appeared on the Detachments Board list. This would be my first real GRIS job! My excitement soon changed to anxiety when I realised I was headed for RAF Ballykelly in Northern Ireland. Of all the places I could have been going to, I certainly was not expecting Northern Ireland, especially with all that was happening at the time. I felt I was going into a war zone and was totally unprepared for it. There again, I wouldn't be going out on street patrols like the Army, so maybe it wouldn't be that bad after all. I consoled myself with this.

I looked down the list of names. There was a flight sergeant, a corporal, a J/T, and two other LACs. It was going to be a quick job, about three weeks to remove an airfield radar system, as the station was closing down. After the Friday one o' clock parade, I packed my holdall with a few clothes and got changed into my best uniform. I walked out, climbed over a five-bar gate, and began hitchhiking my way home for the weekend.

When I arrived that evening, my mum and dad weren't too pleased with the news of my detachment because it was during the time of "The Troubles" with the Irish Republican Army (IRA). Random and targeted bombings were a daily occurrence during that period. Mum had visions of me being shot to pieces or blown up as soon as I stepped off the ferry! I tried to calm her and allay her worry by telling her I wouldn't be going out on patrol around the city streets. I was going to remove a radar system, that was all. The weekend soon passed, and on a sunny afternoon, I was out on the road, hitchhiking my way back to Henlow.

On Monday, our crew met for a quick briefing by the officer in charge of the party, Flight Sergeant Matthews. He told us this job had to be finished in no more than twenty-eight days. The job was going as planned and without any problems until Flight Sergeant Matthews informed us that after we returned to Henlow, all LACs would be transferred into EES until they passed their promotion exams to SAC. Then, if we wanted, we could rejoin GRIS. I and the other two LACs were stunned. This was what I had tried to avoid. However, there was nothing we could do, so we continued with the job in hand and grumbled about it between ourselves. We left Ballykelly with heavy hearts, as we did not want to leave GRIS and join EES.

# Chapter Twelve
## B.B.

B abies don't come with owner's manuals. There were no childcare classes offered to prepare me to take care of a newborn. I had no prior experience with babies. In fact, I had never taken care of a baby on my own in my entire life. I had no sisters, no aunts, no sisters-in-law, or anyone else to teach or help me as I learned how to care for a newborn. My baby weighed close to ten pounds and had a voracious appetite at feeding time. Having had a lifelong struggle with weight, I concluded that feeding her skim milk instead of formula might be a better option. I tried that only once. The incessant crying and tummy ache were enough to teach me I should never do that again.

I didn't understand that a tight tummy and crying meant I hadn't adequately allowed my baby to burp and expel extra gas after feeding. I didn't know why it was ill-advised to prop up a bottle during feeding. I didn't know how to swaddle her or how to safely trim her fingernails so she wouldn't scratch her face. Remembering that my oldest brother Freddy had died of sudden infant death syndrome (SIDS), I was a fearful young mother, up and down all night, checking Sara to make sure she was still breathing. Sleep deprivation took its toll, but we both survived those critical first months as I was learning from experience how to be mother.

In the weeks that followed, "baby blues" quickly progressed to depression. At the age of nineteen, I bore the responsibility of cooking dinner for Dad and Steve in the evening, then packing Steve's lunch and getting him off to work at 11 p.m. At 4 a.m., I was up again to cook breakfast for my dad, pack his lunch, and get him off to work at 6 a.m. After that, I tended to the needs of feeding, bathing, and dressing a newborn. Steve would be home from work around 7:45 a.m., expecting breakfast before going to bed for the day. I had the duties of two households and no rest while still deeply grieving the loss of my mother. I had no support, was overwhelmed with responsibility, and had no time to heal.

Occasionally, Steve would feed her or change a diaper. He would hold her in his lap after I bathed and dressed her, smelling her sweet, fresh baby smells. Briefly, he would talk to her in baby talk and bounce her on his knee. Most of the time, he was sleeping during the day, working in the mines, gardening or hunting on weekends, or watching television. His intervals of playing with her were brief. I was never truly off duty because I didn't trust him to watch her alone and keep her safe. He was too inattentive and easily distracted with other things.

Grieving the loss of my mother while carrying the heavy load of added responsibilities eventually took its toll on me. The stress of being a new mother, hormonal changes, and sleep deprivation set me up for postpartum depression. Over the span of several weeks, depression progressed to what I learned almost two decades later (in nursing school) was postpartum psychosis. I was severely depressed, afraid to be alone, increasingly sleep-deprived, and exhausted.

I began experiencing the feeling of a constant formless presence I could not see, with me wherever I went. On several occasions, I saw a fleeting, featureless white figure, darting through the doorway of a room as I entered. It gave me the sensation of goosebumps and filled me with anxiety. This did not make me feel comforted or peaceful and was very disturbing. I did not feel that this was my mother's spirit watching over me. All I felt was fear. There was no one I felt safe enough to talk to about this, so I suffered in silence. I didn't see a doctor for fear he would think I was crazy and have my baby taken away. No new mother should go through such a horrible ordeal alone.

## THE SUBSTITUTE

Dad, now age fifty-eight, became very clingy after my mother died and didn't want me out of his sight. Throughout their forty years of marriage, my mother had managed the household and taken care of all their personal business. He was lonely and missed her companionship, yet declined invitations to go with Steve and I when we visited Steve's family on weekends. He was floundering to know what to do with himself in my mother's absence and I felt smothered trying to manage two households. I was already stretched to the breaking point as a young mother. Still, Dad resented me leaving him alone and accused me of abandoning him. I was doing my best but it was never good enough to escape the implied guilt.

Seeing how lonely Dad was, a friend of his from work stepped up to role of matchmaker and introduced him to a widow he knew. Simply being a widow and widower are not the sole qualifications for an ideal match. Edith and my dad couldn't have been more opposite. Dad was predictably comfortable, casual and simple but his hair always neat and with a clean-shaven face. Edith was style conscious, a very talented seamstress and well-dressed, even at home. Her vast wardrobe was in a wide array of colors with matching shoes and purses. Her hair was usually done at a salon and her nails polished to perfection.

One Saturday afternoon, quite out of the blue, my dad came home and unceremoniously announced they had gotten married. Having never known each other before my mother died, the two had met, courted, and married only four months after my mother's death. Steve and I had been visiting his dad that day. I hadn't been told of their plans and wasn't invited to their wedding. That evening, taking only his clothes, Dad left my childhood home empty and moved in with his new wife about eight miles away. I'm certain their union was the result of Dad's loneliness rather than genuine affection. Whenever I saw him, Dad never missed an opportunity to tell me I had forced him to get married by my unwillingness to be available for him whenever he needed me.

At first, Dad's remarriage meant a huge burden was lifted from me. I was no longer responsible for the role of managing two households. I no longer had to cook for and prepare lunches for two men with different preferences and eating schedules. As it turned out, Edith was a tidy housekeeper but her culinary skills left much to be desired.

Several months later, Edith and my dad decided to sell her property and move back to my dad's home and begin interior and exterior renovations. The changes were esthetically good but my childhood home was no longer the same. Few of my mother's things were offered to me but many were discarded without my knowledge.

Now as close neighbors, if Dad came to visit us too often or got too close to me, he would experience Edith's fury once we were gone. She was extremely hard of hearing, whereas I believe my dad might actually be able to hear a pin drop. Consequently, Dad always got the last word in any disagreement between them (and there were many), whether Edith heard it or not.

It was quickly obvious she felt threatened by my relationship with my dad and didn't want me around. I saw no warmth or love in this woman, not toward me, not toward Sara, and not even toward my dad. By all appearances, this had been a marriage of convenience. She was my mother's polar opposite and I could not bring myself to refer to her as my stepmother. Still, she relieved my burden of responsibility for managing two households.

Despite the relationship challenges, the break was good for my mental health. Six months later, with more sleep and rest, but still lacking grief counseling, I was able to recover from depression. Sawyer came along in 1972, just 18 months after Sara. This pregnancy was completely different. Sawyer wasn't as active, but I would later laugh as I realized he was just saving up energy for his tireless childhood shenanigans. Edith commented that he was "the ugliest baby she had ever seen." She said he looked like a little old man, but that must mean he was going to be really handsome when he was grown. Some people just have no clue how to give a genuine compliment but she was right about him becoming a handsome young man.

Having two children so close together meant I had two in diapers at the same time. Everywhere I went, I now had a baby to carry and a toddler to lead. Steve worked nights and slept during the day, so there was little opportunity except weekends to venture out.

The '70's were anything but carefree for me. I rarely ever tuned in the radio to listen to music. My days were filled with the cries of babies who needed my attention when they were hungry or had a boo-boo while playing. I had little time for myself. Occasionally, in the evenings when Steve was gone to work and my toddlers were tucked away in bed, I would sit alone and reminisce by going through boxes of family photos. Seeing photos of my mom always make me miss her even more. She left me at a critical time when I needed her to teach me how to be a mother.

As I sorted through those photos, memories flooded back while my mind was transported to different places and times. Mixed in with all those treasured family photographs was the two photos Jim had sent me so long ago. I picked up the photo of Jim standing in the doorway of his home, gazed at his image, and wondered how different my life would have been if we hadn't been separated by oceans and the span of thousands of miles. In the other photo, Jim was with a group of fellow Marine Cadets. I wondered whether he had made it to sea and whether he had achieved his dream of being the captain of his own ship. Either way, I was sure his life was far more glamorous than my own. The illusions of daydreaming with open eyes are soon shattered by reality. This was my reality and I had no idea what Jim's reality was like at the moment.

# Chapter Thirteen
## J.D.

Arriving back at Henlow, I reported to Radar Flight, where I was given a choice to either stay in Radar Flight or join a small section that would refurbish a mobile search radar. I looked around me and saw groups of men working around a large table containing a huge cable form. They were fitting connectors, plugs, and sockets to the appropriate ends of the cables. There were printed sheets in what appeared to be organised chaos. Some spoke amongst themselves very quietly, with the occasional muted laugh. Apart from this group, the large area was mainly empty except for a couple of mobile radar wagons and offices. Not one of them looked happy. Nobody was really smiling or regularly talking. I had been told it was like hell working there. They were checked in on their entry and their time was logged (especially if they were late). There was a fixed time for morning and afternoon breaks. Being away from there couldn't be any worse, so I opted to join the smaller section. I was shown where I was to go, and to whom I was to report.

After introducing myself, the flight sergeant said a few words, then picked up the phone and made a call. "I have a new man here for you. I'm sending him your way now."

I reported to a massive old hanger housing odd bits of radar gantry, beams, and trusses. A couple of men were cleaning, and others were painting. To one side, part of the hangar was partitioned off. Behind the partition, I could see a lot of really old historic aircraft.

"Are you the sprog?" I was asked.

"No!" The term "sprog" was military slang for a "new boy" or new recruit. I was certainly no sprog.

A door opened, and a J/T came out and greeted me.

"I'm Phil, and this motley crew are my lads." He was rewarded by a number of choice phrases. I introduced myself.

"Come with me," said Phil. Phil was short and quite rotund. He had thin slits for eyes. His dark hair was slicked back. He showed me into the office from where he had come. The office was small. Just enough space for a desk, a single chair, a couple of cupboards, and the inevitable clipboards hanging from the sides. A single, narrow metal-framed window allowed a bit of daylight.

"This is the office, where you will do any paperwork that needs to be done." He showed me some of the forms. "You are here to clean and paint the radar-supporting framework you can see outside. Plus, any other part that requires seeing to." I felt disappointed at this prospect.

Without any warning, Phil asked, "Do you play pontoon?"

"Yes," I replied.

He then told me how things really worked here. Two lads would be outside working while the rest of us played pontoon in the office. There would be no money on the table, just sheets of paper with such lists as "Al owes Bob," "Bob owes Al," "Bob owes Chris," etc. On payday, everybody settled up. It was a system that worked. If anybody came near, one of the working parties outside would enter the office to alert those playing. All cards and slips would hastily be put away, and paperwork would appear.

One day, we all got called in to see the flight sergeant. One of the forms (Form 720C) we used came with built-in carbon in the top sheet, and on the inside was the impression of "Bob owes Phil" followed by a list of numbers. Somebody had written out a tally sheet on top of one of those forms. The evidence was there for all to see. Sadly, Phil received a serious telling off and got transferred. We all got a good telling off as well. A new J/T was placed in charge of us.

After a month or so of tedious work, one of the LACs, a former roommate on GRIS, told me he was being detached to RAF Masirah in Oman for a couple of months. They needed more people, and he advised me to see the radar flight commander about volunteering. I made a mental note to do this first thing the next morning.

Early the next morning, I went to see the flight commander, explaining the reason for my visit. He phoned GRIS, spoke a few words, then nodded a number of times. At the end of the conversation, he said, "I'm sorry, all the places have now been filled. However, as soon as any other positions come up, they will let me know, and I'll let you know." I thanked him, saluted, and returned to the hangar to continue cleaning and painting. The days dragged by endlessly with the same boring routine.

Another couple of months of painting and cleaning had passed when I got an urgent message to report to the radar flight commander. One never gets summoned urgently to see the flight commander for a petty reason. Upon arrival, I knocked on his door, and his voice called out, "Come in." I entered and saluted.

"You wanted to see me, sir."

"Ah yes, Aubrey," he began. "Regarding your request for temporary transfer to GRIS a couple of months back. Are you still interested?"

"Yes, sir. Of course."

"Good. I have had a call from GRIS about a job going out to RAF Gatow, Berlin, in a couple of weeks. Unfortunately, it's only 'humping and dumping,' and it's for six weeks. Are you interested?"

"Of course, I'm interested, sir! I'd rather be humping and dumping in Berlin than painting and cleaning here." He smiled, then told me to return to my section while he made appropriate arrangements.

A few days later, those of us going on the detachment were briefed about the job, the expectations, and the restrictions we would be under. The job, we were informed, was classified as was the building in which we would be working. We were not to mention any part of this to anybody. It all sounded intriguing. Before we left, we were required to sign a copy of the Official Secrets Act, even though we had signed it when we joined up. Transport would take us to RAF Cottesmore, where we would be catching a flight to RAF Gatow. We would be leaving the following Monday.

I went home for the weekend to tell Mum and Dad where I was going. Dad wasn't happy about my detachment in Germany. He had had a brother killed in the war and cautioned me to be careful who I trusted.

Monday arrived, and the bus arrived to take us to RAF Cottesmore. The next day, we boarded an Argosy transport aircraft. This was my first time in an RAF aircraft. It surprised me that the seats were facing the rear. As I made myself comfortable, I was both excited and a little nervous. It was my very first flight, and I had no idea what to expect. As the aircraft moved off, I looked out of the window. The aircraft vibrated, and we finally turned onto the runway. The engines revved up for a few seconds, then were powered down again. This cycling continued three or four times more before the engines revved up more than previously as our speed increased. The aircraft seemed to bounce along the runway until the bouncing stopped, and I saw the ground slowly drop away. I knew then we had taken off and were on our way to RAF Gatow. I settled down to read my book, moving the bookmark that Beth had sent to me all those years ago. The noise from the engines stopped my concentration, so I placed the bookmark between the pages and put my book away as I continued looking at the ground passing below.

After we landed, the aircraft stopped outside a hangar, and a squadron leader entered. He firmly instructed us concerning our behaviour upon exiting the aircraft. We were to look straight ahead and not to talk and not to look around, but walk briskly towards the hangar where we would be directed where to go.

It all seemed very James Bondish, but we did as instructed and were ushered into a room. Again, the squadron leader entered, explaining to us in no uncertain terms what we should and should not do. There were areas in Berlin where we were not permitted to go under any circumstances. Being apprehended there or reported as being in any of those areas would lead to serious consequences.

The initial job description was correct. The first weeks were spent moving cabinets and relocating them. The highlight of the mornings was when the food van from a Methodist church arrived, and we indulged ourselves in ham rolls made with fresh-baked bread rolls and home-cooked ham, all washed down with a litre of farm-fresh full-cream milk.

After a few weeks, the site was ready for the main installation. Two members of our party were told they were no longer needed, but I and an SAC, Grant Tunstall, would be remaining. When they had left, the second group of half a dozen arrived to carry out the main installation. They were all ex-apprentice J/Ts. The final party consisted of fourteen altogether.

Grant, I soon discovered, was a good artist. He had created a number of pictures and drawings during the evening and on weekends. At school, I had really enjoyed the art classes, but was never allowed or encouraged to focus on creating art. Once again inspired, I, too, began to focus on drawing in my spare time with Grant's help and tuition. Soon the pair of us had quite a gallery of art taped on the wall. The pictures ranged from cartoon characters to abstracts and portraits. He taught me a great deal, rekindling my love for drawing and painting.

At the conclusion of the installation, I had been there for four and a half months on an initial six-week detachment. During this period, I celebrated my twenty-first birthday. Unfortunately, there isn't much I can remember about it! I do recall a large birthday cake being brought in, bottles of German sparkling wine (Sekt), and the presentation of a wristwatch, all paid for by the lads in the installation party. I was very grateful for their generosity. I wouldn't say it was a raucous party. From what I was told, it was quite boisterous, but well-behaved.

Just before Christmas, our part of the installation was complete, and it was time for us to return to Henlow. I was saddened to be leaving.

By the time I returned to RAF Henlow, it was time for Christmas leave, so I felt there was no need for me to return to my old section, a decision the flight sergeant did not like. To be honest, I didn't particularly care if he liked it or not. We had worked hard when we were there and deserved our TOIL (time off in lieu—time off given for extended work hours or reward for good work) and annual leave.

Once the holidays ended, I reported to my section, where I was confronted with yet more cleaning and painting. I had hoped it would all be completed by the time I returned. What a comedown from what I had been doing!

A few more weeks passed. I had had enough of this tedious job. So, after a morning break, I went to ask the flight sergeant for a word. I told him about my experience at college and my qualifications, and that I was not being used to the best of my ability, just cleaning and painting. He reminded me that I was a leading aircraftman and that was the scope of the work for that rank in his section. I began to argue, believing I was making a good case, especially when I began to talk technically at a deep level. Still, he sent me back with the others.

A few days later, I got called in to see the flight sergeant. "Come with me." He showed me into a room where a corporal was working. "This is Corporal Harris, and this is his lab. You will be working with him from now on. He'll show you what to do." With that, he walked out.

Although I had seen him before, he always sat on the NCO's side of the break room, so we rarely had any interaction. We introduced ourselves informally. I was told that here they tested thyratron valves (a gas-filled electronic valve used as a high energy switch) and ascertained their condition. They also refurbished the pulse tanks (high energy transformers). This was now my job. I quickly learnt it and was able to carry out the task unsupervised.

By early May 1972, I had attained proficiency at my job, and once again, I was summoned to see the flight commander. There was a request for further GRIS assistance on a job going out to Malta in a couple of weeks. The duration of the assignment would be for around six months. He must have seen the excitement in my eyes as he pointed out that the assignment period would overlap my promotion exams, due in July. Without hesitation, I agreed to be included, fully aware my promotion would be delayed. I was instructed to return to my section and the arrangements would be made.

A week later, I reported to GRIS for the job briefing. There were two other LACs there from EES Radar Flight. We would be assisting a team from RAF North Luffenham to install various systems at a place called Madliena. It was a radar site built in an old Victorian fort by the coast.

Upon arrival, we were then allocated accommodation, and we unpacked. It was a basic room with a bare tiled floor, four beds, a metal locker for each bed, and a ceiling fan. Soon, two SACs, both permanent staff, entered the room. We introduced ourselves. However, one was not very sociable and left me alone. The other became more sociable as we found we had similar tastes in music.

The next day, our party headed for the sergeant's mess, as previously instructed to wait for our transport to Madliena. Waiting with us were three other SNCOs and a corporal. "Madliena?" I asked. One of the SNCOs nodded. "You must be the Henlow boys." We nodded. A chief technician then came over and made the introductions. Soon, we were driving through Sliema and up a hill to the site. It looked old. We could see a couple of old, motionless radars. "Is this what we're fitting out?" I asked. A couple of the NCOs laughed. "Just wait until you see them!" That sounded ominous. The sight that confronted us was one of destruction.

"Don't worry about this. You'll be wiring up the control room."

As it turned out, none of the equipment had arrived, so after our look around, we were assigned to do the dishes after the Luffenham guys had cooked lunch.

A few days later, I was asked by another Henlow lad (who was part of another installation team on the airfield) if I fancied a trip to Pretty Bay. I had never heard of it, so I agreed. After swimming and sunbathing, we decided to go for a meal and a beer in a local bar/restaurant. It was a place the others were familiar with. They joked with the girl behind the bar (her family were owners), and a couple of waitresses. I found one of those waitresses very attractive. We talked a bit, then left and headed back to camp.

That restaurant soon became our main destination. I became very fond of the place, and particularly that waitress who I found out was American. I really wanted to ask her out but was afraid of rejection, especially in front of the others. Somehow, I just couldn't get away from the group to ask her. I had not had much luck dating girls in the past, just the odd night or two. Also, one of the lads I was with tended to be sarcastic. Had I asked the girl whilst he was around and had she turned me down, he would have had no problem humiliating me, or anybody else had it been one of them. Yet he never tried to ask himself.

## THROWING DOWN THE GAUNTLET

One evening, while still at Malta, a small group of us were having a quiet drink in the club when a dozen or so raucous guys came in. They immediately began singing bawdy rugby songs, one after another without a break. It destroyed the quiet of the evening. We discovered from the barman they were from the Royal Navy Fleet Air Arm. Apparently, they were in transit to join their ship. I had consumed a few beers at this point, so after about an hour, I decided somebody needed to throw down the gauntlet.

I stood up, put one hand on my waist, limp-wristed the other, and began singing,

"All the nice boys love a sailor. All the nice boys love a tar!"

Immediately, they all rose as one entity and headed my way. My so-called comrades in arms had suddenly abandoned me. So much for esprit de corps. I was cornered, surrounded by a bunch of matelots.

"You're in the Air Force, right? If you can't sing us a song we've never heard before, we'll see how well you can fly through that window!" We were on the second floor, and from their muscular appearance, just one of them could have picked me up and pitched me through the window with little effort.

I thought for a moment, then remembered a song we sang at college:

Puff the magic dragon didn't have a mate.
He frolicked in the autumn mist, accustomed to his fate.
Then at last he found one, a cracking bit of stuff.
But didn't know what to do, that's why they called him *Puff!*

They just burst out laughing, patted me on the back, dragged me to their table, and bought my drinks for the rest of the evening. I never saw them again after that.

83

Another day, we were in Pretty Bay, and I saw Francesca, the waitress I liked, cradling a baby. "Oh no!" I thought. This was my clue that she was married, and it put an immediate end to any thoughts of asking her out. I just said, "Hello," then sat down with the rest. I abandoned any thought of a relationship with her other than friendship after that.

A couple of weeks later, when we arrived on site, we were called together and told, "The equipment we were supposed to be receiving is not coming. It is staying en route to the UK, where it will be fully refurbished and modified. This will take a number of months. Consequently, you guys from Henlow are now RTU'd" (returned to unit). We were thanked for our help, and a couple of days later, we were headed back to RAF Henlow. Before that, I headed out to Pretty Bay to say goodbye to everybody in the restaurant/bar. I signed the obligatory visitor book. Francesca told me she would be returning to America in a few weeks too. For some reason, she asked me for my address. I gave it to her. A good, long job had only lasted a month, but at least it was a month away from Henlow.

On my return to the section at Henlow, they wanted to know why I had come back so early. However, they were pleased to see me, especially as I would now be available to take my promotion exams. Around a week or so later, I received a letter with a Maltese stamp and postmark. It was from Francesca. I opened it and avidly read it. She had enclosed a photo of herself. This surprised me. She wrote that the other girls were going out with some of the boys from the other party, and she had nobody. This really surprised me, as I thought she was married. I wrote back in the hope she would receive it and reply.

Some weeks passed, and I received a familiar blue airmail envelope from the US. This time, it was from Francesca. She told me she had returned with her parents to New York. She also clarified the situation with the baby. It was her cousin's baby. I could have kicked myself for being such a fool by not asking her out when I had the chance. We continued writing to each other, and we became good pen pals. It was like writing to Beth again. At least this time, I could put a face behind the letters. We wrote about general topics: our jobs, what we were doing, the weather, and such. Just a general talk in letter form.

The rest of my time in the section passed quickly. I took my promotion exams, passed, and was anxious to return to GRIS. The jobs on GRIS at that time were scarce, and only small crews were needed. I spent a lot of time at

Henlow, doing little more than menial work. I was assigned to a couple of short jobs installing additions to radio beacons in Scotland.

Finally, I received notification that my Fitters' course would begin in February 1973. With Christmas and the New Year pending, there were even fewer jobs going out. I tried to get one, but was told that because of the length of jobs coming in, they would interfere with my Fitters' course. I was effectively "grounded." After New Year's, I complained bitterly about being stuck in camp week after week. They looked at the board and asked whether I would object to helping out on a transmitter communications installation for a couple of weeks. Soon, I was away again, just to fill in time before beginning my Fitters' course.

When it came time to depart for Henlow for the course, I had to go round with my blue card to get myself cleared from all the various sections. As I arrived at the GRIS Section, I looked at the jobs board. It was nearly full with destinations such as Cyprus, Malta, Germany, and Hong Kong. I looked down at my blue card, then up at the board repeatedly. A voice behind me whispered, "It's not worth it. You'll never know when you'll get another chance at a Fitters' course." It was one of the old hands, a corporal.

The next day, I got a lift to RAF Locking. This time, I would be there for a very long twelve months to complete the Fitters' course I had so long anticipated.

# Chapter Fourteen
## B.B.

## MOTHERHOOD 101

From April 1971 through 1975, I was totally consumed with taking care of my two children. I traveled only with Steve's help, when we were going grocery shopping or visiting Steve's family. At home, my days were filled with the never-ending monotony of diapers, bottles, cooking, cleaning, and watchful supervision to keep both children safe. My friends were those whose children were close to the same ages as my own. Playdates were a chance to get together for adult companionship.

Since I had no mother, aunts or sisters, I often sought the motherly advice of a lady named Maria. She had lived next door to my parents throughout my childhood. She was only one year younger than my mother, with two daughters of her own as well as a host of grandchildren. She was my trusted source for information on childcare and childhood illnesses. She was my resource for cooking as well as food preservation from our backyard harvest. I doubt she ever knew just how much I loved and relied on her. I hoped her own daughters didn't resent the time she took to teach me. She was like a surrogate mother. Her daughters, near my own age, felt like my sisters.

I had to learn how to be a mother in the months and years before my babies were old enough to talk to me and tell me what was wrong or what they needed. Maria was the one who taught me that a baby who is pulling on its ears has an earache. She taught me the benefits of vaporizers when treating respiratory problems in children. Carrying a baby to full term and giving birth is the simplest part of becoming a mother. Protecting, caring for, teaching them, and providing for their ever-changing needs were the skills I had to learn from experience.

In the midst of my homemaking and mothering, Steve's show of affection toward me was usually short-lived and for a self-gratifying purpose.

I was just there, fulfilling a role rather than being a loved companion. Frankly, the ability to father children seemed more important to him than actively parenting our children. The contrast between the selfless love and fierce protectiveness my dad demonstrated and the coldness Steve showed was striking. His words "I love you" had a hollow ring. They were simply words without demonstrated action.

# Chapter Fifteen
## J.D.

## FITTER'S COURSE 1973 TO 1974

The Fitters' course was much the same as the Mechanics course, except in much more detail. The course was almost as intense as my Radio Officers course. There were lighter times, such as the day that Kevin Adams got his divorce through. It was payday and "Pig's Night." This happened once a month where we would just drink and have fun, playing silly, stupid games. That night was absolutely crazy. The next morning, we had only been in class for about an hour when the disciplinary sergeant came into our classroom and gave us all a real telling-off and lectured us on how to behave. We were ordered back into the club bar to clean up the mess we made the evening before. It was so bad, the club's cleaners refused to do it.

As we walked into the bar area, our feet made a sticky sound. There were beer stains on the ceiling. How they got there, I don't know. It might have been due to Slattery shaking his bottles of beer to create a fountain. I cannot recall the height of the beer getting as high as the ceiling though. Outside, there were plates "Woody" had thrown out behind him through a partially open window with the cry, "Look out! UFOs! Wheeeeee!" How those plates didn't smash or break the window is a miracle. There was a pile of chairs stacked up in one corner where we had "enthroned" Kevin on his freedom. How he didn't fall off or the stack didn't collapse is yet another miracle. We spent the next few hours cleaning up our mess. It was a fun night that was well worth the telling-off and this cleaning detail. The manageress wasn't happy with us, but as she turned away to head back to her office, she shook her head, and I am sure I saw her smile.

One of my friends, Matt, and I had managed to find a couple of girls at a dance and had been dating them for a while. Matt saw an advertisement for a day trip to Ilfracombe, North Devon, on a vintage excursion ship, the

MV *Balmoral*. He asked if I would be interested in going with our girlfriends. I jumped at the chance.

As we embarked, I began explaining the parts of the ship with details about the lights, flags, etc. They were very impressed. The sail to me was perfect. Once we had returned, Matt turned to me and said, "You know, Jim, as soon as we got on the boat, I noticed a big change in you. As though you were another person." I remember thinking, "What you saw, Matt, was the *real* Jim Aubrey."

I was still writing to Francesca, and like with Beth, I looked forward to seeing the familiar blue envelope. This time, most of the envelopes had little stickers on them. They were flowers, cartoon characters, or anything else she could find.

Later, she wrote, saying she would be visiting relatives in London. I replied, asking if we could meet. She agreed.

I spent the weekend in Paddington, London. I wasn't familiar with this part of London. I needed to find a hotel. I had been told there were plenty in the area, and there was no need to book. I walked around and finally found one. It was a really low-end place. I didn't mind as I had anticipated this weekend would be very expensive.

Francesca had given me the address of where she was staying. We met and talked a lot. I then took Francesca into the centre of London and showed her some sights. This included a river trip from Westminster to the Tower of London. She wanted to see the Crown Jewels; I had never seen them either. As we walked around, she was asking questions I didn't know the answers to, so I did my usual by giving silly answers. This annoyed her, and I felt that the prospect of any future relationship was receding rapidly. On the return boat, I asked her about seeing her again the next day. She told me that she was spending the day with family, so she couldn't. Francesca must have seen the disappointment on my face.

"I'm meeting a friend tonight, but you can meet us at a local pub, the Red Lion." We arranged a time.

We met with her friend, and we talked a bit, but she seemed to be talking more and more with her friend. Later, Francesca and her friend told me they were going to a nightclub and asked if I would like to join them. I would have liked that, but my money was really getting low. The amount I had already paid had broken me financially for the rest of the month. I just couldn't afford it. I made some excuse not to go. Before they left, I leant over to thank Francesca for being with me and attempted a kiss. She turned away and said, "I don't want you to kiss me." I was downhearted. They walked away, and I went to the bar and ordered another beer.

Francesca and I kept writing, and she wrote to say how much she enjoyed being with me. This really surprised me, considering the way she had been with me.

The days of the course dragged on, and the theory and electronics content got deeper. I was again dreaming of being away on installation jobs. I felt myself sinking deeper into a state of depression. At one time, I became very isolated; I ignored any social interaction with my course mates. I became a recluse. Even in the bar, I would sit by myself and decline offers to join the company of others. Thoughts of what I was doing here kept running through my mind. I should have been at sea, not here. I slowly sank further. In an attempt to focus on positive thoughts, I kept writing on some of the pages of my text the amount of pay increase I would get once I got through and passed the course.

I wrote to my brother and sister-in-law, Natalie, explaining how I was feeling. Just writing about my feelings seemed to help a bit. Natalie replied and encouraged me to get through this phase by reiterating I only had a few months left and to consider my future. Eventually, I snapped out of it and returned to normal. It was as though a light had been switched on. I began to see a bit more clearly and returned to my old social self. I still hated being there and longed for the course to be over so that I could get back on GRIS again.

At the request of another friend on the course, I joined the Station Rugby Team, playing as a second row forward. I really enjoyed playing and the social activities afterwards. The team captain, Robbie, was a flight lieutenant who had the smelliest socks that it had ever been my misfortune to smell. After a game, he would force the person who he considered to have had the worst game, or to have made the stupidest mistake, to hold his socks on their lap.

On returning back to Locking after an away game at Bristol, we got held up by a swing bridge that had the road closed to allow a ship to pass by. Robbie got up, took his socks, and told the driver to open the door. He then got out and ran alongside each of the cars in front of us, holding up his socks. Apparently, he was asking the people if they wanted to smell his socks. When the bridge reopened and the traffic began slowly moving, he ran back towards our coach. We told the driver to keep the door closed as Robbie was hanging onto the door with one hand and his socks in the other. "Open the door, you bastards!" was all we could hear. When we let him in, he found out which of us told the driver to keep the doors closed, and *he* was one "in charge of the socks" for the rest of the journey back.

The time eventually came for us to put in for postings. We could list three stations where we would like to be posted. There was also a space for a place we didn't want to be posted. My first choice was Henlow; the others also involved some form of travel. Most on the course put Henlow as the posting they did *not* want. When I told them I had put in for Henlow, they laughed, but I knew what I wanted.

The day came for the postings to be announced. Henlow was announced frequently, usually to a forlorn cry of "Nooooo!" When my name was called for Henlow, I was extremely happy, and I was preparing myself for another tour on GRIS.

## GRIS (SECOND TOUR), 1974 TO 1977

Soon, I was heading back to RAF Henlow with shiny junior technician rank badges on my sleeves. It had been a long, hard year, and I was glad it was finally over.

Eventually, we entered Engineering Headquarters only to be confronted by the bane of just about everybody in EES, Jed Middleton. Middleton hadn't changed. His hair was very short cropped around the side of his balding head and above his skeletal face. His uniform trousers and shirt sleeves were pressed into a sharp line, and his shoes gleamed in the light. He was immaculate as always. He was well-known as a strict disciplinarian. I walked in with the rest of the group. When he saw me, he pointed toward me.

"Well, well, well. Who do we have here?"

I told him who I was, and he replied, "Oh, I know who you are, Aubrey! You've come back here in the same state that you left. Unpressed trousers, dirty shoes, and in dire need of a haircut!"

I replied, "At least I'm consistent, Chief."

Middleton gently shuffled his arm.

The round badge of a four-propeller blade above the three stripes had been replaced by a brass crown. Middleton had been promoted from chief technician to flight sergeant.

"Sorry, Flight! Congratulations on your promotion." I looked at him and smiled.

"Thank you," he responded impassively as he looked at me. "I suppose you'll be wanting to get back with that bunch of scruffy undisciplined rabble in GRIS, will you?"

"Of course, Flight. You've noticed I'm dressed for the part," I said, noticing a slight change in his mood.

Middleton laughed. A very rare sight. "You certainly are!" With that, he made a phone call. "Anybody else want to go into GRIS?" Two others raised their hands. Like me, they were both single. The others were married or about to get married, so they opted not to be on GRIS.

Walking through the entrance of GRIS was like arriving home. Nothing had changed since I left a year ago. The highly polished brown lino corridor, affectionately known as "The Golden Mile." The PWR and Detachments boards, offices to the left, the tool store on the right with more offices on either side. I walked along the corridor to the main office and greeted everyone there. After dinner, I took myself to the Bonanza Club for a beer. I was looking forward to seeing old friends, but there was nobody there I recognized. They were all strangers. I stepped towards the bar and got served by somebody I didn't know. I sat, drinking my beer.

I looked up and saw a familiar figure. Gwen, who worked in the NAAFI, walked in from a door to the right of the bar. "Jimmy! How are you? What job have you come from?" We were old friends, and she was genuinely pleased to see me. I was glad to see a familiar face. Gwen and I talked for a long time. I asked where everybody was. Quite a few had been posted, and the place just wasn't the same. She mentioned a number of familiar names who were out on jobs. It was usual to be gone one day and not see a familiar face again for a number of months due to the nature of the work.

The following Friday morning, Steve Tennant, Bob Sanders (we were on the same course and arrived together), and I were told we were going to RAF Brawdy in South Wales on Monday to assist with the installation of the communications equipment in the control tower.

After only ten days at RAF Brawdy, Steve, Bob, and I were heading up the stairs of the control tower when Steve and I were told to pack our bags. We had been reassigned to RAF Machrihanish in Scotland.

As we walked away from the tower, I turned to Ted and said, "Shit! We've got one helluva journey ahead of us now!"

It was about a twelve-hour journey by rail just to reach Glasgow, including a four-hour wait in Crewe. The next morning, we caught the early bus to Campbeltown, an approximately four-hour journey. It was bitterly cold when we arrived in Campbeltown. We found a phone box and called the station. We were told there wasn't any transport available. I informed him that we were from the Henlow fitting party, and we had been traveling since yesterday morning from RAF Brawdy. We were tired, hungry, and freezing our nuts off, I said, "so get some transport here sharpish, or there will be a strongly worded signal addressed to Strike Command!" He told us to hold the line for a minute.

A few minutes later, he returned. "There'll be a vehicle to pick you up in half an hour." He told us where the transport would be, and we made our way there.

It was a freezing and draughty drive in a Land Rover with a canvas cover. We asked to be dropped off at the mess as it had gone past dinner time by now. The driver told us the mess was closed. We didn't care; they surely had something we could eat, even if it was only bread and jam. We entered the mess and were looking at the opening times when a short, stocky cook came over to us. He was wearing cook's whites and had a thick leather belt around his waist full of knives, butcher's steel and a meat cleaver. He looked frightening.

"Wha' ye lads after?" he asked gruffly.

I told him, "We've just arrived; we're cold, hungry, and tired. We were hoping to see when the mess was open next."

"We'er ya' come frae?"

"Yesterday from South Wales, overnight in Glasgow, and bus to Campbeltown."

"Hmm…Follah me." He made a quick motion with his head towards the dining room, indicating the direction we were to go. We followed him into the kitchen, where we had some bread and cheese. It wasn't much, but it was something.

When we went to get a room and bedding, we were told there wasn't any actual accommodation available. We were placed in temporary transit accommodation. Due to the extremely cold condition, we were allocated a second thick white blanket.

This was February 1974, and the country was on a three-day week. During this time, companies had restrictions on electricity use because of a miners' strike. Unfortunately, this included our RAF station. At 5 p.m., all heating and hot water was switched off on the working part of the station. The transit accommodation just happened to be linked to the working area. As soon as it became too cold, we headed for the shower and ran hot water to get warm, which was fine until the hot water ran out. Then we had to get dried, get dressed, and go where it was warm, the NAAFI.

The next morning, we reported to the fitting party in the control tower. Although we were to help install the Precision Approach Radar, I ended up helping another who introduced himself as Mark Cassidy wire up the base of the Airfield Control Radar Consoles. This was simple enough, but time consuming and repetitive.

After about three days, we were transferred out of the transit accommodation into the standard accommodation, located on the domestic site. It had permanent heating, hot water, and single rooms. I had been there for about three weeks when I got a call to get cleared and make my way to RAF Honington in Suffolk, where they needed somebody with PAR experience. The fitting party was installing a brand-new air traffic control tower including displays, recorders, communication equipment, and ancillary equipment as well as an updated PAR. This was a huge task.

## THE CHALLENGE

After around four months, the job was coming towards the end, so we had an impromptu but lively party. The party took a strange curve after a fair number of pints were consumed. Somebody suggested that there should be a race between the radar side and the comms side. We were up to the challenge.

I was chosen to be the radar runner, and one for the comms side was chosen. The race route was quickly mapped out: to run from the NAAFI to the guardroom, wave at the orderly sergeant, and to race back again. The first one back was naturally the winner. Simple as it sounded, there was a twist. Keeping with the craze of the time, we would be "streaking"! Due to the graveled car park being part of the course, we would be allowed to keep our shoes on. Off we went! We started running, but soon decided running was stupid if we didn't really need to run, so we walked most of the way. As we approached the guard room, we looked at each other and yelled, "Go!" Immediately, both of us took off running as fast as we could up to the window of the guardroom, where the orderly sergeant was reading his newspaper. We jumped up and down a few times and waved our arms. We certainly did get his attention! At that point, we turned and began running as fast as we could back toward the NAAFI.

We were confronted by the whole fitting party cheering and urging us on. Unfortunately, the comms guy was a faster runner than me, so he got to the group first. His reward was to be drenched in beer. I, on the other hand, skirted around the cheering mob and entered the bar area. No beer was thrown over me, but I was the first one back in the bar, so I quickly went into the toilets and got dressed. The comms lad came drenched with beer, and the NAAFI manager handed him a towel to dry himself as he headed toward the toilets. By the time the rest settled down, the orderly sergeant arrived, demanding to know who the streakers were. Everybody denied all knowledge.

"I know it was your lot!" he called out. "Now, who were they?"

Frank, our SNCO in charge of the installation, stood up, emphatically denying that it was any of us. We were just having a quiet drink after a hard day's work. The NAAFI manager confirmed that the streakers were not part of the group there. With that, the orderly sergeant stormed out. Technically, neither Frank nor the NAAFI manager actually lied. The streakers were not in the group that was sitting there. We were still in the toilets getting dressed and keeping out of the way until the fuss died down.

When we reentered the bar, there was great cheering. The result was decided to be an official draw, as both sides claimed victory. I claimed victory because I was first back in the bar, and the comms lad claimed victory because he was the first to make it back to the party. He and I didn't have to buy another beer the rest of the night.

During my time at RAF Honington, I received a wedding invitation from a friend who was in my Fitters' course. He was marrying the girl he met whilst stationed at RAF Hartland Point, in North Devon.

I met up with other wedding guests at a hotel near Hartland Village. We were all congregating in the bar when somebody in a full cowboy outfit walked in. He was wearing a Stetson, check shirt, bandana, waistcoat, cowboy boots complete with spurs, and a gun belt with a pair of "six guns" around his waist. The groom laughed, then introduced "Kipper" Clark to us. Apart from being a Western buff, I discovered that Kipper was currently detached to a civilian research establishment, working out of uniform with civilians. It sounded idyllic. I pressed him for more information and then decided that I would love to go there. Unfortunately, the job at RAF Honington was still in full flow, so the civilian place had to be put on the back burner until the current job was finished. I knew I wouldn't get transferred whilst I was there.

The Honington job was finally finished. I was ready to leave. I paused to take one last look in the equipment room. All the equipment was humming away. All the cabling was secured neatly in looms around the wall behind the bulk of the equipment. It was a great feeling of job satisfaction, knowing I helped complete this huge project. Initially, we started off in a completely empty room and left it a few months later fully operational. This is why I loved my time on GRIS.

On my return to Henlow and GRIS, I went to the office to say I would like to volunteer for RRE Malvern when a position came up. He informed me that Steve Tennant had already applied, and there weren't any current vacancies.

I made the journey home by train to spend Christmas and New Year's with my parents. It wasn't much different from any other festive occasion at home. Our Christmases were very quiet. We watched the programmes on TV, Mum cooked, and we had a few drinks at home. Nothing remarkable, just routine.

Back at Henlow, there were a couple of months without any jobs going out. My name and a couple of others were called to remain behind after one eight o'clock parade. I hadn't seen my name on the jobs board, so I reckoned we'd been lumbered with a "gash" job, something I wasn't too keen on. We were to go to another building and to report to a corporal; we would be sorting radio crystals.

After a week or so of being there, I was summoned to report to GRIS HQ. I was confronted by comments such as, "You jammy bastard!", "Lucky you!", "What did you do to get this?"

I had no idea what they were talking about. They pointed to the jobs board. I noticed I was being detached to the Royal Radar Establishment (RRE) Malvern. The job would be for six months.

The following Monday, I was all packed and heading in a Land Rover that would drop me off at Malvern.

On arrival at my lodgings at Malvern, the driver helped me with my luggage. After checking in, I was shown my room. This was down some flights of stairs into what must have been the basement of the building, then along a couple of dimly lit corridors. As I was shown into my room, I noticed it was shared with two others.

"Your companions are also from RAF Henlow, so you might know them." The room, apart from the three beds, had the old-style wooden lockers, a bureau with a wooden chair for each bed, and a wash basin. It was very basic. Plain brown lino flooring with bedside mats. The windows were very large and gave plenty of light despite the room being down in the basement.

I dropped off my bags and asked if there was a telephone. I was shown the location on the ground floor. I called the number I was given. Soon, a car arrived to take me to the Establishment.

On arrival, I was met by Steve Tennant.

"Hi Jim, welcome to RRE Malvern," Steve said. He was smartly dressed in civvies: light brown trousers and a striped shirt with a plain dark brown tie. His hair was longer than regulation. He beamed. "Good to see you here."

With that, he took me to the lab where I would be working. It was a small room with a long bench extending nearly the length of the room. The bench was covered with various circuit boards and components. There was a shelf above the bench. Nailed to the front of it were a few hand-drawn circuit diagrams and reels of wire. I noticed Mark Cassidy sitting at the bench. He was working away but stood and welcomed me. "Good to see you again, Jim." He looked at his watch. "Just in time for tea break. Come on, I'll introduce you to everybody down there." I was led along a corridor, down some stairs, and into what looked like a workshop. There were a number of men sitting around talking and drinking tea. Introductions were made and a spare cup found for me.

After tea, Mark took me around the remainder of the site, including the various stores, library, and stationary office. He told me as long as I had a valid list of items, I could get anything I needed. It would all be marked down to the project. When we got back to the lab, Steve took out a form and started to fill in various mechanical tools.

"You're going to need a toolbox and tools of your own. Here's what we'll get for you." Mark and Steve began making the list. "When we get to the tool store, we'll wander around and see if we can come up with anything else whilst we're there. We need to be fully kitted when we go out on trials."

"Where's the tool store?" I asked.

"It's over on the North Site. I'll book a car for us in the morning." Mark then picked up the phone, dialed a number, and booked a car to take us to another section of the Establishment.

I could not understand how Mark could just call for a car and it would arrive without any problems. When I asked, he told me the Establishment had its own carpool ready to drive anybody who needed a ride, provided it was for official use.

"Come on, Jim. We're going to see the Mechies."

The Mechanical Engineering block was a short drive away, but on a different part of the site.

"In summer, this is a decent walk, but not at this time of the year," Mark explained.

Mark introduced me to the mechanical engineers we would normally be working with.

Our role was to build the circuits for the scientific officers (design engineers) and get them working as required. We would then redraw the pencil sketches into something the mechanical engineers could use to create the schematics for tests and trials equipment. The mechanical engineers would then send the schematics to produce the printed circuit boards, if any were required. Most of the time, only the rough boards would suffice.

After work, we made our way back to the lodgings. We walked into the dining room and round to the servery. I chose something and went back to the table where Mark and Steve were sitting. I looked around at all the others. "They're all civvies here, apprentices mainly. They all worked in or retired from RRE." I had noticed a few older men and women there. Apparently, this was their only home.

That evening, we lay on our beds and talked. Mark went into more detail about the job, our role, and the town itself.

"There's not much to do here. There's a few pubs and a theatre. Worcester has some shops and some good pubs."

"Not many 'birds' either," interjected Steve. "You'll see them in the day, but they must get locked up at night."

Soon after, Mark said, "Come on. Time to go to the pub."

When we arrived, it was as Steve mentioned earlier. There were no young single girls my age, just the occasional older women who seemed to be out with their husbands.

# Chapter Sixteen
## J.D.

*THE PICK UP*

L ater the next morning, Mark escorted me to meet the senior RAF officer, a wing commander. By the time we got back, it was getting on towards lunchtime. Tom, the officer in charge of us, was in the lab waiting for us, tapping his watch. Both Mark and Steve knew what that signal meant. We drove to the local pub. Being the new boy, it was my turn to buy the first round.

During our meal, Tom kept asking me questions about myself. One of the first things that struck me was how pleasant and civil everybody had been towards me. Even the officer who had been put in charge of us was pleasant. I felt comfortable and at ease, as though this was the place I truly belonged.

Some months later, I felt I had reached the point in my life when I wanted to settle down. The other lads were away for the weekend, and I was in my room reading a magazine when I ran across an ad from a computer dating service. For a twenty-pound fee, they would find prospective matches based on my answers to a questionnaire. I felt I had nothing to lose, and at least it would pass the time. A few days later, a letter arrived with a list of six potential matches.

I wrote to all six. I received an actual written response from only one, Mary. She didn't include a photo, but she sounded reasonably nice, and we exchanged letters at first.

One Saturday night, Mark and Steve were away again for the weekend, and I decided to go to a different pub, The Unicorn, for a drink. I felt like having a quiet night and was happy sitting at the bar, alone in my thoughts, when a soft voice beside me said, "Hello."

I turned and replied, "Hello."

"My name's Anne." She was short and wore dark-framed glasses with shoulder-length, mousy hair. She wore a pale blue top and jeans. She looked pleasant enough and had a nice smile.

"I'm Jim." With that, she extended her hand. We talked for a few minutes, and I offered to buy her a drink. It was a lager and black currant. I cringed inwardly; I could not even contemplate such a mixture. She accepted, and we talked a bit more.

"I noticed you sitting here on your own and thought you might like some company. I'm with some friends. Would you like to come and join us?" she continued.

I turned around and saw a group sitting by a window, all looking in my direction.

"Why not?"

I bought another beer. The group made room for me and introduced themselves. One girl there had the most beautiful eyes and mousy-coloured hair that fell just past her shoulders. She had a radiant face that beamed when she looked in my direction. Her eyes were blue. She was slightly bigger in build than Anne, but she seemed to carry it well. She really looked lovely. She was Anne's sister, Christine. As it turned out, both girls and their friends were employees of the same hotel. We all got talking and laughing. At length, the pub closed, and we all started to go our separate ways. Anne was the exception. She held onto me, saying, "No, you don't!" Then she leaned over and gave me a long, passionate kiss. She was a smoker, and I remember that her kiss tasted of stale tobacco. She and I left together and headed back to where I was staying.

I kept writing to Mary, and within a few weeks, we arranged to meet in her hometown, just over thirty miles away. I had to take two buses to get there and spent two nights in a hotel. I waited for Mary at our appointed place about ten minutes before the agreed-upon time. I waited and waited. I then saw this girl heading towards me with a huge smile on her face. She was wearing a dark brown bouclé-style coat and a brown patterned scarf on her head. She wore glasses with wings on the edges where the frames connected to the arms. To me, they looked dated. We shook hands and introduced ourselves. Mary took me to a local pub where we could have a drink and talk. I went to get the drinks as Mary found us a table. On turning from the bar, I looked round and couldn't see Mary. My initial thought was that she had run off. A few seconds later, I saw her waving at me. She had removed her glasses, coat, and scarf, revealing her soft, curled brunette hair. She looked different. She had deep brown eyes. She wasn't what I would call unattractive. We got along and talked for a while, only faltering when I couldn't think of anything to talk about that could possibly interest her. She spoke a bit about her family and their dog and said that she did secretarial work. Afterwards, she drove me back to my hotel. We talked for a short while, and I leant over to give her a kiss. She recoiled with a look of shock on her face. "I'm not kissing on a first date!"

My relationship with Anne went on for about a month. We usually ended up going to her sister Christine's room for a coffee before the end of the evening. It was during that time that I became acquainted with Christine, and the more I got to know her, the more I began to like her. From the very beginning, I had been more attracted to Christine than Anne.

One night, whilst in Christine's room, Anne had to go out. Christine immediately jumped up, locked the door, grabbed hold of me, and said, "Now you're mine!" I didn't complain. When Anne returned to find the door locked, she called out, and with no answer, she called out a few choice names to her sister and walked away. "She's grabbed a few of my fellas before now. She'll get over it." That night started my relationship with Christine. Anne did get over it, very quickly, as it happened. Christine and I stayed together for quite a long time.

I had already told Christine about seeing Mary, but she didn't mind. She was content to have me during the week. Mary, on the other hand, did not know about Christine. Admittedly, my relationship with Christine was very physical, whereas my relationship with Mary was not.

One morning at work, the head of our department came into our lab and informed us that our requirement on the project was extended indefinitely, and we were told we would be remaining there until further notice. This was excellent news.

During a leave whilst walking through Blackpool, I saw a box of paints in a shop window. I recalled the pleasure painting had given me at school, and whilst in Berlin. I bought the set, a pad of oil painting paper, and an instruction book for beginners. The book made it look easy, but it took a lot more practice than just slapping paint around. Back in the lodgings at Malvern, I practised in my spare time.

Whilst reading through some DCIs (periodical instruction documents), I saw a request posted for those interested to put their names forward to be part of an "Exercise Medsailor" on the RAF yacht *Lord Trenchard*. This was a Nicholson 55-foot yawl. Personnel could choose a particular two-week leg of the whole cruise from the UK, round the Mediterranean Sea and back to the UK. I applied for the leg from Gibraltar to Cagliari in Sardinia.

About a month later, I heard I had been placed on the reserve list for this leg. At least I stood a slight chance of going, but I didn't raise my hopes at this point.

A few weeks later, Jim Archer, who was a squadron leader and put in charge of us after Tom's posting, came into the lab, walked over to me, and smiled. "I believe congratulations are in order."

"What do you mean, sir?" I asked.

"You're going on Exercise Medsailor," he said.

"How do you know?" I asked.

He just looked at me, put his head slightly to one side, and said in a low voice, "I had to approve your application, remember? When they confirmed your place, they notified me to get my final consent. Incidentally, I had no hesitation giving my final approval. Enjoy the experience." With that, he left.

I later received official word that my application was accepted for the Gibraltar to Sardinia leg. My flight was scheduled for early January 1976. I would be at sea for two whole weeks, which made me extremely happy.

Now I needed to tell Christine and Mary. The situation with these two was getting very complex. I loved them both, but in different ways. I was glad to have a long break away from both of them so I could think things through. I knew I would marry one of them; I just didn't know which one. My mind was in complete turmoil over this decision. When I was about to choose one, I felt the other was more suitable. This was going to be the hardest decision of my life. I could make one girl very happy but break the heart of the other. I hated myself for getting into this situation in the first place.

The two-and-a-half-hour flight from Gatwick to Gibraltar wasn't very good, as I was in the cramped economy seating of a budget airline. After collecting the bags, our transport to the yacht was a short journey. I was excited to see the twin masts of the yacht by the harbour. There were twelve of us altogether, including two girls of the WRAF, the skipper, two watchkeepers, and nine crew. It was quite packed in the main cabin, but only when ashore as two "hot bunked" when going off watch with two who were on watch. My watch consisted of the watchkeeper who was a semiretired wing commander (Alan Porter), a squadron leader (Colin Baines), a sergeant

(Brian Cookson), and me. Alan was a good-humoured, portly man who wore a massive, well-groomed handlebar moustache.

The weather was good, considering it was the beginning of January. One main problem was we were rapidly running out of fresh bread. We had to cut the mould off and ate the remaining bread available until there was none left. When we eventually docked at Ibiza, our first call, the skipper suggested that as we were now in Spain, we ought to go find a place for some paella. We all agreed and found a restaurant. When we were seated at the table, the waiter began to bring in baskets of freshly baked bread. The aroma was overwhelming. Within minutes, all the bread had gone. We were like a swarm of locusts as arms and hands reached out to get at the baskets of deliciousness. We asked for more bread, time and again, until a steaming pan was brought to the table. It looked and smelt divine. We dove into the pans of hot rice and shellfish, then used more bread to mop up the sauce left on the plate. It was the best meal we had had for days.

The next leg to Palma was lovely, warm and sunny. After we docked, we walked by the harbour and found a bar, where we snacked on fresh stuffed olives and a few beers. The sail from Palma to Mahon was exhilarating. Strong winds were sufficient for the skipper to order full sail. As the wind began to strengthen, we had to haul down the spinnaker. This was done not a minute too soon, for as we were releasing the sail and in the process of hauling it in, a squall hit, and we had as many as we could fighting the sail back on board, whilst others were lowering other sails so only the mainsail remained.

It was during this cruise that whilst on either the middle (0000-0400) or morning (0400-0800) watches, I found time to ponder the burning question: Should I marry Christine or Mary? This was a difficult and life-changing decision. Both had their merits. Mary was the more serious and pragmatic, yet always seemed to keep me at arm's length physically. At the same time, she intrigued me with her elusiveness. Christine was very much a passive person who would be happy to accept whatever life threw at her. She just seemed to shrug off any mishaps that Mary probably wouldn't. On the downside, Mary seemed more old-fashioned in her attitudes, almost prudish.

The only stumbling block with Christine was how we came to be together and how she treated her sister. It was such a difficult decision that I changed the question to "Which girl should I not marry?" One name stood out: Christine. The reason stemmed from when we were in Christine's room and Anne left. Christine locked the door on Anne and took me. I know it's hypocritical, and I agree I was a willing soul, but she proved to be less trustworthy than Mary. I knew Mary would be faithful, but if Christine could do that to her own sister, how would she treat me? The decision hinged on trust. Once I made the decision, I felt a weight had been lifted off my shoulders. All I had to do was to keep seeing them to make sure I was making the right choice.

Far too soon, we were on our last leg at sea. It was sad that it had to end, as I had a marvelous time. I had quite a few talks with the skipper and helped with the chartwork while on board. He seemed interested in how I knew so much. He said I ought to do more sailing and go for watchkeeper training. I would have liked to do that, but due to my current situation, it wasn't really feasible.

We cooked our last breakfast, and the skipper passed out the bottles of duty free we had ordered.

When I arrived back at Malvern, nobody was in the room. I dropped off my bag, picked out the presents I had bought for Christine and Anne, and walked to The Unicorn to see the girls. When I saw Anne, she came straight over and said, "Thank God, you're back! Chris has been like a bear with a sore head ever since you left!" I looked around, but Christine wasn't there. "She's in her room and has been totally antisocial for weeks." I gave Anne her present, finished my drink, and headed to Christine's room.

I knocked on the door. It opened slowly, and I saw Christine through the narrow opening. As she recognized me, her face lit up. She grabbed me, pulled me inside, and gave me a long, passionate kiss. Perhaps I was making a mistake in my decision to marry Mary over Christine.

The following Saturday night, I met Mary. When she saw me, she ran towards me with open arms and gave me a big hug and kiss. I gave her the present I had bought for her, a soft leather beach bag with a native pattern on it. She didn't look that impressed with the gift. Even so, I knew that telling Chris of my decision was really going to be hard.

The days turned into weeks; then Easter weekend 1976 came. Easter was memorable because it was when I got engaged to Mary. Telling Christine had been the hardest thing I had faced. I knew she loved me, but I couldn't get past the trust issue. I had sowed my proverbial "wild oats" and was now ready to make a long-term commitment.

It was a lovely Saturday when Mary and I drove to buy her engagement ring. The one she really liked was a bit over the budget; however, as she loved it so much, I bought it anyway. It was a large sapphire surrounded by diamonds. "It reminds me of your eyes," Mary said to me. We were happy as we drove back to her parents to show off the ring.

When we arrived, we saw a full tea setting being made. There were champagne glasses on the table, so the news was certainly expected. Her brother and his fiancée were also there. I went into the lounge and sat as Matt, Mary's father, came in. We began talking, and I asked him for his permission to marry Mary. He smiled and told me he would happily give his consent. We stood up, shook hands, and then walked out to a prepared meal, already waiting. Mary and I shared a toast to our engagement. As I slid the ring on Mary's finger, I was moving toward her for a kiss when she shied away, coy-like. "Not in front of everyone," she whispered. Nonetheless, we were now officially engaged to be married. After dinner, we took their dog for a walk. As we passed one of the houses, Mary turned and pushed me into a big, bulging bush. "What was that for?" I asked.

"Doesn't everybody push their fiancé into a bush when they get engaged?" We both laughed as we continued our walk.

# Chapter Seventeen
## B.B.

### THE UNRAVELING

During the course of almost ten years of marriage, Steve had had several affairs. The first hint of his infidelity came the night I overheard him on the phone having a one-sided conversation. I heard the phone ring on my nightstand as he was getting home from "coon hunting" very late in the evening. I remained motionless with my eyes closed, even though the ringing had awakened me. He quickly answered and took the phone to the adjacent living room. He lowered his voice, and I was curious about who would be calling at this late hour, so I strained to listen. I heard him say, "I can't tonight, maybe next weekend." I never learned the identity of that late-night caller. I did learn, however, that his older sister had such a dislike for me that she gave out our phone number to other women, encouraging them to call him. Admittedly, our family backgrounds and values were worlds apart, but surely nothing I ever did merited this kind of disdain. That late-night call ended any trust I had left in Steve.

### WHY ME?

In November 1975, when I had a three-year-old son and a four-year-old daughter, I went for my annual ob-gyn appointment and a routine Pap smear. It wasn't until early January that I was called to come back for follow-up because my Pap results were abnormal, with Class IV precancerous cells. My gynecologist scheduled me for a cone biopsy, then recommended a hysterectomy. He cautioned that these were the kind of cells that "would turn into cancer."

Steve was waiting outside in the car for me the day I was given this devastating news. I was already in tears when I told him what the doctor had said, but he showed no emotion. He didn't attempt to console me by taking me into his arms or holding my hand. Through tears, I asked, "What am I going to do?" His response was simply a cold, heartless "Take it like a woman."

I viewed the world differently in the days following that news. I appreciated the moments of my life more. I took time to gaze at the leaves budding on the trees and the spring flowers in bloom. I took a good, long, incredibly hard look at my marriage, what it was, what it had never been, and the total lack of emotional support. I pondered over why my female friends, who were my age, were suddenly at a loss for words and could no longer identify with me. Cancer, after all, is not contagious.

## THE INTERCESSOR

I had gone for a second opinion in Lexington and felt much more confident with the second doctor. He gave me options, whereas the first hadn't. He told me that I could delay the surgery, but to do so could potentially decrease my chance of survival. The cancerous cells had extended to the full margin of the pathology slide. This meant it was ready to become invasive. I had already been blessed with two children. My priority was to do whatever it took to make sure I was around to see them grow up.

In April 1976, at age twenty-four, following a cone biopsy, I left the mountains of eastern Kentucky and headed to a hospital in central Kentucky, wondering whether I would survive this ordeal with cancer. It was one of the toughest things I had faced, and I felt completely alone.

The morning of my surgery, I remember being in the operating room and the nurse anesthetist beginning to administer my anesthesia. I was asked to begin counting backward from one hundred. My surgeon was standing at the foot of the operating table. As I was drifting off to sleep, I remember hearing him saying a prayer for me. God heard and honored his prayer that day.

When my doctor came out of the operating room to speak to my family later that morning, no one was there to hear the news. Steve had already gone. I was in the hospital for six days while he stayed home and continued to work. It wasn't until afterward that I learned he was with another woman while I was still in the hospital. After that, we pulled further and further apart as his affairs continued. Trust was completely gone. Our marriage foundation, weak from the start, had crumbled.

Years later, on a follow-up visit, I had the courage to tell my doctor I had heard him that morning as he interceded for me in prayer. After all those years, I remembered and would never forget how comforting it was to have a praying doctor.

Having never before had surgery, I wasn't expecting such a lack of energy during the postoperative recovery period. There was no such thing as "taking it easy." When I came home from the hospital, I had toddlers, a husband, and household duties to resume. Because I didn't give myself the time to recover initially, and because I had been on a strict weight-reduction diet beforehand, it took much longer to regain my strength.

During a visit to the local library to check out some books, I saw some beautiful pieces of framed embroidery on display. Some were for sale, but the cost made them unaffordable. Handmade items and art always appealed to me as the personal touches that make a house a home. It was clear that if I wanted them, I'd have to learn how to embroider.

A retired nurse named Jean lived close to our home and was the kindest, most loving lady. She didn't have children of her own, but neighborhood children were naturally attracted to her and her husband. She was petite in stature and a bundle of energy. When I was a preteen, I would stop on my bicycle and talk to her when she was outdoors tending her flowers. She had been the one who took the time to teach me (and many other neighborhood children) how to swim.

She was forever doing crafts, and I imagined she could do just about anything she set her mind to. I decided to ask her if she could teach me to embroider. I ordered three beautiful kits, each including a pattern, diagram, and all the embroidery yarn for the project. Each of the kits was well above my skill level, but I imagined how proud my grandmother would be that I had learned how to embroider. Jean taught me first on practice cloth, stitch by stitch, from the simplest to the most complicated stitches.

Over the course of a few months, I completed several large pictures and had them framed. I was so proud to have created something through my own effort that I couldn't afford to buy ready-made. I completed them all while recovering from major surgery. The next time I talked to my grandmother on the phone, I told her about them and how pretty they were. I was sure she would be pleased that I was learning this skill. Instead, she asked if I was making pillows out of them. I was horrified at the mere thought of somebody tossing around and laying their head on something I had worked so hard to create. For me, this was needle art, not a craft.

My grandmother's reaction? "Why don't you learn to do something useful, like quilting?" The creative art of needlework for the purpose of decorating a home was lost on her very practical mindset.

When Sara started kindergarten, I wanted to be that mother who actively participated at school. Mothers alternated bringing treats for special parties, and I was assigned to her class's Halloween party. I was to bring cupcakes for every child and the teachers, about three dozen in all. There were no bakeries or grocery stores in the area to pull off a cheat and buy the treats instead. The night before the party, I sat up all night baking and decorating those cupcakes. Some had jack-o'-lantern faces, while others were cats or ghosts, all painstakingly done as close to perfection as I could make them. I wanted Sara to be proud of her mother's contribution. I finished the task at 5 a.m. the morning of the party, exhausted. Sara was delighted with how they looked, and that was what mattered most to me.

Mothers brought lots of treats that day. When the party started, I watched in absolute horror as some of Sara's classmates took a single lick across the middle of their cupcake or ate a bite or two, then left them on their plates to be discarded in the trash. Lesson learned. Next time, I would put forth that kind of effort only for my own children, not for an entire classroom.

In primary school, the competitiveness began. One of Sara's friends, a little girl named Kellie, was always the best dressed in her school. Her grandmother made sure of that. Sara came home telling me about the kinds of clothes Kellie was wearing and the jewelry she had at the age of only eight. She suggested Sara ask me to buy a rabbit fur coat and real diamond earrings like she had. It was a small town, I was a stay-at-home mom, there was no grandmother to spoil her, and I simply could not compete.

In the months ahead, I learned that Kellie's grandmother was always the one who appointed herself to guard the mothers' purses at school parties. She was an extremely likable person, always chatty with the mothers. One day after dropping Sara off at school, I was in the parking lot, having a chat with her. My purse was on the seat beside me. It was fall and had gotten cool outside, so I invited her to sit in the passenger seat and continue our conversation. Later that afternoon, I discovered money missing from my purse. It was money I needed for essential things. It was only later that I discovered she had a reputation as a notorious shoplifter who had been banned from a number of stores in the area. The school had already been on alert about her because of other missing items, but I had been unaware.

I explained to Sara that I would do everything in my power to provide her with the things she and Sawyer actually needed, but I didn't have the resources to give them everything they wanted or to compete with their classmates. The difference between "need" versus "want" was a hard lesson for them both.

I showed my love for my children not so much through giving material things that were nice to have, but through small gestures. I left them notes in their school lunch boxes, and they in turn left notes and drawings for me, many of which I collected and preserved. One Halloween, I used a cookie cutter with an imprinted design of a jack-o'-lantern face to impress into slices of bread. I trimmed off the outer crusts and made peanut butter and jelly sandwiches. Sara and Sawyer discovered these in their lunch boxes while waiting for their school bus one morning. Lunch never made it to school that day.

## YOUTHFUL IMAGINATION

Of the two, Sara was the most sensitive. She loved music and often held the end of her jump rope, pretending it was a microphone. To this day, she loves to sing and has a beautiful soprano voice. When she was a toddler, she made up her own words long before she developed an extensive vocabulary. One such word, she only used when she was angry. This word was directed at an object that hurt or frustrated her (and occasionally at a playmate who refused to share). Her face became flushed, and her body tensed and trembled as she pointed her index finger and exclaimed, "You're a such-a-bee-my-leez!" I wrote it down phonetically so I would never forget. As an adult, Sara isn't given to using profanity. I believe she got it out of her system as a toddler.

Sara loved to role play. Many times, I would find her dolls lined up against pillows on the sofa or in Sawyer's high chair. Those dolls were her audience, and she pretended to teach them. I never heard those actual lessons and never realized she would someday become a middle school teacher.

Sawyer loved the popular and very addictive video games of the 1980s. One game featured a character grabbing hold of a rope and swinging across such obstacles as a pond filled with alligators, a fire, or a vast hole in the ground. If you were fortunate, you made it across that obstacle and accumulated points. Being an energetic, imaginative, and very impressionable boy, Sawyer often role-played what he watched. On one such occasion, I came home from work to find my five-globed incandescent kitchen chandelier pulled out of its ceiling mount and dangling only by the wiring inside.

110

Stunned, I asked, "What on Earth happened to my light fixture?"

I could almost see the little halo above Sawyer's head as he innocently replied, "I don't know, Mom. It was like that when we got home."

It would be years before he finally admitted he was imitating the video game and thought he'd get on top of our kitchen table and swing from the chandelier across imaginary "threats" on our kitchen floor.

Protecting a son without a dad around came with challenges I never imagined. As soon as his eyes were open in the morning, he was a nonstop bundle of energy. Once, he veered off our one-lane road on his bicycle as a car suddenly approached. He rode his bike over a rock wall, then downhill and headfirst through a neighbor's kitchen window as they sat at their table eating breakfast. Shattered glass was everywhere, but Sawyer didn't sustain a single scratch.

Other such daring feats included the time a friend's grandpa caught him playing with baby rattlesnakes (more venomous than the grown ones). He was amused, thinking worms were striking at the small wooden stick in his hand. Single parenting is certainly not for the faint of heart. My children had many protectors, both seen and unseen.

# Chapter Eighteen
## J.D.

### WEDDING ARRANGEMENTS

The reception venue turned out to be a bigger challenge than coordinating the wedding and church. In the midst of wedding arrangements, we had to find a place to live and get it furnished. We looked at various houses, but most were unaffordable. Those we could afford needed a lot of work or were in undesirable areas. Due to Mary's job as a shorthand typist with the town corporation, she was able to secure a house for us. It was in a new area and would be a new house. She told me it was expensive to rent, but her pay would just cover it. The task of looking to furnish and equip it was interesting. Neither of us had ever furnished a home, but the novelty soon wore off. I looked at furniture until I was blinded. As soon as Mary and I agreed on something we liked, we bought it. We had the money saved, so buying without credit gave us a discount on most of the larger items. We accepted the house and arranged for all the furniture to be delivered on separate days of the week before the wedding day.

In the beginning, all went well, with one exception. The carpet fitter, three-piece suite, bed, cooker, wall cabinet, electric, gas, etc. all came on one very hectic day. Once everything had been taken care of that day, I was able to sleep and live in our marital home. Mary still stayed with her parents and would not move in until after the wedding.

The wedding day finally arrived. On the way to church, my best man and I were engrossed in a conversation about cricket (England v Australia). We continued the conversation inside the church. The vicar eventually came over and informed me that my bride had arrived. I thanked him and continued with the conversation about cricket.

I felt a bony finger jabbing into my back. "You've got to stand up now!" It was my mum. She always used her long, bony fingers to jab when she wanted to get attention. I always hated that habit, but I stood, and the ceremony began.

The ceremony went well, but the person who was meant to drive my family to the reception in my car hadn't shown up. I quickly arranged for somebody else to drive them there. The wedding guests arrived and were waiting whilst there was no sign of my parents. Fifteen to thirty minutes had passed when Mary's mum suggested we proceed without them. I insisted that we wait. Eventually, they arrived, and the driver said they had gone to the wrong venue that had the same name.

When we were seated, instead of having my parents at our table, Mary's mother insisted that Mary's brother and his fiancée be seated with us. It was clear long before our marriage that Mary's mother didn't like my family. By now, my parents were already sitting with my brother and his family, so it was OK. Still, I wasn't happy and remember thinking, "Is this how it's going to be in the future?" It was indeed a foretaste of my future.

When the reception ended, Mary changed out of her wedding dress and into another outfit. I recall how good she looked in that outfit. It was a brown mid-length dress with a flower pattern. We then drove back to our new home. We sat and then lay on the bed together, grateful it was all over. I expected there would be intimacy between us, but Mary refused. Since there was nothing going on between the two of us privately, I eventually suggested we join my family at the hotel later that night, as I was sure they would be having a celebration. There was a resounding "*no!*" from Mary. I respectfully decided to give her time. She said she just wanted to rest as it had been a long day. I had to admit, it had been a long day for me, too, and we were both tired. So, I let it go at that.

We went on our official honeymoon a few days later. We hired a static caravan owned by one of Mary's cousins. It was located by the seaside at Berrow and was ideally situated for us. It was comfortable and spacious. Our honeymoon lasted a week, and at its conclusion, there still had been no consummation of our marriage. Of course, I was upset when she rejected me, but her reasons did seem to be valid. She didn't want to "do that sort of thing in somebody else's bed." So again, she had it her way. Little did I know at that time this would be the first in an endless round of excuses. When the honeymoon was over, it was back to work for us.

## POSTING TO RAF BISHOP'S COURT

A couple of weeks later, I was called into Squadron Leader Archer's office. I had a feeling there was bad news coming. I was right. He told me that he had been informed of my posting from RAF Henlow. I asked where. He replied, "RAF Bishop's Court." My head spun. Northern Ireland! I'd just got married and set up a new home and now I was being posted to Northern Ireland? How would Mary take this news? There were so many decisions to be made about the house. Should I commute back and forth every month or so, or should Mary relocate with me? I felt I could be putting her in danger. I felt my whole world seemed to collapse around me again. I was still stunned as I walked out of the office.

I phoned Mary at work to break the news and she immediately began crying. "What am I going to do? What about the house? What about my job?" After a few days of consoling and reassuring her, life settled down. It was obvious she still wasn't overjoyed. Neither was I.

Several days later, Squadron Leader Archer walked into the lab and told me had been talking to another Squadron Leader. He had arranged for me to meet with him and discuss my posting. The meeting well. He greeted me pleasantly, motioned me to sit down and offered me a cup of coffee. He began telling me he had been told about my concerns regarding my posting. Continuing, he said he had just returned from his posting there, and began telling me about what to expect, places of interest to visit, where we could and could not go etc. It was all very informative. Finally, he told me that neither myself or my wife should be too concerned about the posting. It was obvious this was to allay any doubts and fears my wife would have. He was very relaxed throughout the whole meeting, leaving me feeling better about the situation. How Mary would take this information, I would soon find out.

On my return home I informed Mary about the discussion. It didn't help. If anything, it made things worse. "Why can't you get somebody to change with you? Do you realise what I'll be giving up for you?"

Of course, I could fully understand her misgivings regarding this posting. From then on, there was always a dark cloud hanging over us and our home that never seemed to leave us or the marriage.

If that wasn't bad enough, a few weeks later Archer came into our lab, closed the door and told us to switch off the radio. This sounded serious. He had never told us to switch off the radio before. He cast his eyes over us and told us in a flat, matter of fact voice, "This will not come easy for you, but this job is coming to an end in two weeks. Your services will no longer be required. You will be returning to RAF Henlow. In the next two weeks I expect this lab to be clean and tidy condition with three full toolboxes on the bench. You will NOT remove any tools from this Establishment. I shall, of course be checking up on you as the time of your departure draws closer." He then turned round and walked out. As normal, he left the door open.

As we closed the door, we just looked at each other in stunned belief. This news was hard to take. I had been there for nearly two and a half years. I thought of Mary and the house. It would be very difficult to commute from Redditch to Henlow. It would be a two hour drive each way. I would either leave at around 5:30 A.M. each morning to arrive at GRIS HQ on time or I would remain at Henlow during the week and travel home for the weekend. Neither were good options.

The last day finally arrived. I drove into the Establishment for the very last time. It was as though I had always been there yet now it felt somewhat eerie. A sense of sadness came over me as I drove up to the parking area and walked up the steps for the last time. The walls of the lab once covered with cuttings and pictures were now bare. The bench that had once been a hive of activity of wire, circuit boards, wire and components were now empty, except for three full unlocked toolboxes.

As I was looking around, I heard the cars of my colleagues as they drove in and parked. The car doors opened and closed. Then the tapping of feet on the stairs and corridor floor. The door opened and they entered the lab, ready for the final clean up. I really enjoyed my time here. For the first time in my RAF career to date, I had been treated with respect and not as a second-class entity. It had been worth it all just to have that sense of dignity restored.

Together, we had a final tidy up of the filing cabinets, leaving them neat and well ordered. We were just about to go down for our last tea break when the Squadron Leader entered the lab. "I'm really sorry to see you men go. You have been a credit to the Royal Air Force and your Unit. You never caused any trouble or discredited the Service or yourselves. I wish you all well in your future careers. Aubrey, good luck with your posting, and tell your wife not to worry too much." He then shook our hands in a farewell gesture. On the way out, he actually closed the door.

As I drove back to Henlow, I remembered the good and happy times at the Establishment. I reflected on the people I met there, especially Christine.

I couldn't help wondering how Christine would have taken the news of my posting, had I married her instead of Mary. I felt she would have just shrugged her shoulders and said, "OK. When do we go?" She was so different compared to Mary. Thinking of those girls brought my mind to the pubs, the fun, laughter and conversations. I loved that place, the job, everything. It was now gone forever, like ghosts in the dawn.

We found Henlow basically unchanged as I drove and parked outside the GRIS block. When I walked inside, I was overwhelmed with the strong smell of polish. The GRIS block had never been like this! I made my way to my old room. The door was locked, and my key didn't work. I made my way to GRIS HQ. When I walked into the long, highly polished corridor nicknamed "The Golden Mile," I was almost blinded by its brilliance.

I passed the familiar Detachment and PWR boards and looked to see if there were any familiar names. There was not a single one, except for my own, for RAF Bishop's Court. I received the new key from the office and then drove back to GRIS block. I noticed the cars of the ex-Malverners already there. I parked, got my bag, and went up to my room. This time, the door was open. I walked in, greeted a guy lying on his bed, and threw my bag on my old bed.

"Who the fook are you?" he asked in a thick Liverpool accent.

"Jim Aubrey. Just got back from RSRE Malvern."

"Fookin' 'ell! We've never seen anyone in that bed, yet. I've bin 'ere nearly a year an' never seen anyone there."

"Well, I'm here now," I said as I began to make up my bed and get unpacked. I was in no mood to be sociable or make small talk.

"'Ow long were you on that job?"

"Two and a half years."

"Fookin' 'ell!" He got up and sat on his bed. "I'm Dave Torrance. Everybody calls me Torry."

"I'm Jim. Jim Aubrey. Jimmy."

There was a knock on the door, and Neil and Bob came in. "C'mon, Jimmy, tea! I'm driving," said Bob.

"C'n I cadge a lift, please?" asked Torry.

"Yeah. Get a move on, though. I'm starving, and we need to check out the new mess."

"Wha' new mess? This one's bin 'ere for ages," remarked Torry.

"Well, we haven't seen it yet," I said. I introduced Torry to Bob and Neil.

"'Ow the fook did you get on a job like that?"

We explained to him about the Malvern job.

"Lucky bastards" was all Torry could say.

The new mess was a great improvement on the old wooden hut I was used to. It was nice, airy, and clean, but somehow lacked the character of the old mess.

We returned to our rooms, and I just lay on my bed and got out a book I was reading. The page was marked by the bookmark that Beth had sent to me all those years ago. I looked at it and saw it was now a bit more battered after years of use. I had carried it with me wherever I had gone. I couldn't part with it. It was a reminder of a past time, a lost life, a lost future. I began reading. It wasn't long before it was time for the bar to open.

I kept thinking of Mary and how lonely she must be feeling now. She always hated it when I went away on trials. I got up and headed towards the Bonanza Club, as the old bowling alley had closed with a new build where the old mess had been, not knowing if I would recognize anybody. I found most of them were strangers until I heard a familiar laugh. "Geordie, you old bugger!" I called out. Geordie stopped laughing and looked round.

"Jimmy! Ya boogah!" he replied in his thick northeastern accent. Standing by his side was Arnie, a fellow storeman. They had been here at Henlow since I was first posted, back in 1971.

"What are you doing back here?" asked Arnie in his South African accent. "I heard you'd left and become a civvy."

"No," I replied. "I was on detachment for two and a half years in a civvy establishment, working with civvies in civvies."

The catching up and drinking began. Most of the old faces had long gone. Most were posted, and others demobbed. We continued talking and drinking until the bar closed. Then it was back to our respective rooms.

After one eight-o'-clock parade, I was told to stay behind when the parade ended. I was informed I was the only one presently at GRIS who had experience of a PAR building recovery. As a consequence, I was assigned a recovery job at RAF Benson in Oxfordshire, the following week. We would be dismantling and removing the structure only. The job was estimated to be about a week maximum. The equipment had already been removed. There would be a sergeant in charge, me, and two others. I was given a manual and told to study it. I laughed as I read the conditions specified for the removal of the building. At a previous recovery at RAF Oakington, we had broken just about every ruling specified. This was a textbook recovery, and we finished in just under a week. It would be my very last job on GRIS.

My next official task was clearing from Henlow. I spent so much time there, it had become a major part of my life. This would be my last night there. I went into the club, and there were my old friends Arnie and Geordie, propping up the bar as usual. We drank and talked. Geordie was being demobbed a week later, and Arnie was being posted as well. We talked about the "old times," the characters who had come and gone.

The call came for last orders, so we ordered our last drinks together. "We're the last of the 'Old School,'" said Arnie. We looked at each other and nodded. I raised my glass and said, "To the Old School!" We drank the toast, finished our beer, and left with a strong handshake, knowing we would never meet up again. It was like saying goodbye to my family. We walked, talked, and split up for the last time. This time tomorrow, I'd be at home getting ready to leave for my posting. I knew Mary would be dreading this coming weekend. I would dread listening to her complain about it.

The day finally came for me to leave home and make my way to Liverpool to catch the overnight ferry to Belfast. It was a horrible experience. Mary was extremely upset, with tears rolling down her cheeks. With a heavy heart, I got in the car and drove to Liverpool.

Soon after I boarded the ferry, I went up on deck and leaned against a rail as I watched Liverpool slowly glide away. I imagined the exhilaration and excitement of leaving on my first trip as a navigation cadet on board my first ship, as so many had done from this very port. I stood there watching the lights of the city and docks slip away, deep in my thoughts. I didn't want to leave my home and wife. I told Mary this would probably happen, and she seemed to accept it. Now that it was a reality, she found it hard, as I did. Soon, I would be returning home to pack up the belongings we had lovingly built together. My heart sank as I thought about it. I looked towards the stern and whispered, "T'rah Mary, my love. See you soon." Never "goodbye." That would be bad luck.

We docked the following morning and I drove off the ship and into Belfast. Thankfully, it was fairly early in the morning, and there was very little traffic. I drove cautiously, fully aware that my car had English number plates and that would make my vehicle stand out amongst others. That fact alone could make me a target. I kept looking around, making myself as aware of my surroundings as I could whilst concentrating on where I was going. Soon, I was out of Belfast and heading on a main road to Downpatrick. The sun was rising, and the fields were covered in ground mist. It was a clear, cloudless morning. It looked too peaceful for me to imagine this place being a place of conflict.

The next day, I made my way to the Station Headquarters to begin my arrival. I eventually made it to my section and introduced myself to the flight sergeant. He asked if I played sports. I told him I played rugby. He nodded, signed my blue card, and told me to go into the crew room and have a coffee. I introduced myself to those who were in there as I found the kitchen area and made a coffee. A few minutes after I sat down, a corporal came in and called out my name.

"I understand you play rugby."

"Yes, I do," I replied.

"What position?"

"Second row. Number five."

He raised his arms and said, "Fantastic! Do you fancy playing on Saturday? RAF Valley. Away. A friendly."

RAF Valley is in North Wales and a long way from here.

"Sure. Why not?" I replied.

"Great! I'll get it sorted."

That was it. I was on the station rugby team and going away for the weekend. What a great introduction!

A few minutes later, Flight Sergeant McNemeny came in and called my name. I got up and followed him into his office.

"Interesting," he said. "You haven't been with us more than ten minutes, and you're playing rugby at Valley." He looked at me oddly. Then he smiled. "Good to have you here, and thank you for volunteering for the team. I'm sure we'll all get on well. By the way, your hair is a bit long."

"It's on purpose, Flight," I replied, trying not to blot my copybook after making such a good first impression. "I don't want to make myself an obvious target when I'm not in uniform."

He pursed his lips and said, "That sounds reasonable. Just keep it neat, tidy, clean, and not too long. OK?"

"Thank you, Flight. I won't."

The next couple of days were as expected. I was shown around the section, introductions were made, and I became familiar with the equipment. More would be done on Monday. This weekend, I had a rugby game to play.

I arrived on Monday at the section and was introduced to the watch. J/T Palmer eyed me very aloofly as he showed me around. Most of the equipment I remembered from my Fitters' course. I was shown where all the logs, records, manuals, and service sheets were kept and how to fill them in. It was after lunch that he told me he was going on leave for two weeks after this watch cycle, and he asked if I thought I would be good to cover whilst he was away. I said I would, and he smiled, wryly.

For the rest of the watch cycle, I did all the servicing and any fault finding whilst Joe watched over me like a mother hen. He watched my every move to ascertain just how I would cope in his absence. Towards the end of the last night shift, I heard him talking to the watch SNCO, Sgt. Mills: "He should be OK on his own."

On the next two watch cycles, I learned a great deal. I spent a lot of time studying the manuals and how the equipment was interconnected. The watch cycles when I was on my own came and went. I didn't encounter too many problems, but those I did were readily overcome. Joe and I got along well, worked as a team, and agreed to share the workload. One would do the servicing, and the other would handle any faults. We changed roles every shift day. If there were no faults that needed correction, one had an easy day. Occasionally, there was the odd day when there was a really difficult fault, and we would work together to repair it.

One day whilst Joe was on another leave, I had done all the servicing, and all the equipment was working correctly. I was sitting in the crew room having a coffee when Flight Sergeant McNemeny came in, bade us all a good morning, and proceeded to the kitchen area to make a coffee. A while later, he returned to wash his cup and looked directly at me, then went out. After an hour or so, he came in again to make himself another coffee and saw me. This time, he stopped. "Aubrey! Every time I have seen you this morning, you have been sitting in that same chair in the crew room!"

I replied, "Funny you should say that, Flight. Every time I have seen *you* this morning, *you* have been in the crew room!"

Somebody in the crew room heard the conversation and spat out his drink in laughter. Flight Sergeant McNemeny turned away, chortling and shaking his head, while the rest in the crew room broke into laughter.

When McNemeny came back with his coffee, he looked at me, shook his head and just walked back to his office. I now felt as though I had become a "permanent fixture" and part of the crew.

Mary eventually joined me in an allocated married quarter and had settled in nicely. Our house had a lovely view of the mountains of Mourne in the distance. We tried not to notice the view of a chain-link fence topped with rolled razor wire, but we coped with that. We invited some of my single colleagues for meals, which they greatly appreciated. Mary was able to get acquainted with some of the men I worked with, and this gave her a feeling of belonging.

Finances were really tight. Food and fuel were far more expensive than on the mainland, as were the utility bills. After a number of months there, Mary was feeling she had had enough. Because of the higher cost of living, there was insufficient money to get all the basics we needed. She kept talking about missing her job, family, and friends. She didn't like having to book out and book in as we travelled around. She also didn't like the feeling of being a potential target for terrorist groups. The stress of living in Northern Ireland was beginning to overwhelm her. To a certain extent, it was overwhelming for me too. I had the added responsibility of ensuring Mary's personal safety every time we went anywhere.

Finances played a great part in my own personal stress. Every penny was valuable. I had to think before even considering buying anything, especially if it was a "nice to have" item. Mary was always talking about getting another posting. She made it abundantly clear that she no longer liked being here. The novelty had long since worn off the extended holiday, as had our savings.

One morning, I went in on the first day shift, expecting just another "day at the office," when Flight Sergeant McNemeny entered the crew room. "RAF Killard Point is closing down. Anybody who wants to get short-toured can put their name on this sheet. He will then be transferred to Killard Point until the final closure in four months." I immediately got up and put my name on the form. McNemeny looked at me strangely. We had all got on so well, my quick response must have surprised him. I was later asked by the watch sergeant why I had been so quick to sign up. I told him my reasons, and he understood.

When I got home for lunch, I told Mary. She was very happy. "Where do you think we'll go?" I had no idea, but I told her that I was on what they referred to as a "hardship posting," meaning I could put down three stations where I would like to get posted. This was something I had considered most of the morning. Malvern would be number one, RAF Locking number two, then RAF Troodos. She wanted to know more about Troodos, so I told her it was in Cyprus. Once I told her, she had her heart set on going there. Due to recent changes in trade structure, I was now restricted in my future postings to Air Defence Radar sites only, of which there were very few. Airfields would be out.

Mary and I were anxiously waiting to hear about our posting. We knew it would take a while, but I had already applied to buy myself out. The strain had been very heavy on both of us, and I had had enough.

# Chapter Nineteen
## B.B.

### WORKING MOM

Finances were tough enough as it was. Now, the miners' union was facing a long contract strike. Our family couldn't face the uncertainty of weeks of lost income, so I decided to look for a job. I hired a neighbor, my best friend, to watch the children, now both in grade school, until I could get home in the evening. The job was as a part-time canvasser for an aluminum siding sales company. I would be going door to door to get leads for the two salesmen. The biggest benefits it gave me were the self-confidence I lacked and a bit of independence.

I did a great deal of thinking and problem-solving while I was alone in my vehicle, driving from place to place. I mulled over the details of my life, my marriage, and the affairs Steve had had. We never had an intelligent, meaningful conversation as a married couple. I doubted that he ever really loved me. In fact, I doubted he knew the true meaning of the word "love." His behavior seemed to prove otherwise. Our marriage had reached the point where Steve looked better to me when he was leaving than when he was coming home.

One day, I reached the conclusion that our marriage was dead, and I had had all I could tolerate of the misery. I wasn't willing to settle for the continued infidelity and being made to feel that I never looked good enough and always fell short of expectations. When physical expectations are based on images of women in a magazine who have been surgically enhanced and their photos airbrushed, it is impossible for a real woman to measure up. While I was on a break for lunch, I made the spontaneous decision to drop by the first attorney's office I found. I found one I knew absolutely nothing about, then walked in and blurted out the words, "I want to file for divorce."

He was a tall, lanky man, nearly my dad's age. I sat in a chair across the desk from him and poured out all the reasons I wanted a divorce. My goal was freedom from the hell my marriage had become. I remember feeling very awkward and guarded around him but attributed that to the circumstances of my visit.

In the following weeks, I received phone calls from that attorney, totally unrelated to the divorce, asking me out on a date. Frankly, it made my skin crawl. He was my dad's age. My dad, on the other hand, recognized that this man had both money and power and thought I should accept. I stopped answering the phone to avoid him or unplugged the phone from the wall altogether. This was long before call screening and answering machines were available. My only interest was for legal counsel. Money was tight, but I wasn't for sale.

Some women are drawn to money and power and stay in loveless relationships because of them. From my perspective, this is the same as being for sale to the highest bidder. I would be relieved when my divorce was finalized and I never had to be in contact with him again.

The space between Steve and me had reached gulf-sized proportions. I had moved totally out of our shared bedroom and began sleeping in one of the twin beds in my son's room upstairs. When Steve touched me, I was so repulsed that I felt like my skin was crawling. Regardless of the fact that I had only a high school education and a year of vocational school at the time, I would manage somehow without him. I would rather be a single mom and struggle than live with someone who was unfaithful and treated me the way Steve did. The day the sheriff served the divorce papers on Steve, he exhibited no emotion, so much like the coldness I had come to expect from him.

## THE UNION STRIKE

As expected, the UCWU contract strike came, lasting a brutal 111 days, beginning in December 1977 and not ending until March 1978. The need to travel away from home for work (and get away from Steve) was a blessing, but I missed Sara and Sawyer terribly. Since at least November, my supervisor had known of my failing marriage. For several weeks, my new coworker, Rita, and I worked territories in Tennessee. The weather was bitterly cold that year, and I don't recall a single sale closing. This meant no bonuses for either of us. Our expenses were covered, but beyond that, we earned very little. For me, it was a respite to get away.

I dreaded the thought of going home where Steve was. If it had been possible, I would have had my children brought to me so I didn't have to go back to the same house with this man. He had become like a stranger to me, and my children were the ones I missed. I felt guilty even leaving them with him.

## NO MEANS NO

One Thursday night, I came back home from Tennessee and, as usual, headed upstairs to share my five-year-old son's bedroom. I was abruptly awakened in the night by Steve pushing his way through our son's bedroom door. Soon, he was on top of me, roughly and forcibly trying to strip off my pajamas as I fought him off. My son, sound asleep on the other twin bed in the room, thankfully never knew what had happened.

We barely spoke to each other after that, and I barricaded the bedroom door at night. Unfortunately, because of the long strike, he lacked the financial resources to move out. When the contract strike ended in late March 1978 and he returned to work, once again, I asked my neighbor and best friend to help with childcare. By this time, the weather was bad, sales were down, and the salesmen decided to take a winter break for a few weeks. My supervisor said he would not be coming back to do sales work in the Kentucky area for a while, but offered me a job if I wanted to move to Tennessee. He insisted that business would pick up when the weather was better. I agreed.

## TWO PATHS DIVERGED

There's hardly anything cuter than a five-year-old boy in a miniature mortarboard with tassel and long, light blue graduation gown, reciting the nursery rhyme "Georgy Porgie" at his commencement ceremony. It is a night I will never forget. Neither will the little boy in this story. It was May 1978, the night Sawyer graduated from kindergarten. Steve insisted our children and I go to the graduation early, and he would be there soon to join us. When he finally arrived, he was behaving differently. Unbeknown to me, he had arrived later because he was packing and had no intention of returning to our house.

Once the three of us returned home, I noticed his personal belongings were missing throughout the house. I concluded that he wouldn't be back. That night, I got my first glimpse of the next six years of our lives. Suddenly, our lives were turned upside down. Intuitively, I knew there was another woman involved, again. Soon after, I discovered her identity. It came to me like an epiphany. This other woman was my best friend, Sonya.

For three days, I hardly stopped crying over the deception and betrayal. The tears flowed like a river, and I mourned, more for the loss of my best friend than for Steve. Then, as though the dam had finally run dry, the tears stopped.

Steve remained distant, and the children missed him terribly. Despite the fact that he lived only fifteen miles away, he never visited the children. It was a horrendous situation. The husband of my best friend had also been Steve's best friend, Pete. Once he heard the news of the betrayal, he reacted very differently than me. Instead of tears, he wanted revenge. He put up fence posts and strung barbed wire separating our properties. He even posted "No Trespassing" signs, directed toward our house.

Sara, always a daddy's girl, was devastated. There's really no way to explain the dynamics of a relationship breakup to children as young as Sara and Sawyer, who were ages seven and five. They couldn't understand why this situation had cost them not only a dad, but a playmate they had seen daily before.

The person who actually brought my friend back to reality was Steve. He wanted Sonya to give custody of their only child to her husband so the two of them could start off a relationship unencumbered by children. That was the reality check she needed to see clearly the heart of the man she thought she loved.

Although Sonya and Pete were briefly separated over this ordeal, she quickly came to her senses after she realized Steve didn't want her children. When she returned to her husband, I saw them together and knew they were trying to salvage their marriage. That must have been incredibly hard. Thank God the two of them stayed together, worked through forgiveness and broken trust issues, and made their marriage work.

For years after, her husband, unable to exact his revenge on Steve, banned our children from playing together. The closest satisfaction he could exact to hating Steve was hating the three of us.

One evening, I received a knock on the front door. At first, I was apprehensive when I recognized my visitors were Sonya and Pete.

Pete's calm demeanor soon put me at ease. He began, "Can we come in and talk?"

"Sure," I replied, quickly motioning them to a seat on the living room sofa. I was grateful he had come peacefully after all the animosity previously shown toward us.

"I haven't been fair with you," Pete began. "I've come to apologize for how I have treated you and the kids over this whole mess. I have blamed you for what happened, but I realize this was not your fault. I haven't handled things very well. I've come to ask you to forgive me for the way I've treated the three of you."

Sonya's facial expressions during this interaction were attentive and relieved. Once Pete finished his apology, Sonya gave her apology for the horrible mistake she had made.

"I love Sara and Sawyer," she began. "Our son, Dennis, has missed playing with them. The three of you are welcome in our home anytime. If you need help with them when you have to work, I am happy to do that." Sonya smiled.

Stunned as I was, I responded without hesitation. "Yes. I am happy to put this behind us and do what we can to restore our friendship. My children have missed playing with your son."

Pete continued, "The three of you are welcome at our home anytime. Your children are welcome to come play, and I am taking down that barbed wire fence I never should have put up."

"Thank you," I said, relieved.

"I don't suppose I need to tell you that the same welcome does not extend to Steve," Pete hedged.

"You don't have to worry about Steve being here. He doesn't even come to visit his children," I replied.

That day, we started over as neighbors. After Sonya and Pete left, I watched as he tore down the barbed wire that had separated our property lines for well over two years. The journey to forgiveness is sometimes a slow process. There is no barb or poison worse than unforgiveness. Although I forgave Sonya, it would take years of healing before I would trust having another friend as close as Sonya was to me.

Steve never sent a single check to honor his written agreement to pay child support. To make financial matters worse, the courts didn't force the issue. Eventually, I sought an attorney and brought him to court, but every time a garnishment order came through the payroll department where he worked, he quit his job to avoid paying it.

I petitioned the court six times on behalf of my children because of nonsupport. When that was unsuccessful, child support enforcement intervened in court to obtain a blanket wage assignment. It wasn't until my son was a senior in high school that the children started getting regular child support checks. Together, they received a whopping forty dollars a week of the five hundred dollars per month he originally agreed to pay.

Meanwhile, Steve broke promise after promise to Sara and Sawyer. He never bought a birthday, Christmas, or graduation gift or even sent a card. He never helped buy school clothes. He never called. Emotionally and financially, he abandoned them. Still, I didn't punish Sara and Sawyer by publicly berating their dad. Someday, they would be mature enough to draw their own conclusions.

## SURROGATE DAD

My dad loved children. After Steve left, he stepped up his grandparenting role and became like a dad to Sara and Sawyer. Frequently, they'd find him sitting on his front porch on their walk home from the bus stop. Naturally, they would stop for a chat, and he'd invite them in for deli ham sandwiches, chips, and strawberry shortcakes.

Now in his seventies, some days he would play with them. I remember the day I was in my kitchen and Dad walked inside asking for a bandage, showing me a scrape on his elbow. Concerned that he had fallen, I asked, "What happened, Dad? Did you fall?"

"No," he replied. "I was riding with Sawyer on the Big Wheel" (a low, three-wheeled trike with an oversized front wheel), "and it tipped backward with us."

I couldn't help smiling. Dad grew up in the early 1900s and didn't have many toys as a child. Most were homemade. Now, he was getting to play with his grandchildren. Sara and Sawyer put their papaw on their two-seater go-cart and rode him around. I only heard about this after the fact. My dad was both protector and playmate for my children. I only wish I could have seen him playing with Sara and Sawyer and memorialized it in video or photographs.

My dad taught my children, especially Sawyer, so much more than their own dad had. He took Sawyer in the hills behind our home and taught him how to hunt and safely handle a firearm. He taught him how to identify trees, plants, and bird songs. He also taught him how to raise a garden, maintain a meticulous lawn, and how to sharpen knives and whittle.

Essentially, my dad taught Sawyer survival skills, all things Sawyer would later use in his career as a naturalist.

## DISCO FEVER

The late 1970s was the height of the disco era. Around 1978, just after my divorce, I caught disco "fever" along with most young Americans my age. As a teenager, I had gone straight from the supervision of parents to marriage and parenting. I had no time in between in which I was accountable only to myself. I was late discovering who I was as a woman on my own. At age twenty-seven, I had just shed over a hundred pounds in anticipation of having a hysterectomy. My husband had never paid me a personal compliment during that entire weight-loss battle or close encounter with cancer. Instead, I was told of my shortcomings.

Personal weight struggles had plagued me throughout high school, limiting dating in the simpler years when there were no adult responsibilities. Now, at a proportionate 142 pounds on a 5' 7 ½" frame with blue eyes and short brunette hair, I remember the day I first caught a glimpse of my own reflection when I walked past a storefront window. I had avoided mirrors for so long that at first glance, I didn't recognize this was actually me.

From my perspective, dating paralleled the navigation of a mine field. I was now thrust in a pool of those past the carefree days of their teen years. As a young woman who felt betrayed and unloved, I was among the "walking wounded" maneuvering through a sea of those recovering from broken relationships, the scars they leave and the behaviors that caused them.

It was difficult to find a reputable person to entrust care of my children for even a rare evening out. I had no relatives I could ask. Occasionally, during those first several months after my divorce, I splurged on the cost of a sitter for the evening. I was determined to have a few hours of respite from the weight of my responsibilities. On these rare "Cinderella" evenings, I tried to grab life by the double hands full. I danced some mean disco under dazzling lights in my stocking feet. I laughed, did a lot of people watching and tried to recapture the misspent youth I never got to experience. I saw young men and women behave badly. I saw middle-aged men and women do the same but I never wanted to be one of them.

One amusing evening, I watched a very inebriated young woman climb on a mechanical bull at a club in Pike County, Kentucky. A crowd of cheering onlookers encircled the performance "arena" where the "bull" was securely anchored to the floor. Soon the speed of the bull increased and the woman's hairpins and long curly brown hair were flinging in a dozen directions. She clung on briefly, only to be tossed off like a rag doll onto one of the well-placed mattresses on the floor below. I laughed out loud, and so did everybody around me. I doubt she enjoyed the memory of that ride more than I enjoyed watching her. Sometimes, it's enough to live vicariously and watch someone else look ridiculous.

Every experience taught me a new lesson. I made more mistakes than I care to admit. Many of those mistakes had names, and I'm just going to leave it there. Some of my biggest mistakes were believing people and giving them the benefit of the doubt. I'm not proud of my mistakes, but I own them and I've learned from them.

I remember dancing until closing time at 1 a.m. I remember hearing the clinking of bottles of various types of alcoholic beverages concealed inside brown paper bags beneath the tables in a "dry" county that didn't (openly) serve alcohol. I was never that woman who drank alcohol and couldn't remember what she had done later. If I had a good time, I wanted to remember and savor it. I didn't want someone else to comment "Wow, you were really having a good time last night." Consequently, if I was at a bar that actually served alcohol, I would whisper to the bartender to make mine a nonalcoholic drink but make it look realistic by putting a long-stemmed cherry and a tiny paper umbrella in my glass.

On ladies' night, I got in without a cover fee and one drink was all I ever bought. If a complimentary drink was sent to my table as an introductory token of interest, my secret admirer would usually tell the bartender to "give the lady another of whatever she is drinking." These were typically the same men who needed two to three drinks under their belts before they got the courage to come and introduce themselves personally and ask for a dance. They usually "window shopped" from afar, seated at their tables until they had consumed enough liquid courage to ask a woman to dance. By the time they finally got the courage, I was headed out the door for home. I can't remember all the times I've been asked as I was exiting the dance club, "You're not leaving now, are you?" Incidentally, I fish with the same philosophy. My opportunities without adult responsibility were few. For all the men who see themselves in this scenario, we can laugh together about "the one that got away." I'm a mountain girl. Fish or cut bait!

I spent the first six months after my divorce trying to assimilate my identity as a single parent and forgive those who wounded me. It was a crash course in social behavior. I quickly grew tired of coming home with my clothes and hair smelling like a stale ashtray. I was tired of the "plastic people", the deceit and the games. I was tired of those who temporarily slip off a wedding band and lie about being single. Initially I was naïve and gullible but soon learned that the phrase "in the process of getting a divorce" actually translated to "I'm married but looking for fun." A wedding band doesn't make you married in your heart any more than removing it makes you single. If a man told me he was divorced, I asked him to prove it and produce the court documents. This quickly diverted the liars and saved me the waste of time. One surprised me and actually did produce the court documents, which I thought was refreshing. Soon after, before we really had more than a friendship, he reconciled with his wife. It was quickly evident that he still loved her and I respected that.

The turning point for me came when I was working out of state in Tennessee. One evening, I went to a popular dance club. I was dressed in a beautiful vivid-red two-piece outfit. Red had been my mother's favorite color and I still remembered how it accentuated her wavy jet-black hair, hazel eyes and olive skin. The day I bought it, I hoped I'd look as pretty as she did. The blouse buttoned in a V-neck with wide, crinkled ruffles that flowed from the neckline. The pants were simple but matching. I felt confident even though I was going without another female companion.

I was seated at a small single table having my customary virgin beverage, listening to the band and watching others dance when a fellow approached me. Expecting he was going to ask me to dance or at least attempt some introduction, I turned to face him. Instead, he blurted out the words, "Do you want to f _ _k?" The color of my face instantly matched the color of my outfit and I could feel the heat of my flushed cheeks.

I was too stunned to deliver the actual slap in the face he deserved. My response was an indignant "You've got to be kidding me!" My evening was immediately ruined, so I picked up my purse and left. There had been nothing revealing or provocative about what I was wearing.

Reflecting on that event, I tortured myself with unanswered questions. What "signals" did he mistake because I was alone or even because I was wearing red? Did he think I was an escort for sale, was he impaired or just a complete idiot who had never been taught respect? There was nothing memorable about this man's appearance, but I have never forgotten his words. I never wore that outfit again.

131

That night, having met the harsh reality that I was at a crossroad in terms of my priorities, my "fever" broke and I chose my children. Time with my children was far more valuable than subjecting myself to disrespect and bad behavior. I finally realized who I was and what my values were. As for the men I met during my disco fever era, I was tired of the games. Women play games too. Even if nobody else cared who they hurt, I did. Even though I had been hurt, I didn't want to hurt other people. My own happiness would not come at the expense of somebody else's pain.

## ABSENTEE DAD

Steve never sent a single check to honor his written agreement to pay child support. To make financial matters worse, the court didn't force the issue. He never bought birthday, Christmas or graduation gifts or even sent a card. He never helped buy school clothes or helped with child care expenses. He rarely called and rarely showed interest in visitation. Many times, he promised Sara and Sawyer he was coming to take them for a weekend visit. They were excited, bags packed, only to be disappointed when he didn't show up and didn't call to say why.

This is only one of many occasions when he abandoned his role as a parent. Children are not pawns in a battle between two people that couldn't make a marriage work. I never berated him to Sara and Sawyer. I knew someday they would be mature enough to come to their own conclusions. It was more important that they have security now. We were a small family unit, but together we were a "chord of three strands...not quickly broken." (Ecclesiastes 4:12)

# Chapter Twenty

## B.B.

### FIRST-GENERATION COLLEGE STUDENT 1979

Fifty-seven years after my grandmother found herself unable to care for a three-year-old toddler as a single parent, I was facing the ominous task of raising two small children alone. There were no jobs that paid a livable wage for a woman supporting a family, unless you had close connections with someone influential in the hiring process. I was challenged to do in the 1970s what my grandmother had been unable to do in the 1920s. My daddy's words about the value of an education resounded in my mind over and over.

When the only job I could find was a waitressing job paying $1.90 per hour plus tips, I felt defeated. Tips from waitressing in my area wouldn't even pay for childcare or transportation costs. I had no choice but to swallow my pride and apply for welfare. We received a meager $196 a month plus food stamps to support my children, pay utilities and other household expenses, and buy clothing and school supplies.

Education would be my ticket out of poverty. A college degree would lay the foundation for building a better life for me and my children. The closest college was in Pikeville, a two-hour commute. I visited the admissions counselor there and told him, "I want to go to college, but I don't have any money. Can you help me?" I was thrilled when he responded that I could get a mining tech scholarship, which paid full tuition.

In the spring term, 1979, I began my first term as a college student. When my dad heard the news, he had already retired from the mines, but he was really upset with me. Despite the events leading to the separation and divorce, he felt Steve and I should get back together. Mainly, he just wanted Steve to support the children and me. The same man who sent my brother to college, insisting that an education was the key to getting out of poverty, vehemently opposed my decision. I wasn't asking him for money. All I wanted was his approval and encouragement. His harsh words essentially showed he thought I was a failure. "You're going to spend every dime you've got, and you'll never amount to anything!" At that moment, I felt a deep surge of anger and indignance rise inside me. My mind was screaming, "I'll show you, old man!" Out of respect for him, those words never came out of my mouth.

Coal had gone through a real boom in the 1970s. I learned that the college in Pikeville had received funding for scholarships in mining technology. The program offered such courses as mine supervision, safety and first aid, rescue, law, electricity, coal science, maps, roof control, blasting and explosives, coal analysis, and coal preparation, to name a few. I soaked up everything my instructors taught me like a sponge. The expense of making the two-hour daily round-trip commute was an enormous strain. There were times when money was so tight, I had only enough gas to make it to college and back that day. Many times, I didn't know how I could get the money to buy gas the next day. I didn't have a credit card or a charge account. I couldn't afford one. Eventually, you have to pay for what you charge, with interest. There were several times when I picked up pop bottles thrown out beside the road and sold them back to a local grocery store for the deposit to buy gas to go to school. From day to day, I didn't know where the money was going to come from. I was living by faith, not by sight.

For lunch, I walked from campus down to a little grocery store where nobody knew me and used food stamps to buy a couple of packs of peanut butter crackers. None of my classmates knew why I wouldn't go to the cafeteria to eat lunch with them. I didn't realize that my scholarship paid for my lunch too. Thankfully, I found that out the next semester. I was eventually awarded work-study, and that was a financial relief.

The mining tech program had a career counselor named Howard who was a retired human resources director from a local coal company. He was an older man with a smile on his face, a twinkle in his eyes, a positive attitude, a knack for storytelling, lots of spring left in his step, and the gift of gab. He was blessed with grown daughters and a green thumb for growing prizewinning tomatoes. All the mining tech students loved him. Every day, I went to visit him, either between classes or at lunchtime. He drew students into his office like a magnet, and each one of us left feeling uplifted. Of course, female students in this area of study were still in the minority.

I didn't discuss my struggles at home, and few people knew except my children. There was just not enough money to cover expenses, go to school, and support two children. There were times when there was not enough food for all three of us to be able to eat the same things at the same meal. Sometimes, there was no milk, no bread. Once, I caught my children pouring juice over their cereal because there was no milk. Intense feelings of guilt welled up inside me. I felt I was a complete failure for letting my children down.

Electric heat would be totally unaffordable in that drafty old coal camp house, so I had a fuel oil furnace. Our home provided basic shelter, but the construction was cheaply and quickly done at the turn of the nineteenth century. The exterior was constructed of wood siding with plaster over lattice boards inside the walls. There was no insulation apart from what I had blown in the walls and attic. There was certainly no air conditioning to ease the heat and humidity of a 90-plus-degree Kentucky summer.

When it was bitterly cold outside and fuel oil was low, I could use the oven and elements on my electric stove, while boiling a kettle of water on a burner, to add warmth. Of course, that increased my electric bill. My children would never know how many times I lay awake in bed at night, crying quietly with my stomach feeling like it was in knots and my throat tight and choking with worry. This is not something you burden young children with; they need to feel secure. I was the parent, and this was my problem to solve. I prayed to see just a small glimmer of light at the end of a very dark tunnel. More than anything, I needed hope and encouragement. The task before me seemed insurmountable.

I needed that hope when our fuel oil tank was empty on a below-zero winter night, and I had no money to fill it. There was just enough money to buy kerosene for a small, portable kerosene heater. I needed that hope when my children and I huddled together in the same bed for warmth, with quilts over the doorways to hold the heat just in the room where we slept. I piled multiple blankets and quilts on top of us to stay warm. We could still see the fog of our breath in the cold bedroom. We were spared asphyxiation from carbon monoxide fumes from that kerosene heater because our old house was so drafty. For that, we have all lived to give thanks. With our limited resources, we never splurged on nonessentials. I bought foods that would provide the most meals.

I got exactly two new outfits, bought at bargain prices, at the beginning of each new school semester. Instead of buying more clothes, I chose to give all I could to my children. If, out of desperation, I asked my dad for help, he always made me feel like an unworthy beggar. This was his way of punishing me for the divorce, as though it were all my fault. He used those occasions as opportunities to lecture me about my failures.

One day, the electric company came to disconnect our electricity. Since my dad lived only two houses down from me, I asked the utility worker who had come to do the disconnection to please wait and let me see if I could get the cash from my dad while he waited. Dad refused, reminding me that I shouldn't have divorced Steve. As I was walking back up the road with tears in my eyes, the neighbor who lived in the house above me (who also had daughters and grandchildren) said he would give me the money. That day, I was spared a disconnection. To this day, decades later, I struggle first to do things on my own, rather than ask for help. I am still learning to ask for help when I need it.

When I was on campus and feeling especially discouraged, I visited my career advisor, Mr. Brown. I waited patiently until the other students had gone, and then I poured my heart out to him.

"Mr. Brown, you know some of the challenges I am facing financially as a single parent. Do you really think I can do this?"

Without hesitation, he responded, "I know you can! All it takes is determination." With that, he handed me a quote by Abraham Lincoln:

"Determine that the thing can and shall be done and then...find the way."

He divvied out just the right amount of encouragement day by day until I finally began to believe in myself. He imparted his favorite quotes to me. I still read them daily and treasure them after all these years. Here is one:

The Bridge Builder by Will Allen Dromgoole

An old man going a lone highway,
Came at the evening, cold and gray,
To a chasm, vast, and deep and wide,
Through which was flowing a sullen tide.

The old man crossed in the twilight dim;
The sullen stream had no fear for him;
But he turned, when safe on the other side,
And built a bridge to span the tide.

"Old man," said a fellow pilgrim, near,
"You are wasting strength with building here;
Your journey will end with the ending day;
You never again will pass this way;
You've crossed the chasm, deep and wide—
Why build you this bridge at the evening tide?"

The builder lifted his old gray head:
"Good friend, in the path I have come," he said,
"There followeth after me today,
A youth, whose feet must pass this way.

This chasm, that has been naught to me,
To that fair-haired youth may a pitfall be.
He, too, must cross in the twilight dim;
Good friend, I am building this bridge for him."

I was determined to be a bridge builder for my children and make bridge building my lifelong pursuit.

# Chapter Twenty-One
## B.B.

## THE TESTING

In the summer of 1979, Mr. Brown persuaded a coal company to grant me a four-month internship. Most of my meager student's salary went for childcare and gasoline for the seventy-mile daily commute. Since coal mining was a male-dominated environment, most men were smiling and welcoming on the exterior, but some were determined to "break" me. I had just begun to learn the grit I was made of, but they had no idea. I had overcome much already. I had something to prove, but it certainly wasn't about being liberated. It was about surviving as a family unit. I was learning self-reliance while earning the income to provide for my children. More than anything, I wanted to be a positive role model; I wanted my children to be proud of me. I had my dad's deep sense of pride and strong work ethic, and I had no intention of raising my children on welfare.

A mining engineer and his transit man first took me underground to help with an off-shift survey. Surveys provide strategic information to the mine managers to help them determine the direction active mining should take place, to stay within the property boundaries and the coal seam. The height of the coal seam where we went that evening was under 50 inches high. I was 66 inches tall. I stooped over as far as I could, but my back was still hitting the ends of the roof bolt heads and their surrounding metal plates (used to bind the roof strata together and prevent a roof fall). Soon, I began to notice that the back of my coveralls was no longer getting caught and ripped on the sharp edges of the metal roof bolt plates. When I looked up, we were already headed through an underground intersection, headed toward the working coal face. The previous shift had stopped the mining process at the conclusion of their shift but failed to set temporary roof safety jacks. When temporary roof jacks are not immediately put in place and permanent roof bolts are not immediately installed, the roof strata begin to sag and separate. This is against mining regulations because it increases the risk of a roof fall. I was just an intern, but I knew this was wrong, and I knew I was in immediate danger.

The smirks on their faces quickly let me know they thought this "test" was pretty funny. Miners take risks all the time, by the nature of their hazardous jobs, but this was not a risk I was willing to take. I had two children at home depending on me for their security. Immediately, I turned around and went back beneath the roof supports. I learned to watch out for myself rather than trust my safety to others.

The next day, I was assigned to the safety department. The safety director and his assistant took me to non-active areas of the mine where the ventilation was poor. There was so little air movement that I could see the particles of dust, still suspended in the air, illuminated by my battery-powered cap light. I wasn't sure which of them had a death wish, but I didn't. If they were trying to scare me, I didn't waver. My fear of not being able to provide for my children was far greater.

A few days later, I was once again assigned to the engineering department to conduct a survey on the remote surface areas of the mine property. It was while working with the engineer and transit man that I became aware of the subtlety of being ignored and "talked around" in conversation. Perhaps they thought, if they ignored me, pretending I wasn't there, I'd eventually just go away. The term "inclusion" certainly was not in anybody's vocabulary in that era.

The survey site was in a hilly area, so overgrown with vegetation that we used machetes to hack our way through it. I helped them clear areas to set up the transit and observed while they plotted a survey. We encountered several snakes in the process of clearing vegetation. I quietly distanced myself from my slithering foes. I wondered whether the engineer and transit man were disappointed when I didn't scream or run.

Our jeep broke down that day while we were inspecting huge ventilation fans extracting air from active mining areas to the outside. We were in a jungle of rugged overgrowth. The engineer remarked that he and his transit man were going to begin walking back to the mine office. I had the option of staying there alone, not knowing when (or if) anybody would come back to get me, or I could join them and hike the twelve miles back to the office. There were no cell phones then, and I concluded this was yet another test I had to pass. Fear hadn't worked. This was a test of endurance.

That evening, after I got home and bathed, I don't even think I ate. I was so exhausted I went straight to bed, long before dark. Still, I was back at work the next day. After that, they gave up trying to "break" me. They must already have played their full bag of tricks.

## THE GRADUATE

In May 1980, I was awarded an associate of applied science degree in mining technology. Denny Zigler, the region's most notable coal superintendent, was at my graduation to deliver our commencement address. My dad was absent, still boycotting anything to do with his daughter working in the coal industry. That day, it was Denny, a well-known and well-respected mining engineer in my hometown, who realized my determination, accomplishment, and the obstacles I had overcome as a single mom. He was the one who told me how proud he was of me.

## CARBON CANARY COAL

On May 27, 1980, I began my first mining job postgraduation as a respirable dust sampler in the safety department at Carbon Canary ("Triple C") Coal. In 1975, Triple C had two separate methane gas explosions that killed twenty-seven miners. One of the first mines I was assigned to was in a known gassy coal seam where both of those methane explosions occurred. I descended in an elevator cage through a borehole 380 feet below ground level, roughly twenty breaks from the source of that tragic first explosion. A coworker named Kyle directed my attention towards a barrier wall made of concrete blocks used to direct mine ventilation toward the working face of the coal. Kyle pointed out the still-visible remnants of a blue sweatshirt worn by one of those miners, blown through the concrete blocks. The miner had been communicating on a mine phone when the explosion occurred. Kyle remarked, "You are looking down the 'gun barrel' of that explosion." I redirected my gaze as a wave of sadness came over me. I observed a moment of quiet reverence for that lost life and all the others who lost their lives in that horrible, needless tragedy.

I expected to find a company now devoted to safety after those two explosions. Instead, I found that the mine managers had learned very little, and safety was still not a priority. Like electricity, methane gas is a danger you can't see. I could hear a sizzle (similar to the sound of bacon frying) as methane gas emitted from the active face where the coal was being mined.

One single spark could cause an ignition. Miners who exited that section came out with their faces blackened with coal dust. The only visible parts of their body that weren't covered in coal dust were the whites of their eyes and their teeth. Those facts alone were evidence that the flow of ventilation was inadequate to sweep away the dust generated in the mining process, as well as the accumulation of methane gas.

Huge external fans ventilate the mines by drawing in fresh outside air and directing it toward the active mining areas (known as the "working face" of the coal). Fresh air is directed underground to the working sections by a series of concrete partitions and temporary brattice cloth "curtains." These cloth curtains, constructed of woven polypropylene fabric with an anti-static grid and flame-retardant coating, separate the contaminated air from the fresh air after it passes across the working face. Contaminated air is directed down a return airway and exhausted back outside the mine. The volume and velocity of that fresh air is measured by an anemometer and must be maintained at an adequate level. (Reference: Mine Safety and Health Administration 30 CFR §75.371.) The explosions that killed those miners occurred because methane gas concentrations rose to an explosive range of 5 to 15 percent. This was caused by the failure to maintain adequate ventilation. Coal production still took priority over safety.

It was public knowledge that major explosions had happened at the mine where I was working. It was also a fairly recent victory for women to attain work in male-dominated environments, especially one as potentially dangerous as coal mining. No other mothers in my children's school worked in the underground mining environment.

One day, I was notified by the school secretary that Sara had been sitting in her classroom crying. When asked why she was crying, she told them, through tears, that she was afraid something bad would happen to me at the mine. Later, Sara told me I was the only parent she could depend on, and she was afraid she and Sawyer would lose me. This ripped my heart. Children so young should not have to bear the worries of adults or feel insecure. I had no idea she realized I was in such danger. All I could do was reassure her that I looked out for my own safety every single day and that I would be extra careful.

In June 1980, I received my first paycheck. Having started work in the middle of a pay period, I was paid for four days plus two hours of overtime. With a two-year associate degree in coal mining technology, my next paycheck was exactly $163.69. One of the industrial engineers who worked across the hall from me asked me how much I was being paid. Foolishly, I told him. His nasty and disrespectful response was to ask me whether I was sleeping with my boss to earn those wages. I quickly learned to keep income information private.

One day in late June 1980, a safety office coworker named Lyle remarked, "Men are superior to women, and women have no right to a man's job." This remark totally caught me off guard since this topic had never even come up in conversation. He went on with his rant, saying he "didn't like my women's 'libber' attitude." Surprised by his candor, I asked him to give me an example of why he thought such an attitude was evident in my behavior. He could give no response other than to mention my membership in Coal Employment for Women, an organization promoting the hiring of women in nontraditional jobs in mining.

## A MATTER OF INTEGRITY

One day, I walked into the respirable dust lab office and caught one of my coworkers forging a miner's signature to a respirable dust sample card. In violation of federal regulations, he was also running the dust pump inside the mine office instead of having it be worn by the coal miner who was supposed to have his exposure to coal dust sampled underground.

Stunned, I asked, "What are you doing?" (although the answer was evident). I continued, "Don't ever ask me to do that because I won't!" He replied, "If you intend to continue to work here, don't tell me you won't do this!" I never compromised.

Every miner has the right to access and review their mine's roof control plans. Since I was working in the safety department, I asked to see a copy of roof control plans for a specific mine. My request was flatly refused by the safety director himself, and shortly thereafter, I was fired. Three lame reasons given for my termination were: 1) "Complaining about the taste of the bottled water," 2) "Running off safety meetings on legal-sized paper instead of standard-sized paper" (the copy paper was actually kept locked up in a safe), and 3) "Asking to see a copy of the roof control plan." I could have contested the firing in court, but being terminated actually came as a huge relief. I had been looking for a job elsewhere anyway. Every day, I went to work with my nerves on edge, in fear for my life. The day I drove out the gates of Triple C property, a huge burden was lifted. I didn't even fight the termination in court. Two days later, I was called to work as a safety inspector at Sedona Coal in Pike County, making almost double the wage and in a non-gassy mine. (Triple C was eventually closed and sealed.)

## HAZING

Regardless of company policy against it, many coal miners participate in the practice of hazing. As a woman in the coal industry, I was threatened with hazing by male coal miners on more than one occasion. They wanted to know exactly what they could get away with. A very clear and distinct boundary had to be drawn. While I was a good sport and could take a joke, the type of hazing I was threatened with was very personal and bordered on assaultive behavior.

One evening underground, a couple of the miners said, "It's time for you to be initiated just like the new guys are when they come to work here." After a couple of subtle comments, they voiced their intentions. One of them would hold me down while the other pulled my pants down. I had heard from Steve several years earlier that the next step in this hazing was the act of "hairing." This involved actually pulling the person's pubic hair. An immediate and firm boundary had to be established. The same laws apply underground in the darkness that apply above ground in the light of day.

"No! You will *not* be putting your hands on me, holding me down, or pulling my pants down! You are threatening me with physical assault. This is not funny, and I take your comments very seriously. Before you take another step toward me, you need to know that I will report you, file formal charges against you, and have you in court so fast it will make your head spin!" Immediately, the threats stopped, and they left me alone. Word soon got around. It must have been the glare from my eyes. They knew I was serious, and I received no further hazing threats.

## THE COURT OF PUBLIC OPINION

In my small town, I was shunned by some women and disrespected time and again. I was accused of "taking a man's job." One snide remark led to another from women who knew nothing of my character and seemed to think I was underground for the sole purpose of "husband shopping." Their disapproval of me as a person was obvious. I didn't have my fingernails polished or wear nice clothes like many working women "enlightened" by the women's

143

liberation movement of the sixties and seventies. While I was worried about how I was going to feed my children their next meal, I fielded such petty, ridiculous questions as "How do you get your bras clean?" I pondered how these refined, "kept" women would react if I simply responded, solely for the shock factor, that I didn't wear one. Would they have an instantaneous meltdown? Of all the questions they could have asked, that question was most demeaning.

I encountered this criticism in local shops such as the grocery store and even from other parents at my children's school. I was judged by men who were superstitious of any woman entering a coal mine as being "bad luck." The most humorous thing happened the day I was running an errand to the local Mine Safety Administration (MSA) office to submit roof control plans for approval. I was wearing my usual work clothes, including hard-toed boots, when I decided to stop for a bathroom break at a popular restaurant. Men wore their work clothes out in the community every day, and nobody seemed to notice. When I went into one of the stalls in the women's bathroom, I was amused by the deadly quiet that came over the neighboring stalls. My stall mates apparently noticed my work boots beneath the stall and thought a man had wandered in. Neither person came out until I was gone. It was unforgettably funny.

Those who were critical didn't know about all the times when my children and I went to a near-empty refrigerator. They didn't know about the heartbreak I felt when my children had no milk, and I had no money to buy it. They never knew about the times when I went into the grocery store with under twenty dollars and had to decide which things were most important, most nutritious, most filling, and would provide the most meals. They never knew about the times when I had to have a "family meeting" with Sara and Sawyer in the car before we went into a store, just so there wasn't the awkwardness of having to say "no" over and over again as they ran to the toy section. I had to tell them we only had money for food but not for toys.

My motives for working in the coal industry had nothing to do with "women's liberation." Jobs offering a livable wage usually went first to wives, sisters, and those otherwise well-connected to the employer. Apart from a local waitressing job that paid one dollar per hour plus tips (in an area that wasn't in the habit of leaving good tips), the next available job was in a fast-food restaurant. They paid only $1.90 per hour, and the job required a twenty-eight-mile commute. It would require me to pay more for childcare than I would earn. For me, working in the coal industry had everything to do with survival.

When two people become parents, they each have an obligation to provide for their children. When one parent neglects or abandons his or her obligations, the other has to step up and take on a dual role. This role was one I never expected and was certainly not prepared for. One parent was never meant to be both mother and father to their children. However, sometimes, the most broken homes are those where couples stay together in a toxic relationship caused by adultery, mental and/or physical abuse, and/or substance abuse. I was determined that as a single parent, I would make sure our home would not be broken. We would struggle, but we would have a strong bond as a unified family despite it all.

# Chapter Twenty-Two
## B.B.

### LATCHKEY CHILDREN

Sara and Sawyer were self-reliant Gen Xers before anybody even labeled their generation. They were as different as two children could be. Sara was very sensitive, nurturing, and affectionate. She took her role of big sister very seriously and was always the peacemaker. Sawyer was an inquisitive explorer, always energetic, adventurous, and methodical. Both had sandy blond hair, blue eyes, and a sprinkling of freckles across their noses and cheeks. Sara was Sawyer's self-appointed protector, even though she was only eighteen months older. I remember many times seeing her struggling to carry him to me when he hurt himself while playing.

At best, the business of survival was hard for the three of us. By the time they were in grade school, Sara and Sawyer had to learn to contribute, according to their capabilities, to simple tasks like picking up after themselves and hand washing a few simple dishes. They learned what it meant to have a schedule and the importance of sticking to that schedule. Every task they didn't complete meant the chores just kept piling up.

I stressed time and again that the three of us were a family, and that our survival as a family depended on us working together and contributing whatever we could to get the daily chores done. When I came home from work, I had hungry children to feed and was already exhausted. They were my strength and my motivation, but I also needed them to do as much as they were capable of doing to help.

Every morning, I got up at 3 a.m., packed my children's school lunches, and carefully laid out their school clothes. I set out their cereal bowls and cereal, leaving them only to pour their milk. Next, I packed my own lunch, bathed, and dressed for work. Around 5:15 a.m., I woke my sleeping daughter to fix her hair for school. She soon drifted back off to sleep afterward. I made sure the alarm clock was set on the nightstand right beside their beds. I wrote a note, listing the chores they needed to complete after school while waiting for me to get home from work. I always emphasized, "Stay in your own yard and don't have our house full of neighborhood kids!"

Around 5:30 a.m., I began my one-and-a-half-hour commute to work. My workday started at 7 a.m. There was a lot of time to think and problem solve on that long commute. On weekdays, when I had already arrived at work by 7 a.m., the children's alarm clock sounded at 7:30 a.m. The two of them, ages seven and eight at the time, had a well-established routine. They dressed in the clothes laid out for them. Next, they poured their milk and took their cereal to the living room to watch television. When a certain program ended and another started, that was their signal it was time to head toward the school bus stop. Only once between 1979 and 1983 did the two of them ever miss the bus. When they did, their papaw (who lived close by) took them. They were accountable not to miss school.

For me, the term "latchkey children" was laden with connotations of judgment and accusations of neglect and parental failure. I was doing all I could to provide for my children while teaching them to be self-reliant. I was teaching them what it meant to work for the things you needed rather than depend on the welfare system. My dad modeled working hard and having a sense of pride and accomplishment in his work. Likewise, while teaching Sara and Sawyer work ethics, I was teaching them to be survivors.

Despite my instructions not to leave our yard, my children exerted their independence and usually did. The simple chores I assigned them didn't always get completed. My intent was to teach them responsibility while keeping them out of mischief in the one- to one-and-a-half-hour wait until I got home from work. Theoretically, once the chores were done, they could either play in the yard or watch television. First, we work, then we play. That was a simple concept.

There was no need for wristwatches. I think they developed radar for when I was due home from work. Upon recognizing the distinct sound of my compact car's engine, I usually caught a glimpse of them making a mad dash through our front driveway headed for our back door. When I finally pulled in our driveway and walked through the back door, they were like little angels and "busy" as worker bees, doing the chores I had assigned them to do.

I held dreaded family meetings when they were not making an effort to help by doing their chores. At these mini meetings, I reemphasized how important it was for the three of us to work as a team. Our survival depended on us working together, being there to support each other, and sharing the chores. They were children, but they understood. Their cooperation always improved afterward, and sometimes, I even got an apology. Sometimes, it came in the form of a sweet handwritten note with their own artwork adorning a piece of folded notebook paper. I have kept and still treasure many of those notes they wrote to me.

From the beginning, I established a secret emergency code word known only to the three of us. This code word came with instructions for their response in the event a stranger approached our driveway. Those instructions involved turning off anything that made a sound, making sure the doors were locked, and hiding where they could not be seen through the window. This had to be done quickly. They did not come out until I gave the all-clear signal, or the stranger was gone. They were never, under any circumstances, to go to the door for a stranger.

Unfortunately, as a single mom working in a predominantly male industry, there were times when we had to actually carry out this procedure. There were incessant and inappropriate requests for my personal phone number at work. In a small town where everybody knows everybody, all a stranger had to do was stop at a business in town and ask where a certain person lived. The locals were trusting and divulged information that should have been kept private. I had many uninvited male visitors appear at our front door, usually on weekends since I worked Monday through Friday. Knocks from strangers went unanswered, and I was home whenever the code word was needed.

One day, I watched them carry out the procedure we had walked through many times. It began when I spotted an unrecognized vehicle with an unrecognized male driver backing into our driveway. Immediately, I called out the secret code word. The two of them quickly sprang into action. All sound was turned off. Door locks were quickly checked. The three of us disappeared from view and remained silent until the "threat" had passed. They had been well-trained.

# Chapter Twenty-Three

## B.B.

### SEDONA COAL CORPORATION

I accepted a position as safety inspector at Sedona Coal just two days after I left Triple C. I was thirty-one years old, the first and only female to work there in a nontraditional role. Most men there respected me for not being on welfare and choosing to work to provide for my family. Some miners even held the mine doors (metal trap doors in the concrete barriers used to direct ventilation to the working sections of the mine) open for me, much as a gentleman would open the door for a lady. That simple courtesy always made me smile, and I always responded with a "thank you."

One day, I was underground, conducting a routine inspection, when one of the more macho and vocal miners in his thirties remarked, "I have more respect for a woman who works in a massage parlor than one who works in an underground coal mine!" By that point in my life, there were no tears left to cry, and I was numb to insults.

"I'm sorry you feel that way," I responded. "I have never done anything to earn that kind of disrespect from you."

The other miners and the foreman heard what he said and immediately called him out for it. This conversation was quickly reported by the foreman to the mine manager. The other miners immediately began to tell him how inappropriate his comments were, then voiced their support for me. "You could have been sitting home drawing a welfare check, but instead, you are working to support your children. We have nothing but respect for you." He was sent immediately to the outside mine office to meet with the mine manager.

Clyde, the mine manager (who had only daughters at home and always treated me with the utmost respect) delivered his reprimand at such a volume that I heard him two rooms away. I was defended like a daughter that day. The mine manager made it clear that showing disrespect for me was not acceptable behavior and would not be tolerated. Later, I received a formal apology from that miner. Word travels fast on the company grapevine. From that point forward, no other miner ever disrespected me there.

I occasionally had to redirect married men back to their wives and children. One was persistent. His name was Charles. I was a safety inspector, and he was a mine maintenance foreman. He was accident-prone as well. It happened to be one of my job duties to take workers not seriously injured to the emergency room of the local hospital for treatment. He had become a "frequent flier" to the ER. One Christmas, all the salaried employees exchanged names to buy each other gifts. After some trading around, Charles managed to make sure we got each other's name. I bought him a St. Christopher medal, symbolizing his need for protection. How this man managed to love me, I don't know. It certainly wasn't because I was a flirt. I was definitely not dressed for "husband shopping" at work. I wore coal- and rock-dust-laden coveralls, hard-toed boots, and a hard hat with the nappy hair it caused. I wore no fingernail polish. What did I have for lure? I wore a smile, and I treated people with respect. I listened when they talked to me. Most important of all, I was a good sport and could take a joke. I suppose that was enough, regardless of the environment.

One Sunday afternoon, Charles showed up at my house, decked out in his full National Guard uniform after a "weekend warrior" exercise. He was the ranking officer in command of his unit. I didn't really care about titles. I just know he looked very handsome decked out in his military uniform, standing there on my front porch. I had never told him where I lived, and he had never asked. We had a good working relationship, so I invited him in. There had never been any indication of personal interest from him, and I certainly hadn't expressed any. After all, he was married. His conversation, even with my children present, soon told me he had a more personal interest in me. I had never detected any flirtatious behavior at work. But then, I wasn't looking for it either. I was the mine safety inspector, writing all the inspection reports that he and his evening-shift maintenance crew were responsible for correcting. Yet here he was now, sitting in my living room, respectful, a perfect gentleman and all smiles. I didn't encourage him but listened to what he had to say. There was mutual respect, and I remained polite and kind.

He was a college graduate, intelligent, and hardworking. He was a good man, not what I'd call a typical cheating husband out looking for a good time. We saw each other only in passing at shift changes. There was friendly chitchat, but then I was friendly with all my coworkers.

I continued to create work for Charles and his crew with every daily inspection report I wrote. He was always smiling when I handed those reports to him, and the necessary repairs always got completed.

One day, I came home and found a single white rose he had left for me at my back door. I had never received a flower of any kind without a special occasion. Later at work one evening, he told me how many florists he had gone to in search of that perfect white rose, a symbol of pure love.

About a week later, he showed up at my house again. This time, he was accompanied by his two small daughters, saying he wanted them to meet me. I was stunned, and I couldn't understand what I considered to be very reckless behavior. "What are you doing?" were the only words I could think of in response. Innocent children speak in innocence. Surely, they would say something to their mother. This time, I emphatically but kindly redirected him home. A few days later, Clyde, the mine manager, called me into his office. "Don't you know that man is crazy about you? He would leave his wife in a heartbeat if you would have him."

"That's not the way I roll," I explained. "I know how that feels. I don't want a man with half his heart ripped out. He loves his little girls. I don't know anything about his relationship with his wife, but I could never find happiness at the expense of somebody else's misery." Soon after, Charles walked over to my office and told me he was leaving. He had gotten another job because it was just too hard to see me every day. We both did the right thing. He was a kind man and a wonderful daddy who loved his little girls. Of course, I missed him at work, but I had no right to miss him any other way. His family needed him, and I had no right to need him.

It was eleven years later when I picked up a newspaper and ran across his name in the obituary. The words leaped at me from the newsprint like a lightning bolt through my chest. He had been killed underground in a mining accident while working on a piece of equipment. I turned white and was choked up with tears. "What if?" I asked myself. I could never have lived with the guilt.

## SAFETY FIRST

My role as a safety inspector took me from mine to mine, section to section. Those inspections included all the surface areas of the underground mines, such as the coal preparation plant. Among my duties was assessing for adequate ventilation, electrical hazards, accumulations of combustible materials, proper roof support, functional fire sensors, water sprays (to wet the dust) on the continuous mining machine, proper guarding of moving conveyors and equipment, and compliance with Title 30 CFR Mine Safety and Health Administration Department of Labor regulations. Every time I conducted an inspection, I thought of my dad. He had been injured many times, knocked unconscious, and even trapped in a roof fall. My mission was to make the underground workplace safer. When I was conducting an inspection, I was mindful that identifying and eliminating safety hazards would be protecting somebody else's dad, brother, husband, or son. It was a role I took very seriously.

Annual refresher training and new hire orientation were also among my duties. Instead of imagining a pristine, air-conditioned classroom, visualize instead coal miners sitting underground on stacks of fifty-pound bags of "rock dust." (Rock dust is powdered limestone, applied to mix with combustible coal dust to prevent flame propagation in the event of a methane ignition.) By contrast, those employees who worked at the surface areas of the underground mines would perch themselves atop equipment such as a D-9 bulldozer. Think of the vantage point of stadium seating. I found it amusing. There was no perfect classroom for instruction, and every time, the setting was different.

Flexibility and adaptation were necessary assets for a mine safety instructor and first aid instructor. A sense of humor always helped. Teaching coal miners was like having a group of brothers together. They laughed, teased, and joked as they participated and learned. Miners work as a team. They look out for each other. They develop strong bonds with each other because their lives depend on it. For many of them, I was like a sister.

One day, I was at the coal preparation plant in my coveralls, hard-toed rubber boots, and hard hat. I approached the back side of the plant and could see miners waving frantically at me from the top of the plant. I thought they were just being friendly. Because of the noise, I couldn't distinguish what they were saying. When I took the next step, I was stuck. Both feet were submerged in the muck and sludge by-products of coal washing and preparation. It was like quicksand, but fortunately only went to the top of my boots, making it nearly impossible for me to take the next step. Instead, my feet came completely out of my boots, and there I was in my stocking feet, struggling to pull myself and my boots out of the muck. It must have been a comical sight from their vantage point. What can you do but laugh when you look that ridiculous? My boots, socks, feet, and the legs of my coveralls all had to be hosed down. This was my initiation to becoming one of the crew. We all laughed about it, and my reaction proved I was a good sport. I'm sure that story hit the company grapevine and caused a good many belly laughs.

## CREDIBILITY

To gain further respect and credibility, I took a required exam through the Kentucky Department of Mines and Minerals and became one of only 136 women who were first class mine foremen in Kentucky in the 1980s. This certification qualified me to supervise and lead a crew of underground coal miners during the active mining process. Still, I had no interest in actually becoming a section foreman. My primary focus was mine safety and first aid training.

# Chapter Twenty-Four
## B.B.

## THE NEW GENERAL MANAGER

Everything was going well in the workplace until the day a new general manager named Brent came from West Virginia. He was married and in his fifties. His initial greeting was overtly friendly toward me. Every time he came to the mine offices, he sought me out.

Then, as weeks and months passed, he tried to get me alone in the back areas of the engineering office. He would come within inches of me while I was duplicating my safety inspection reports for distribution. He managed to get as close to me as he could, under the initial guise of conversation, then eventually brush up against me, putting his hands on my arm or back. His touch was unwelcome, and it made my skin crawl.

There was only one other female onsite, Cindi, the mine secretary. She was petite with long, strawberry-blonde hair, wearing snug low-cut blouses and 2 ½ inch heels. She was the temperamental sort, and all the men knew to approach her cautiously. She would bite your head off in the morning, but drip sugar in the afternoon. All her smiles were for one particularly suave, smooth-talking mine foreman, married, of course. I often wondered why the new GM didn't choose to pursue this femme fatale wearing high heels instead of me, wearing the hard-toed work boots and coveralls.

In subsequent visits to the mine office, he tried to put his hands on me again, but I managed to dodge him. If I heard he was on his way up from the main office, I made sure I was underground. This means of escape at least gave me an advantage over the mine secretary.

I reported his stalking behavior to my immediate supervisor, the safety director, Nathan. There was little Nathan could do to help me since he reported directly to Brent. My report put Nathan in an awkward predicament. Although he lost respect for Brent, there was nothing he could do to help me. Soon after, Nathan accepted a job elsewhere and left Sedona. For me, things soon progressed from bad to worse.

I began logging these sexual advances in a diary. On one rare occasion when I had to miss work because one of my children was ill, Brent called me at home to express his "concern" for my child. I tried to be pleasant since I wasn't sure how else I should handle such an awkward conversation. Eventually, he asked me to meet him at a motel. I made an excuse. Thankfully, it was a long commute from the worksite. I started leaving my phone receiver off the hook. That didn't work so well when I was on the job and he called me from the main office. I found his propositions sickening.

I thought about my grandmother, a divorced woman, working in a logging camp in the 1920s. I wondered what her life must have been like there. I wished I could talk to her and hear her stories.

# Chapter Twenty-Five
## J.D.

It was now 1979, and I had already transferred to Killard Point. There was still no word of postings. The days on site were now just tedious.

One morning, I arrived early at the Armoury and was sitting in the crew room waiting for the others to arrive. The police flight sergeant came in and asked where I worked. I told him. When I answered, he asked who was in charge of me. Again, I told him. Then he asked, "Is there a reason why your hair is so long?"

I looked him straight in the eye and replied, "Yes, Flight." Then I looked away.

When the rest of the group arrived, we went to the Armoury to pick up our rifles and ammunition. As I was signing for mine, my beret fell off and landed on top of the counter.

"That's what happens when you let your hair get too long," remarked the flight sergeant.

I picked up my beret, put it back on, and then took my rifle and ammunition. "Don't worry, Flight. I'm going to clothing stores this afternoon," I replied casually.

"Clothing stores? Why?" asked the flight sergeant.

"To get myself a bigger beret!" With that, I turned and walked out of the Armoury to the sound of the flight sergeant bawling something in my direction. I didn't even stop to listen. At this point, I was past caring. I climbed into the back of the Land Rover, rifle across my chest in the "ready" position, and headed towards Killard Point.

The days dragged on. Life was monotonous. I was heartily sick of playing bridge, darts, and Scrabble most of the day, every day. Lunchtime became a welcome relief. Mary always had a hot meal ready for me, and I was always met with the same question: "Have you heard anything yet?"

Each time, I replied, "No. Not yet."

"Is there somebody you could call to get it sorted out?" She just couldn't understand how the RAF operated. I could appreciate her frustration, but the situation was completely out of my hands.

One morning, the engineering squadron officer arrived. He told us some of the postings were in. I hoped to be one of those in the first batch. He read out the names, then their postings. I and a few others were not included.

"Any word when our postings will come through, sir?" I asked.

"No. Sorry. This is all I have at the moment. It shouldn't be too long now, though," he replied.

"Oh, great!" I said to myself. "How the hell am I going to explain that some had got their postings and I hadn't?" I knew exactly what Mary's reaction would be.

When I got back to the house, I found I was dead right. All the questions came: "What about us? When are we leaving? How come so-and-so got theirs and we didn't? When will we be hearing?" These were all questions I couldn't answer, but she just never stopped bemoaning the fact that we hadn't got our posting. We met one of our neighbours as they were going to the Families Club. Mary told them that we still "hadn't got our bloody posting yet, but others had." The neighbour, a corporal, told her these things happened, and at least things were moving. That seemed to temporarily pacify her.

Soon, the engineering squadron officer arrived with more postings. Again, my name hadn't been called. When I asked, the officer said, "Ah, Aubrey. Yes. There seems to be some delay with your posting. I don't know why, but don't worry, it will come soon."

My mind was racing as to what I was to tell Mary when everyone got their posting except me.

I arrived home, told Mary about what happened, and got the reaction I was expecting. She persistently asked the same old questions she already knew I couldn't answer. I just ate my dinner and tried to ignore her.

Eventually, my posting came through. Neatishead! Mary seemed happy to finally know where we would be going, but it was too far from her parents and hometown. A short time later, we were watching a news bulletin and saw roads thick with snow, cars stuck in the snow, and snow ploughs doing their best to keep the roads clear.

"Where's this?" she asked.

"Where we're going in a few days' time! Norfolk."

By this time, we were busy cleaning the house and making it ready for inspection in preparation for our departure, termed "march out."

The constant upheavals in military life are huge stressors. A family crisis just magnifies that stress one hundredfold. Two days prior to the march out, Mary received a telegram that stated she should call home immediately. No further details were given, and she was frantic with worry. Her parents had been involved in a serious car accident, and she was to get home as soon as possible. We talked between her outbursts of tears. As we were leaving in a couple of days, and neither parent was in a life-or-death struggle, we decided not to change our plans. Of course, Mary's heart was no longer into the cleaning and polishing that needed to be done; she was more worried about her parents. The furniture had already been readied to be sent on before us. It would be in storage until we got a place at Neatishead.

The march out was disastrous. So many failings, but I didn't care. Mary wasn't permitted in the house during this process, thankfully. I knew she would really tear into them, especially considering the situation with her parents. I just shrugged off all the negative pettiness of the housing officer. I was long past caring.

Finally, we arrived at the ferry and were just relieved to finally be on our way. The journey back to Mary's parents was uneventful. Her father was out of hospital, having sustained only a broken ankle. Her mother's condition was a lot more serious. As she had severe head and leg injuries, she would be in hospital for quite some time. I called RAF Neatishead, explained the circumstances, and applied for some leave. I was granted a week. I was also told to go directly to RAF Coltishall, where I would get my accommodation sorted out. That week off was beneficial, as I could at least help Mary and her father.

Once the week was over, I drove to RAF Coltishall, got allocated a place in the transit block, and settled in. Mary stayed at her parents' home to be available to them when her mother came out of the hospital.

Upon my arrival at RAF Neatishead, I pulled up at the locked gate, where I was met by guards eyeing me with suspicion. My car, purchased whilst in Northern Ireland, had Northern Ireland registration plates. They must have thought I was an Irish terrorist!

As I got out of the car and approached the gate, one guard levelled his rifle towards me. "Get your hands up!" he called.

"That's not the correct procedure," I thought. I already had my ID card in hand and called out, "I'm J/T Aubrey, just posted in!"

One guard checked my ID, then commented, "You've chosen a helluva time to arrive, mate." He continued making conversation whilst a corporal was talking on the phone. "Where'd you come from?"

"Bishop's Court and Killard Point," I replied.

"Bloody hell! What was it like?"

"OK. I came out of it."

Once inside, a J/T escorted me up to the engineering warrant officer's office, where I was questioned sternly regarding why I hadn't arrived a week earlier when they expected me.

I explained the circumstances and that I had received permission to arrive late. He looked at me, then began shuffling through papers, no doubt checking to see if my story matched. "Very well. As you can see, we are in the middle of an exercise, so there is no point in you even attempting to arrive today. J/T Evans will be your guide for the day, and he will show you around and get you oriented."

Evans showed me around and explained what the main pieces of equipment were. "Are you 'Q'd'?" Meaning if I had "Q-annotation" equipment specialisation.

"No. Displays and back-up," I replied.

Evans asked me about my experience. I told him about Malvern.

"Do you know Mark Cassidy?"

"Mark? Dark hair, sort of curly, loves cars?"

"Yeah, that sounds like him. He says he was at RRE Malvern as well. I wondered if you knew him."

"We worked together in the same lab when we were detached from GRIS, Henlow. Why?"

"He's here on B watch. He should be around somewhere. He's on light rescue somewhere."

This was good news, to have a familiar face around.

We all went to the mess together. It was a combined mess: officers, SNCOs, and airmen's messes all in the same building, but segregated.

The next day, the arrival process was the usual. As I walked into Engineering Wing Headquarters and past the wing commander's office, I heard a voice calling, "Aubrey! Is that you?"

I turned back and looked in disbelief. It was Wing Commander Simpson from RSRE Malvern.

"Hello, sir. How are you?" I asked.

"Come in, Aubrey. Sit down. We've got some talking to do." I always liked him, even though he thought drinking more than half a pint of beer a week was drinking to excess.

He asked me how my posting to Northern Ireland was, then went on to ask about my wife and how she was doing (they had met at a wine and cheese party one evening when we were at Malvern). He even asked how my leave had gone and how my wife's parents were. He had obviously been well informed. This was typical of Simpson. He always seemed to care.

The next day after my official arrival, I reported to the control room. I met the watch commander and watch chief, then was taken to the crew room and introduced to the rest of the watch. My friend Mark was also there.

I was allocated to B watch. Their first day was the next day. I was told to go back to Coltishall once I had arrived and report the next day.

The following day, I was called into the watch office, where both the watch commander and watch chief were waiting for me. They both looked quite stern. I wondered what the problem could be as there were papers on the desk in front of them.

The chief spoke, saying, "Here are your assessments on posting. They are appalling, all threes!"

I sat astonished. Threes were scores indicating well below average performance. We were scaled one to ten, with ten being exceptional.

"For somebody with your experience and time served, these ratings should have you called in front of a trade retention board. You understand what that means, don't you?"

I was almost speechless. I couldn't believe it. Then I realised the person who assessed my performance was Chief Tech. Ronson, who always had it in for me whilst at Killard Point. The chief continued, "Looking back at your previous assessments, you have always been marked very high. These indicate that something has changed drastically. Do you have any reason for this?"

I responded, "Chief Tech. Ronson. For some reason, we never got along well whilst I was at Killard Point."

There was a discussion, and they decided to retain me for a probationary period of a couple of months.

I agreed. With that, I was dismissed. I was furious. How *dare* that bastard screw me up like this! I walked into the crew room and tried to calm myself. Mark was there and asked if I was alright. When I told him what happened, he couldn't believe it and was very supportive.

Later, whilst on a watch cycle, I was walking by some equipment when

I saw one of the back-up guys, a J/T, working on a display power supply. I stopped and bent down to ask him what the problem was. He explained what the fault symptoms were. This was a fault I'd seen a number of times at Bishop's Court. I told him just to change a certain valve and ensure the anode cable was securely connected to the top cap. He responded with a puzzled look. I nodded and said, "Trust me."

He got up, returned with the valve, and then fitted and checked the connection. Once he switched it on, it worked.

"Told you," I said as I walked away towards the crew room, satisfied that I had helped.

That evening, after the day workers had left, I was called into the control room.

"Ah, Jim. Corporal Eastman told us that earlier today, you were able to diagnose a fault correctly without the aid of a circuit diagram. Is that right?"

I thought back and realised it must have been when I helped out J/T Walker with his power supply fault. "Well, yes, Chief. I suppose I did."

The chief continued, "Corporal Eastman was watching you, as he has been on my instructions since you joined the watch. If you can find a fault on a piece of equipment without using a circuit diagram, then that's good enough for me. As far as we are concerned," he gestured to the watch boss and corporal, "your probationary period is over as of now. Welcome to B watch, full time."

I didn't have the heart to tell them it was a common fault that I had experienced a number of times.

During my days off, I drove back to see Mary. Her father was getting better. Her mother was still in the hospital but making good progress. As they both progressed in their recovery, Mary began asking me to get a house. She said she didn't care where or what type, as long as we were together. I returned and applied for a married quarter but was informed I'd be placed on a waiting list. We'd have to wait anyway until Mary's parents were better, and she was ready to move.

Eventually, I received notification that an unfurnished married quarter was available for me. When I went to see it, I couldn't believe my eyes. It was a pre-World War II two-bedroom house, with exterior camouflage paint that had faded over the years but was still discernable. It was tiny and cramped, with only one large electric storage heater in the living room to heat the whole house. The interior "décor" was horrendous and tasteless.

Mushroom-coloured walls, green-and-yellow-patterned curtains, bright red lino with an ochre-and-gold carpet on top. Nothing matched. I was told frankly that it would be this or nothing. I was given one day to make up my mind. I called Mary, and she agreed to take it. She'd had enough and just wanted us to be together again. I signed the paperwork, and the process of moving in began. When she finally saw it for herself, she was shocked. She had no idea it was as bad as I described. She thought I was exaggerating so I could keep living "the single life."

The furniture we had would barely fit in the tiny rooms. We had just enough room to fit the armchairs, settee, and coffee table in the living room. There was barely enough space to walk around. At one time, there had been a fireplace, but it had been blocked off and a very large storage heater fitted. I could barely imagine the cost of running it in the winter. We were grateful for the portable gas heater we bought in Ireland.

Mary compared ours to some other houses in the area. She remarked how much more modern they were and wondered why I didn't get one of those. Once again, I explained to her that none were available, and my choice was either take it or leave it. She was not very happy. In retrospect, I believe this contributed to how our marriage began to fall apart. She loved the area and going out to the coast. However, she was always ashamed of listing our address and telling people where we lived. The whole married quarters area seemed to have a stigma attached to it, an air of depression and gloom. People looked down as they said, "Oh, you live there, do you?" I hated it for her. We had once had a lovely house but ended up way down-market in this dump.

Using the gas heaters had only produced damp conditions in the house. I once retrieved my uniform jacket from a peg by the back door one morning and found the side closest to the wall covered with green mould. I first reacted by throwing the jacket down on the floor in disgust. I ran upstairs to find my uniform jersey and to tell Mary I had found mould on my clothes. She began ranting that she was sick of this house and asking whether I could get an exchange. I tried but was told it was my fault for using a gas heater when there was perfectly adequate heating already installed in the house. No amount of arguing my case would get the housing officer to change his mind. I regretted agreeing to tear up my option to buy myself out of the RAF, yet being at work was the only real bit of peace I got.

Mary told me she would never have children in that place, so any form of intimacy was totally out of the question. This was nothing new; I had become used to her excuses. I was given similar reasons whilst at Bishop's Court. "I don't want to have my babies in a Northern Ireland hospital." Before that, when the subject came up, she would go off on a tirade. "You want babies? We can't afford babies! Look at your bank balance, then tell me you want children. How are you going to support them when you have nothing to support them with?" I became used to Mary's physical refusals to be my wife. She was perfectly content with a platonic relationship. We had a marriage in name only. I finally got tired of the rejection and just gave up and left her alone. Still, I remained faithful to her. This house was another excuse. I wished many times I could turn back the clock and revisit the time I made that decision to marry Mary instead of Christine. I felt I had made a mistake, yet I could not bring myself to leave Mary. I had made a commitment to Mary and her family, and I wouldn't renege on that commitment. There were many times I wished I had married Christine instead of Mary.

During this time, the watch commander obtained his promotion to flight lieutenant, and the watch chief was replaced. This new chief told me I was to train the new LACs, but I was not to touch any of the equipment. My role was to train, watch, and supervise them. As I had always been a hands-on person, it was hard to watch them struggling when I already knew where the probable fault was. I wondered why the new lads were taking such a long time to arrive at that same conclusion, despite my prodding and coaxing them.

Mary liked my being on watch. This gave us four days off each cycle so we could drive to the coast or just drive around the lovely countryside and walk our dog, a beautiful yellow Labrador. These were happier times. We were together more. However, she still missed being close to her family. The days off came as a welcome relief from being on her own for a lot of the time.

It was now late 1980, and I was looking forward to leaving the RAF in eighteen months' time when I received a call from the watch chief. I had been selected to go on a radar specialist course. This would last five months at RAF Locking. I thought it was ridiculous to start a five-year qualification ("Q") after taking a five-month course when I had just over one year left to serve afterwards. He just shrugged his shoulders and said he couldn't do anything about it.

When I returned home that night and told Mary, her reaction was as expected. "What am I supposed to be doing whilst you're away? Does this mean we'll get uprooted again? If you think I'm going to stay here on my own, you can think again!" I tried to console her by saying the chance of being posted afterwards was very remote as there were only three sites containing that particular radar system. There had been no indication of being posted after the course, so I tried to console her with that. It was flimsy reasoning, but it helped. Mary decided that she would stay with her parents, and we would get a flat for the period of the course. Other wives managed quite well there whilst their husbands were on courses or exercises abroad. As usual, I let Mary's condemnations flow over me.

Mary, at heart, was a homebody, even though she and her mother could not get along. Mary was a daddy's girl, and her dad was a fine man. He was humorous, hardworking, loved his family, and was a great storyteller. Mary's mother, by contrast, was very volatile and moody. I felt I was wrong for marrying Mary and taking her away from her hometown, family, friends, and all she had become used to. She had not settled into service life, and it was evident she never would. I vowed I would make it up to her when I came out of the RAF by moving her closer to her family.

Mary stayed with her parents, and I was happy for her to do that. Still, there were the phone calls, asking, "Can we get a place to stay ourselves whilst you're on that bloody course?"

During the phone calls to Mary, she kept asking if I had found something. Every time I told her I hadn't, I got still more questions. "Are you looking in the right places? Are you sure you're really looking?" Every time I heard this, I just wanted to put the phone down. I kept giving her the same answers. I really was trying to find a place. I hated being in the single accommodation and all the pettiness we had to put up with.

I did searches for rental property in the area, but nobody would accept a short-term rental; they wanted a minimum of six months. Some didn't even accept servicemen as tenants. When I heard that, it disgusted me so much that I just hung up on them. This was yet another reason I wanted out. The lack of respect for servicemen was disheartening.

On one call with Mary, she said she had found a farm that had converted a stable and other outbuildings into holiday apartments. They were very amenable to having us stay in one of their apartments for a relatively long rental. For them, it would be considered a long-term lease. We agreed to go see them on Saturday, meaning I would drive to her parents' on Friday evening, travel to the farm on Saturday, and then return on Sunday. That would mean a lot in terms of petrol expense, but as long as it made Mary happy and kept her from complaining, it was worth it.

The rental contained the very basics you would expect from a holiday rental, but Mary was happy with it. It was only a few minutes' walk from the beach. We agreed there and then and would be moving in the following weekend. We signed the paperwork and paid the deposit, and we were done. Moving in was easy, just clothes and no furniture, so it was all done very quickly. We soon settled in and were happy. Each evening, we walked over to the beach like we were on holiday. The mood changed dramatically. Mary was more or less at home, as she had spent a lot of time in the area. It was the closest seaside resort to where she lived. I drove to the course every morning and returned in the evening to pleasant walks with Mary on the beach with the dog. Mary was finally happy and not incessantly complaining.

Then, I learned that the course would be extended because there was a scheduling conflict. A higher-priority course interrupted our course midway through, resulting in a six-week break in the middle of training. We would be returning to our respective stations during this break. Mary wanted to know why she couldn't just stay at the rental we had. We discussed this with the owners, and they said that a second stay would be agreeable to them.

Eventually, the first part of the course ended, and we returned to Neatishead. I was told I would be on permanent day watch for the period, something I didn't relish. I much preferred being on watch working two twelve-hour days, followed by two twelve-hour nights, then four days off.

The time before the resumption of the course was unremarkable. I missed those four consecutive days off, and so did Mary. "We don't get time to do anything or go anywhere now," she protested. No matter what I did, it never seemed to be good enough.

Finally, we returned to the farm for the recommencement of the course. The rental this time was a bit smaller, but comfortable. At least we would be together and have nice walks in the evenings. Then it was back to Neatishead for the practical and final parts of the course.

The time was rapidly approaching for me to leave the RAF. I only had a few months left to go. It was the time of a depression, and companies were cutting down on recruitment. I was feeling more and more apprehensive about finding a job. I bought as many electronics magazines as I could find to search for any suitable jobs or electronics companies who might be recruiting. On Mary's advice, I went to the library and searched various publications for electronics companies. I also registered with a number of employment agencies. I couldn't think of anything else to do. The alternative was to stay in the RAF, despite Mary's deep misgivings. This time, it would mean another ten years of service life for her. There were a couple of positives with this backup plan. I would be employed for a further ten years, and I would get an immediate promotion to sergeant. However, that would also involve a posting on promotion, meaning yet another upheaval for her. I was in a real quandary.

Mary worked hard typing out the application letters for me to find employment. I was on the night shift, and Mary had them ready for me to sign when I woke up. I appreciated how much effort and enthusiasm she put into this task.

One day, I received a message that an education officer wanted to talk to me. He would meet me in a separate building from where I worked. We met, and he began talking about how servicemen were greatly appreciated in the civilian working world, how there were always jobs for ex-servicemen. He just kept going on about all this. I was feeling okay about it until it became clear he was talking about jobs as a security guard. I have nothing whatsoever against that line of work, but I reminded him that I had twelve years of electronics experience and some valued civilian technical qualifications. I should not be in that type of job. He looked indignantly at me as he said, "Well, what are *you* doing about getting a job?"

I told him I had registered with half a dozen employment agencies and obtained addresses of electronics companies, plus my wife was busy writing applications. I didn't get a chance to say anything more. He just slammed his folder shut and threw it into his briefcase. "Then you don't need any of *my* help!" he spat out. With that, he got up, put on his cap, and stormed out.

If the only job he could find me was a position as a security guard, then I didn't need his help. That was the last time I saw him, and that was all the "help" I received from the Royal Air Force to return to civilian life. With this attitude, I was more determined not to stay in the RAF.

There was another problem at this time: the invasion of the Falkland Islands by Argentina. It had been reported in the media that many newly retired servicemen who had been in their reserve period had been recalled into their respective units. Mary was afraid that my discharge would be held up during this period. I felt much the same. I reassured her that as I had completed twelve years of service, I would not be recalled, and due to my equipment qualification, I wouldn't be required. This calmed her down. What I did not mention to her was that I had been cross-trained on a mobile radar that was being shipped to the Falkland Islands and that my name was on the list to go. I later discovered that my name had been struck off the list as somebody who had been fully trained and had practical experience and was detailed to be in readiness. I felt safe and would be leaving on my due date.

A few weeks later, I checked with the general office to see what leave I was entitled to upon discharge. When I was given that information, I realised that my next watch cycle would be my last. Despite all the letters of application Mary typed for me, I kept receiving rejections. I got the usual negative responses. Eventually, one of the agencies contacted me regarding an interview. The position involved testing a radar system. I was surprised, yet pleased to learn it was the replacement for the systems I used to install.

The interview went well, and a few days later, I received a large package from the company offering me the position of systems test engineer. The location wasn't exactly where we would like to settle as it was a long way from both our families. Mary was pleased I had found a job, despite the location. We both felt we would make the best of it.

# Chapter Twenty-Six
## B.B.

*To the root of the mountain I sank down;*
*The earth beneath barred me forever.*
*But you, Lord my God,*
*Brought my life up from the pit.*

—Jonah 2:6 (NIV)


## A PROPHETIC DREAM -1982

As a safety inspector, it was my job to travel to all the working sections of the underground mines and make routine inspections as well as inspect them prior to the state and federal mine inspectors' visits. Once I completed my inspection, I wrote up a list of corrections that needed to be made. Some were safety-related, while others were regulatory violations.

One afternoon, an evening-shift hourly employee named Howard came up to my office for a visit. He was a simple, uneducated, slight little man with a heart of pure gold. He approached me timidly, not knowing how I would react to his message. He had had a disturbing dream. He asked me to let him know if the mine foreman or safety director asked me to go to the number two mine conveyor beltline for an inspection. He went on to say that once I told him an inspection was needed, he would make sure everything was in order, so I didn't have to go. Since he was already assigned to work in that area, he would make sure the fire sensor system was in working order, the belt head was properly guarded, and all the accumulations of spilled coal along the beltline were removed.

"Whatever is wrong, I will fix it, but please don't go there!" he implored. When he didn't think I was taking his warning seriously enough, Howard reluctantly told me about his dream that I was killed in a roof fall accident along the conveyor beltline in that mine. I smiled, thanked him for his concern, and politely responded, "Howard, I will be okay. I will be safe. You know This is my job, and if I am assigned there, I have to go. I can't let you do my job. This is my responsibility."

Weeks later, it was approaching time for a quarterly Mine Safety and Health Administration (MSA) surveyor visit, and I forgot all about Howard's visit and his dream. That memory wasn't even triggered when the new mine manager assigned me to go to the number two mine to conduct an inspection.

I boarded the supply tram on a cold early spring day for a long ride into the number two mine. I asked the motorman to drop me off near the head drive of the number two conveyor beltline. While in this mine, I was completely alone, inspecting the length of a very long, isolated conveyor beltline. There was no way to communicate with the mine office outside.

Slowly, I made my way through the mine, parallel to the moving conveyor beltline. The height of the clearance was only about forty-two inches. I maneuvered by "duck walk," a partial squatting position, for as long as clearance height allowed. When the roof height dipped lower, I had to crawl on my hands and knees over the uneven accumulations of coal and rock on the mine floor. Unfortunately, I was not blessed with great knees. I have had valgus deformity (knock-knees) my entire life.

Weighed down by heavy coveralls and a heavy leather mining belt containing my battery light, anemometer, slate bar, and a W65 Self-Rescuer, I crawled without knee pads over the jagged loose coal and rock. Maneuvering in the low clearance was brutal and slow. I had traveled some distance when I realized I was feeling very tired and decided it was time to stop for a break. I was still catching my breath when, no more than five seconds later, a huge rock dropped straight out of the mine roof and onto the mine floor directly in front of me. The rock was so close, I could feel the whoosh of air passing by me as it dropped and felt the hard concussion as it landed on the uneven, rock- and coal-strewn surface beneath me.

My heart was pounding in my chest. Instinctively, I wanted to run from danger and never come back. In the very next thought, I realized if I retreated in fear, I would be giving up the income my children and I depended on. Instead of trying to escape, I stayed exactly where I was.

I wondered why I stopped to rest when I did, at that exact moment. Then I remembered Howard's dream and his prophetic warning. I would have been killed instantly if I had not stopped precisely at that moment. No one on the mine surface would have known until I didn't come back outside at the end of the shift. Most importantly, my children would have been without a mother. I thought about all this in the moments afterward as my heart continued to race.

Suddenly, I felt compelled to turn off my cap light, leaving me surrounded in total darkness. I couldn't see my own hand in front of my face. The analogy came: this was what my life was like, total darkness. I could have gone to face eternity in that same darkness, but God, who has never abandoned me, showed me grace and mercy. His timing was perfect. God loved me enough to send His Son Jesus Christ, but he also loved me enough to send a prophetic warning. He loved me enough to stop me and to spare my life.

Time passes differently when you're underground. I thought of my children, sitting innocently unaware in their classrooms at school, never knowing any of this. Children need to feel secure, but so do adults. Eventually, I used the sounding (metal) bar I was carrying to check the safety of the roof in front and on the sides of me, and completed my inspection. Once I cleared the mine portal and was safely outside, I told the safety director about the roof fall so additional roof support could be installed.

The next day, I sent a message to Howard, asking him to drop by the safety office to see me. When he came, I told him what happened. God had sent me a message through an angel. My angel was named Howard. Message received and understood.

The following Sunday, I went to the church I had been invited to many times by a couple of men at work. As I stood at the pew, watching the reverence of those around me and listening to the worship songs and music, I felt the powerful presence of the Lord with me there. Without a doubt, he had extended grace and mercy to me. I knew he had warned me, protected me, spared my life, and given me another chance. When the congregation joined together, singing "Just as I Am," I was compelled to take that first step in the direction of the altar. I don't even remember the steps that followed. My feet felt like they had wings as I all but ran to the altar that day, making public my decision to accept the sacrifice Jesus made for me. The weight of my past mistakes was as heavy as the boulder I had almost been beneath underground. That very moment, the weight of my past mistakes was erased, wiped clean. I felt nothing but relief, joy, and love at that altar. I was welcomed with outstretched arms. I was a new creation (2 Corinthians 5:17).

Later, I told Howard about that decision, and he was invited to my baptism the very next Sunday. He came, along with the other men who had been persistent in inviting me to church. They all had beaming smiles to greet me that day. I had already accepted the sacrifice of Jesus on the cross at Calvary, alone and on my knees in the pitch-black darkness of an underground coal mine. Jesus gave his life and took the punishment for all my mistakes, past, present, and future, at the very moment I accepted him. By following through with baptism, I followed the example of Jesus, who was without sin. It was a symbolic washing away of the burden of all my past mistakes, leaving my tarnished life with a clean canvas.

One evening, I explained to Sara and Sawyer why I had gone forward to the altar during the church service. I explained what it meant to change direction from my former path and follow Jesus. I explained to them the sacrifice Jesus made for each of us, but it is up to each of us to accept that sacrifice for ourselves. Jesus had forgiven me for my mistakes, and being baptized was the way I would show the world I accepted that sacrifice and show I am proud to be His daughter. Once I explained this message of salvation, Sawyer said he wanted to follow Jesus too. Sara made that decision shortly thereafter. God rescued our whole family through the prophetic words of our angel, Howard.

# Chapter Twenty-Seven
## B. B.

## THE TROJAN HORSE

When we point our feet in the right direction, there are always obstacles and snares thrown in our way to test us and knock us off course. Eventually, these challenges teach valuable lessons. Sometimes, they bring us to our knees. My next challenge came when my only vehicle broke down. For a while, I had been raising my car's hood, then tapping on the alternator with a slate bar to get it to start. One time, I forgot and left the driver's side door open. The car started with the gear still in reverse and started rolling backward, and the open car door took out the post on my back porch. I must have been a comical sight as I went chasing after my car, jumped in, and put on the brake. Eventually, that slate bar trick quit working, and I didn't have the money to pay a mechanic. I started hitching a ride to work with a coworker.

The Trojan horse came into my life under the façade of a Good Samaritan. My dad had just hired a contractor to do some work on his house. The contractor's son, Daniel, who happened to be a decent self-taught mechanic, was helping his dad. Sara and Sawyer met both these men while they were visiting their papaw and while I was at work. The son heard of my predicament and offered to fix my car if I'd just buy the parts. Vulnerable woman equals huge mistake. After repairing my car, Daniel availed himself of every opportunity to appear helpful. What I didn't know until I was already involved with him was that he was running from financial obligations and a past relationship in a neighboring county.

## PENALTY OF REFUSAL

One day, the GM called me to come down to his office. When I walked in, he immediately closed the door behind me and motioned for me to sit in the chair near his desk. Using a remote control, he drew the window curtains closed. The situation felt almost predatory, like I was an insect caught in a spider's web.

After initial pleasantries, he became much more direct about the intended focus of our meeting. He went on to say that he "would have been willing to send my children to college, but it was obvious that is not what I wanted."

I left his office. That day was the last time I ever saw him because soon after, I lost my job. My termination was concealed in a layoff of many other hourly employees. I happened to be the only person remaining in the safety department when I was laid off. The safety director hired after Nathan left didn't last long. He had been fired for leaving a federal mine inspector unaccompanied underground while he rode outside on the supply motor to avoid the inconvenience of walking the low clearance of the return airway out of the mine.

I was certain I lost my job because I had refused the advances of a person in a position of authority over me, not because the coal company had no need for a safety inspector. I walked away from the coal industry with the knowledge that coal dust is the kind of dirt that will easily wash off with soap and water. Selling yourself for money, personal gain, or power is the kind of inner dirt that stays with you. I wasn't for sale.

## MISTAKES THAT LEAVE SCARS

When I first met Daniel, it was quickly evident that he was a charmer, but I had never interacted with a sociopath. He was intelligent, quick-witted, and a verbose talker who never seemed to meet a stranger.

I happily gave him the money to buy the auto parts needed to repair my car. It was repaired within two days. Unfortunately, the relationship didn't end there, as he found more and more things that I needed help with. This kept him around. In hindsight, I should've found another auto mechanic to repair my car. It would've been far less costly in terms of money and regrets.

This happened at the same time I was fending off unwelcome advances from the general manager at work. I was somewhat relieved to have someone else in my life because it gave me a viable excuse to refuse those advances, hopefully without consequences. I hoped that knowing there was someone else in my life would discourage the GM, and then he'd leave me alone. It did far more than that.

Very shortly thereafter, there was a huge layoff at work. The safety director had taken another job, and I no longer had a buffer between me and the GM. I was a salaried employee, the only safety inspector, and the only remaining person in the safety department. I lost my job during that layoff. For me, at least, the reason was clear. I didn't lose my job because I wasn't essential. I lost my job because I refused the advances of the GM.

At the time of that layoff, there was a major collapse in the coal industry following the coal boom of the 1970s. I applied for job after job without success. Daily, I was job seeking, using my limited unemployment benefits to try to find a new job. Coal miners whose unemployment benefits were expiring were considered dislocated workers. If unable to be reemployed in the coal industry, they were encouraged to be retrained for jobs in other industries. In a region where coal is the primary industry, it was never clear where those new jobs would be. Eventually, I filed a lawsuit due to sexual harassment, discrimination, and retaliation.

Once Daniel was allowed into our lives, he became controlling, aggressive, and belittling toward my children. He picked at and bullied my ten-year-old son. He eroded my eleven-year-old daughter's self-confidence, much like he did my own. He managed to isolate us from our support network, both church and friends. First, he refused to attend church with us. If we went without him, we would return and find him gone, driving one of my vehicles. He would be gone until late evening, as though to punish us for going to church and leaving him at home.

He was manipulative, and when he didn't get his way, he had an explosive temper. Once, he even tried to force my son to eat the fat trimmed off a piece of steak. He yelled at my son, pointing to the fat and commanding, "You eat that, now!" I upheld my son, telling Daniel if he wanted to eat it, then help himself, but my son wasn't going to. There was an explosion of temper, and he started throwing things in my kitchen. I stood there, defiant and provoked, in defense of my son. I told him in words I don't care to repeat (possibly implicating his mother) what a total jerk he was. This was no way to earn my children's respect, or mine.

Sometime later, Daniel actually hit me. When he aggressively put his hands on me, he crossed the line. I snapped. He was an evil man and brought out dangerous, destructive rage I didn't know I was capable of having. At that moment, with adrenaline in high gear and my heart racing, I looked him straight in the eye and said, "Just remember, you have to sleep sometime.

You might want to think about that before you ever lay your hands on me again." He never did.

He flirted with other women right in front of me. His chief enabler was his mother, who excused every bad behavior and mistake he had ever made. "Poor little Daniel" was her only son, and in her opinion, always the victim rather than the victimizer.

I married Daniel of my own volition and have nobody to blame but myself. I was lonely and needed a companion. He was a buffer between me and the men in my nontraditional workplace. Having him around would keep the "wolves" away from my door. Daniel was very intelligent and seemed eager to help at first. In the beginning, my children seemed to like him, and that was important to me. I didn't marry him for financial security, although I thought he might at least contribute to household expenses instead of expecting me to support him. I was deceived on all counts because I didn't want to see who he really was. I believed who he told me he was.

To this day, I have a hard time even thinking of him because of the hell he put both me and my children through. He had been married before, in fact more than once. He had become very astute at presenting the misleading facts in his favor, exonerating himself time and again. The red flags were there, yet I chose to ignore them. Within three months of our wedding, he was already having an affair.

When I lost my job with Sedona Coal, he still had not found even part-time work. I bought a new vehicle shortly before I lost my job because of high mileage issues and high maintenance costs on the car Daniel had repaired. While I was spending every day out searching for a new job, driving my old car, he was driving my new car and (reportedly) doing likewise. I had seen enough of his behavior to know I couldn't trust him. The odometer readings on my new vehicle never coincided with the story of where he claimed he had been searching for a job. I will never forget the evening I smelled another woman's perfume on the collar of his shirt.

I began to notice he was making an unusual number of trips down to our basement. Curious about his sudden change in behavior, I went down to the basement one day while he had gone to the post office. Almost magnetically, I was drawn to our 200-amp electric breaker box. I went directly to it and flipped open the door, and a small booklet fell to the concrete floor near my feet. It was a personal savings account booklet in his name, with his mother as his beneficiary. He had contributed little to nothing to our household expenses, yet he had started a savings account at the local bank. Red alerts were going off like rockets in my brain.

Daniel insisted he be the one to check our mailbox, and now this insistence also became suspect. One day, I decided to check that mailbox myself, and in doing so, intercepted a personal letter addressed to him. Because of the cursive style with a distinct flair, I concluded the letter was from a female. I had never invaded his privacy before, but his behavior caused my curiosity to outweigh my guilt. At this point, I felt no shame. I was the one being violated by his continued duplicity. Her letter read, "It felt so wonderful feeling your warm body next to mine." My face burned as I read those words.

One late night, when he was reportedly taking my old car to sell at an auction, he didn't return until the wee hours of the morning. According to the content of this letter, he had been with this woman.

I should have kicked him out then, but I didn't. Being jobless with two children who had a non-supportive, absent dad was a tremendous weight on my shoulders. However, I decided he had a decision to make. He would tell this woman that evening that their affair was over, or he would pack his belongings into trash bags and get out of our lives. The stipulation was that I was going with him when he told her. This would be his last chance. If he had another affair, there would be no coming back.

At first, he insisted he would go alone. I stood my ground. Those were the nonnegotiable conditions. "I'm going with you when you tell her, or you're out of here tonight." Reluctantly, he agreed. He called her as I listened and arranged to meet her at a local pizza place. She knew I would be with him. I had no idea she was someone I had met until I saw her later that night.

As Daniel drove up the mountain, crossing over into Virginia toward our agreed rendezvous site, he told me he only married me because I "had two kids," "was all alone," and he "felt sorry for me." My throat tightened, and I found it hard to breathe. I could barely speak through tears. Nothing he could have said that night would have hurt me more than those words. Those words left scars.

Our meeting with "the other woman" was completely civil. There were no unkind words spoken between us. That was never my intention. Daniel was the habitual womanizer, and this was his fault. She could have done nothing if Daniel hadn't agreed. Daniel told her it was over between them while I listened.

Alice was at least fifteen years Daniel's senior. Her skin had that damaged, leathery look from years of over-tanning. Her straight, shoulder-length hair was bleached blonde, brittle, with an inch of dark roots showing. Her makeup was applied thickly, as though to cover a very badly scarred or deeply wrinkled complexion. She was about fifty pounds overweight. She worked in a jewelry store, and her body showcased her trade. She wore multiple rings on every finger and multi-strands of gold necklaces and bracelets. Her ears had at least three piercings each. So, this was my competition?

I learned something valuable that night. When someone chooses to have an affair, it is not necessarily because the other person is more beautiful or handsome than the partner they had. A person who is intent on having affairs doesn't stop just because they are caught. A person who has affairs has a heart problem that is not cardiac in nature.

# Chapter Twenty-Eight
## J.D.

### THERMEON ELECTRONICS, 1982-1996

I left the RAF to take my new job, but it was still around six weeks before I officially left the Royal Air Force. I had already cleared everything and handed in my uniform and ID card. To all intents and purposes, I was now a civilian, although I was still being paid by the RAF.

I was very familiar with the principles of the equipment I would be working on, as this job would entail replacing those I had installed whilst on GRIS. The more up-to-date technology was different, as was the terminology, but I soon got used to it.

Mary was happy I was finally out of the RAF, and she was looking forward to returning to civilian life and a sense of stability. She would be allowed to remain in the married quarter until I was able to secure a place for us to live. She didn't mind that as she had made friends during the time we had been there. I was in lodgings whilst Mary stayed in the married quarter.

During the weeks that followed, I was looking for a place to live. We both wanted to buy a house. Unfortunately, nothing was available within our price range. After discussing this with Mary, I went to the local council housing to apply for a house. I was informed that as we did not have children, there would be no possibility of a house, but a flat would be more likely. A few weeks later, I received a phone call from the housing office and was informed there was a flat available; I could pick up the keys to take a look. When I mentioned the address to colleagues, I was told I was very fortunate to be offered a place in that area, as it was in the older and better part of the town.

I looked at the flat with the landlady of where I was in lodgings. She, like me, liked how spacious it was, even though it was on the fourth floor with no lift, so it would be a hard climb up the stairs. She, too, told me I was fortunate to be offered this place, so I made notes, called Mary, and gave her the details about it that evening. She agreed with me that we should take it.

We could now feel settled and make a life, and hopefully, Mary would be happier than she had been for the last number of years. We made the flat into a home, but the stairs would be a major obstacle for Mary. As her brother said later, these helped us to keep fit. Even so, carrying the groceries up the stairs was a hard task. Sometimes, it required around four trips to and from the car. I had to admit, it was gruelling.

There were occasions when either Tim Coulton (who had left the RAF and had joined the company a week before me) or Dan Blackman (the antenna site supervisor) was on leave, and I would go to the antenna test site at the old RAF station at North Weald. In Dan's absence, I would assist Tim in tuning the antenna.

Before the equipment was shipped to the RAF station, it had to go through a process of automatic testing, controlled by a computer. I was intrigued by how this worked. Tim, who was a serious home computer user, showed me how to access the code and how to interpret what was going on. This fired my interest in computer programming.

After checking our finances, I decided to buy a computer. After research and a frank discussion with a salesman, I decided upon the Commodore 64. On this computer, I began writing programs of my own as well as using it for relaxation in playing games. Mary wasn't too keen on this at first, but once I showed her how this could help me in my work, she was happy.

At this time, Mary had work as a temp. She was getting used to various word processing systems in different companies. Some infuriated her as they expected her to know their system from the offset. "Every typewriter was the same, but these bloody machines are all bloody different!" was her usual response when she got home after another frustrating day. I bought myself a cheap word processor, spreadsheet, database, and graphics package. It was very basic but gave me a solid grounding so that I would know how to use more professional packages and know the terminology. At last, I could relate to Mary's work.

When the project eventually concluded, we were transferred to Production Test, located in the main factory area. This was a transfer I was not looking forward to. After a while, I was temporarily seconded to the R&D Lab to work on a new method to test a receiver system. From there, I relocated to the RF and Microwave Group to learn and introduce the new radar system into the Production Test.

Later, I applied for and attained a position as a test applications engineer in a new group and building especially designed for the RF/Microwave Department. This role would make good use of my programming and graphics knowledge. Although my knowledge and experience were basic, it was a good grounding for this new job.

Mary once told me there was too much clutter in the flat, so I began sorting through some old boxes, and I had to throw out anything I didn't need. This included the letters and photographs from Francesca. We had both stopped writing when we got married. I had kept them because I remembered how my mum had destroyed the ones from Beth and how it had upset me. Reluctantly, I tore them up and threw them out, along with several old exercise books from college and my Fitters' course. During this clearout, I found my old box of oil paints and my pad; I went into our spare bedroom and began painting as a means of stress relief. It was a still life of a bowl of fruit. It was the first painting I had done for many years, and admittedly, it was not that good. I was still pleased because it was something I created.

A few weeks later, I heard about an art group that met close to where I lived. They met on Tuesday evenings, the same evening that Mary helped out at a local Brownies group. I decided to join. I enjoyed painting in oils: the aroma, the feel of the paint, and the colours. I had never painted on canvas, only on oil painting paper. I had mainly concentrated on portraits but decided to paint landscapes.

The first meeting I attended was a bit intimidating. I looked in and at first glance saw the array of lovely tabletop easels; all I had was a homemade lash-up. I asked, "Tuesday Painters?" Some of the occupants looked up and beckoned me to come in.

"Find a chair and set up somewhere." As I settled in, we began to introduce ourselves. A kindly man with a goatee and piercing blue eyes came over to me. "I'm Les. Who are you again?" he asked.

"I'm Jim. Jim Aubrey."

He looked at me blankly. The man sitting beside me told me I would need to speak up as Les was profoundly deaf. I spoke up and told him again who I was.

"Can you draw?" he asked.

I showed my current work. He waved his hands at the painting. "No. I can see you can use paint, but can you draw?" He told me to put my paints away and to use a pencil and paper to draw the painting I had nearly completed.

He later came back to see how I was progressing. He looked over my shoulder. "Switch the light on. Use your tones. What you have drawn is tonally flat." He then pointed at various parts of my drawing. "Put your darkest darks here, and here and here." I thanked him and followed his instructions. The drawing looked much better. I could now see how my painting could benefit from this exercise. I really enjoyed being part of that group and being taught by Les. He was inspiring.

In time, I began using watercolours, but I had a very high "mortality rate" with this medium. Looking at videos in the local library, I took home a video explaining soft pastels. This medium looked so much easier. No mixing and easy-to-make corrections. I bought a set of soft pastels, a pastel pad, and an instruction book and started experimenting. After a few hours, I had created my first pastel painting of a bleak landscape with a figure huddled up against a strong wind as he walked on an old path, surrounded by bare winter trees. I was extremely happy with it, as a first attempt anyway, and titled the piece *Windswept*.

At around this time, I joined a National Art Society group called the Society for Amateur Artists (SAA). They soon organised an art exhibition in a prestigious London art gallery. I entered my first pastel painting because I liked it so much. Nine hundred paintings were exhibited, and I later found that mine had been awarded a runners-up prize. I was really pleased with that, especially as it had been the local newspaper that had told me. They interviewed me for inclusion in a column. I was extremely proud of my achievement.

I exhibited with the SAA on three further occasions, twice in prestigious London exhibition galleries and once at a local exhibition hall. Eventually, I began selling my art. All these paintings were landscapes in soft pastels.

Despite being more settled, Mary was still missing her family. It hurt more at Christmas, Mother's and Father's Days, and birthdays, when she could see other families getting together and enjoying themselves. I felt sorry for her, but at the time, there was very little I could do. We did, of course, spend as much time away with both sets of family, hers and mine, and did try to even out the time spent with both families without favouring one over the other. During my single time in the RAF, I had got used to being away from family. Mary did not feel the same way.

By now, I had really improved my computer and programming skills. When my position became redundant, I was transferred back into Production Test as a senior systems test engineer. I was put in charge of a small group responsible for testing special RF circuit boards. Eventually, due to restructuring, that group was absorbed back into the main production area. Once again, I was back in the regimented life of production.

Some months later, I applied for and was accepted in the RF and Microwave Group again; I was developing and assisting the design engineers with new product designs. Mary was still missing her family, who lived about 150 miles away. We had made some friends here, but very few, if any, were what we would call real friends. They were very much family-centred, and we were always the outsiders. This deeply upset Mary. The only ones we were really friendly with were the couple who lived in a ground-floor flat in our stairwell, Andrew and Jean Zahra. They were a wonderful couple. Andrew was the caretaker for the flats. He was due to retire a few years after we moved in. Joan had already retired from her job as an office cleaner for the council. She always referred Andrew as "He's my bleedin' 'Andy Andy, 'e is!" They treated us as if we were their children. Had it not been for them, Mary would have felt even lonelier. Despite the goodness of these neighbours, Mary kept complaining about the stairs (which I could understand), the cliquishness of others, the lack of money, the missing of her family and friends, etc., the usual complaints I had been listening to ever since we had our posting to Northern Ireland. In the interest of peace, I began the search for another job, closer to some of her family, or mine if necessary.

Reading through a magazine, I finally found and applied for a position in the same town as Mary's favourite aunt. Even though I didn't have all the necessary experience or knowledge of the products, I applied for the position and was later invited for an interview. I didn't think the interview went very well because it lasted little more than half an hour. I was surprised when, on the following Saturday morning, there was a heavy thud from the letter box in the front door. Stamped on the large envelope was the name "Salco." Rejection letters are not sent in such large envelopes, so I knew it must be a letter of acceptance. I called out to Mary, and she couldn't believe it, either. I hurriedly opened it and discovered I had been hired as a test development engineer. I would be responsible for the design and development of software to test the mobile phones Salco produced; I would also be a liaison between different R&D areas and suppliers and would travel as required. The salary was a lot more than I was already receiving. All removal fees and legal expenses involved with the move would be covered by the company, including the cost of new lodgings. Even though the job required some overseas travel, Mary felt it would be alright as she would have family nearby. This was something we had discussed before I applied for the job. We called up her aunt Molly and told her the good news. She sounded happy, but to me, she seemed a bit distant. However, she did say she would send us a list of estate agents and property pages from the local newspapers. My next job was to write my letter of resignation from Thermionics, then wait for the information to come from Aunty Molly. Mary was thoroughly overjoyed at the prospect of moving away from the flat and closer to some family, especially her favourite aunt.

# Chapter Twenty-Nine
## B.B.

## LOSSES AND BEGINNINGS

U nemployment compensation expired without a single extension, and I was unable to find another job. At that time, Kentucky had an incentive program to help mothers on public assistance further their education. Education programs were mandatory if you resided in a county where there were offered. I lived in a remote county where no education programs were available. I had completed first aid, cardiopulmonary resuscitation (CPR), and emergency medical technician (EMT) training. These were all stepping-stones to the healthcare profession.

One day, it struck me like an epiphany: I no longer had any real roots in my hometown. I began to take mental inventory. My high school friends moved on when they left for college and didn't return. My only sibling was one of those who never returned. My dad had moved away to a senior citizens' housing complex and rented out our old homeplace. I didn't have a single relative living there anymore. Why was I still there when I couldn't even find a job to support my family? It was time to move on.

Even the trains I used to daydream about so long ago no longer came into my hometown. I no longer heard those five-chime steam locomotive train whistles blowing in the distance. The collapse of the coal industry had taken its toll. My opportunities were elsewhere, and I needed to either go find them or develop new ones.

## BREAKING AND REBUILDING

In 1985, I volunteered for a training program in nursing and moved into subsidized housing fifty-five miles away to attend classes. When I drove away from the house where I had spent the past fourteen years of my life and the town I was born in, I didn't look back. The hardest and most formative years of my life and my children's lives had been spent in that small town. The most painful memories of my past still haunted me there. I didn't even leave a forwarding address when I moved. That day, I burned bridges.

The practical nursing program was very difficult. It was a process of breaking and rebuilding. The stress level was incredibly high. The instructors were strict, all business, and rigid, barking instructions like drill sergeants during clinicals. I began to feel like I was in the military rather than a school. Our initial class enrollment was thirty-three students. Only eleven of us completed the program in 1986.

That same fall, after completing the practical nursing program and passing my state board exam to become a licensed practical nurse (LPN), I enrolled directly into an associate degree (RN) nursing program in Hazard, Kentucky. I had just settled the case against Sedona for harassment, discrimination, and retaliation in an out-of-court settlement because I wanted to move on with my life and quit looking back at the past. Now, I had a profession and was employable. The foundation was being laid.

## GRAND OLD HOUSE

Daniel was still around when I received the modest settlement of my harassment and retaliation lawsuit. I was able to make a down payment on a nice, older home in a more rural area of Perry County. It was a two-story wood-framed house. The large columns in front and the windows and door trims were painted beige, and the rest colonial blue. Twin, custom-built curved metal stairs descended from French doors off the main family room down to ground level. It wasn't grand like my grandmother's historic townhome with a spiral mahogany staircase, but nevertheless, it was grand to us. At the back was a carport with a metal roof. There was an air of mystery about the house that charmed us. The previous owner had been a spy during WWII. The house was built with unique passageways that connected from each of the second-floor rooms. These passageways fed the imaginations of my teenagers.

On the hillside above stood a grove of white pine trees that greeted us with a wonderful fresh fragrance as we approached our house from the long driveway. Their fragrance was enhanced by fresh rain. When the wind blew, they seemed to sing in the breeze. Beneath them, the ground was cushioned with a blanket of fallen pine needles. We were surrounded by mountains on all sides. Below the house was a stone-bordered path leading down to a small post office. That first fall, the three of us planted a border of tulip bulbs along the path to give it our personal touch of home.

Across Kentucky Highway 7, the road below our home, was a small grocery store. Behind that grocery story was the North Fork of the Kentucky River. Nearby was a railroad track. Just as in my childhood, in the wee hours of the morning, I could hear the train whistle blowing in the distance. Even at the age of thirty-six, the childlike wonder returned with the same unanswered questions: "Where did that train come from? Where is its final destination? Will I ever see what is on the other side of those mountains?"

## THE LEOPARD

Leopards don't change their spots, and Daniel continued his flirtatious behavior. My nursing classmates had seen him flirting with some girls in the cosmetology program at the same school. He would leave for work on a Saturday morning, telling me he'd be going straight to his mom's house afterward to cut her grass. He began returning in the wee hours of the morning. Each time, he had prepared an excuse. Either he and his mother had "gotten into a long conversation," or she had asked him to do another chore that detained him.

One Saturday, I went to my part-time job teaching coal miner's first aid and mine safety training. (By now, I was working three part-time jobs while going to school full time.) Daniel went to his part-time job as a clerk in an auto parts store. After that morning, he never called, and he never came back.

The following Monday morning, I found an attorney and filed for divorce. I would make it on my own without him. His biggest contribution to my life had been the never-ending emotional battering. He had managed to isolate and alienate me from friends and family and had bullied my children.

I was within one semester of graduation from the associate degree nursing program. Upon completion, I would be able to sit for the State Board exam to become a Registered Nurse.

I never knew until my son was grown that Daniel had once choked him until he passed out. My son had carried the hurt all those years of believing that I knew and hadn't defended him. Even now, I feel anger for what Daniel did, and I ache for my grown son. When he finally told me, all I could do was tell him I was sorry. I was heartbroken that he was put through that physical and emotional trauma because of my poor decisions. I was always a fierce protector of my children, and I don't even want to think about what I might have done to Daniel if I had known when it happened. My children were elated when they realized Daniel wasn't coming back.

## OF MICE AND MEN

Especially in the fall, some of God's less-desirable creatures were seeking a homestead for winter shelter. That was the case at our grand old rural home. Its location near the river and farmland made it even more attractive to them. My son, ever the curious, adventurous one, discovered the telltale signs of new occupancy of some furry, four-legged critters at the foundation of our home, near a side porch. Upon making that discovery, he alerted me, and I considered what I might do to eradicate the problem. Rodents can quickly increase their population, chew wood and wiring, and become very destructive.

That Saturday morning, I left early for the one-and-a-half-hour commute to my part-time job as a mine safety and first aid instructor. My teenagers were left at home and usually managed well on their own. Sawyer, age fifteen, ever the resourceful problem solver and critical thinker, began to consider how he might solve our new rodent issue. He began to inventory the possibilities from the things we already had on hand. He was, after all, the man of the house now. We had a lawnmower, so we had a can of gasoline readily available. We had a wood-burning buck stove; therefore, we had an abundant supply of matches. Soon, Sawyer developed what he thought was a perfect plan. It involved fuel, heat, and oxygen, creating that "big triangle" that spells trouble.

While his sister was indoors and unaware of the plot, Sawyer was busy implementing his plan. He would pour gasoline down each of the rodent holes that went beneath the foundation of our side porch. Once the holes were full of gasoline, he would stand at a safe distance and toss a match.

WHOOOOOOOOOMMMMMMMMMMMM!!!!!!!!!!!!!!!!    The concussion of that ignition shook the entire house, amplified by the attached metal roof on the carport. The explosion separated the blocks at the foundation of the house. Fire shot out of each of the holes. Sara ran out of the house, frantic and screaming at Sawyer. "What are you doing? Are you crazy? I'm telling Mom!"

When I came back home that day, sure enough, there were cracks in the foundation at the side porch. Mortar had been blown out. The most important thing of all: both my children were uninjured, and the house wasn't set on fire in the process. A valuable lesson was learned that day. As for the rodents? We never saw them again. Despite a near-positive outcome, I cannot recommend this particular method of rodent eradication.

# Chapter Thirty

## B.B.

### FROM BANJO TO STRADIVARIUS

Wrapped within the isolation of the eastern Kentucky mountains, I remembered my teen years, when I lay across my bed and heard the train whistles blowing in the distance. Back then, I longed to get a glimpse of the world outside. It was a world with possibilities I couldn't even imagine, except for what I gleaned from reading books and watching television. As much as I wanted to see the world for myself, I also wanted my children, now in their teens, to see and experience it firsthand. I wasn't going to miss an opportunity to open windows for them to see the world, and to walk through doors to experience it with them if I could.

My first exposure to the real world of classical music came when I was only twelve. A touring Russian violinist, David Rubinoff, performed for our two-roomed Catholic school in Jenkins, Kentucky. It was to be a short sampling of his full performance that evening at our local high school auditorium. Convincing my mother to allow me to go to a night performance in early February was out of the question. She didn't drive, and Dad worked evening shifts.

I remember my excitement when Mr. Rubinoff was introduced to our class. I had a sense that this was a rare once-in-a-lifetime opportunity to hear a special and talented musician. Until then, I had only heard the private family performances by my dad, a self-taught musician, on his inexpensive and unsophisticated five-string banjo with hide-skin head.

Mr. Rubinoff, dressed formally in a two-piece charcoal-gray suit with matching tie and a crisp white shirt, had been a child prodigy. He had convinced his parents to buy him a violin when he was only five. I had never seen a classical instrument, much less a Romanoff Stradivarius violin. I understood how special that instrument was when I learned it was made in Italy in the early 1700s. It was insured for $100,000 back in 1964 but is worth millions now. As untrained as my ears were to the beauty of classical violin music, I remember sitting quietly, mesmerized by the richness and purity of the sound, even in a classroom with poor acoustics. I was struck by the tender way Mr. Rubinoff caressed his violin as he drew the bow across the strings. There was no jig, no foot tapping, no vocal accompaniments. His performance was all about the love of the violin and the music. The music resonated sweetly in my ears, evoking a sense of calm and peace. I had never witnessed this kind of passion for music.

In contrast, my daddy's performance attire was a pair of faded jeans and a well-worn plaid, double-pocket shirt with long sleeves. He was cold-natured, and unless it was mid-summer with scorching hot weather, he always wore long sleeves. His shirts always had double pockets to accommodate his Prince Alfred tobacco, crooked stem pipe, and eyeglasses.

Instead of a bow, he played with his thumb and right hand, clawhammer style, strumming downward. Often, he would dance a jig to particularly lively tunes as he serenaded us with traditional bluegrass music. His stage was usually our kitchen floor. We were his only audience, but we were seated with attentiveness, often tapping our feet in tune with the rhythm. I cherished the rare occasions when Dad was in the mood to pick up his banjo and perform. My favorite bluegrass song he played, sang, and danced his jig to was "Groundhog." The memorable lyrics to his rendition:

Yonder comes Sal with a snicker and a grin.
Yonder comes Sal with a snicker and a grin.
Whistlepig grease all over her chin.
Groundhog.

As much as I loved to hear my daddy play his banjo, nothing I ever heard from him could compare with the beauty of the sound of that violin. The printed flier distributed to our class that day is still a cherished keepsake, safely tucked away in my memory chest.

When they were old enough to sit still and listen, I explored every opportunity to expose Sara and Sawyer to the performing arts. We began our exposure in a small roadside theater in Letcher County, where two incredible male storytellers brought the scenes of *Red Fox/Second Hangin'*, the story of M. B. "Doc" Taylor (known as "the Red Fox") to life on stage. Their only props were two chairs and a small table where each of them had a glass of water. My children and I sat spellbound as they created incredible scenes with their words, emotion, and theatrical passion. We needed nothing more. The door to the world stage was officially opened, and we never missed a chance to enjoy live performances.

# Chapter Thirty-One

## B.B.

### FRIENDS AND NEIGHBORS

We were still living in our grand old house in Viper when a young couple, both attorneys in their early thirties, moved into the house next door. Randall was from Iowa, a fiery redhead of Norwegian ancestry. Irene was a slight Jewish girl who weighed less than one hundred pounds. They were a strange union of fire and ice.

Randall had already passed the state bar exam while Irene was studying in preparation. She had gone home to Chicago for a review course and to visit with family. During this time, we got well-acquainted with Randall, who had become like a big brother to Sawyer. They teased each other, debated popular topics, and even wrestled together like brothers. Since Randall was there alone and had become like family, we often invited him to share dinner with us. We got into a fairly regular routine in the evenings. He introduced us to our first cups of espresso and cappuccino, along with Mediterranean dishes like falafel and hummus. In turn, we introduced him to Southern cuisine.

One evening when I extended the usual dinner invitation, Irene had just returned from Chicago. That evening I planned to serve a meal of very tender sliced calf liver, sauteed in onions. It would be a rare treat, but certainly not to Irene.

That evening would be a hostess's worse nightmare. When Randall and Irene arrived, I learned that a) Irene was vegetarian and b) Irene's sister had recently had a liver transplant. The evening meal was a disaster but we have had a good many laughs about it since. I never again served liver. You can't make up faux pas stories much worse than this!

## BROKEN AGAIN

It was 1987, and my children were away with their high school marching band at a competition. Band consumed my children's after-school time and weekends during marching season. Sawyer played trumpet (with braces on his teeth), and Sara was in the color guard. I was glad they were involved in something positive and something they loved to do.

As for me, I was a thirty-six-year-old woman, often home alone in a huge empty house that was as hollow as my life felt. I was overcome with fear, despair, and the complete loss of hope that my life would ever be better. I wanted it to end. Apart from my children, my life was not worth living. My burden had once again become too heavy to carry alone. I fell to my knees, my spirit completely crushed and devoid of hope. The tears came in a flood as I cried out to the Lord in desperation. He heard. I felt my burden lighten almost immediately, but I wasn't yet sure why.

My children and I had been invited to church, ironically by the attorney handling my divorce. I didn't think a lot about it until the evening a pastor and a deacon (a band parent) from a different church surprised us with a home visit.

Pastor Ed explained the strategy of the enemy, Satan. He loves to isolate and sidetrack believers. Once he gets them isolated from the flock, sidetracked and out of fellowship with other believers, he starts working on them even harder. Bit by bit, he is able to creep back in with his influence. When you are a sidetracked believer, you don't have the support and strength that comes from being in the flock. Remember, the good shepherd left his flock to rescue the one sheep that was lost. I recognized that the "lost sheep" in the story was me. I was in a place of danger because I wasn't connected with my source of encouragement and strength, Jesus. This was what I had allowed Daniel to do. That night, Pastor Ed was a true shepherd, seeking the lost sheep who had strayed from the fold.

From that point onward, the three of us were once again in church as a family. Pastor and his wife, Ellen, became like watchful, loving grandparents to my children. Sara and Sawyer would attend youth meetings hosted by Ellen in their home while the adults attended Wednesday night prayer meetings. Knowing how tight finances were for us, Pastor and Ellen would recruit Sara and Sawyer to help them. Sara helped Ellen around the parsonage while Sawyer helped Pastor do chores around their family farm.

Countless times, the three of us would find money that had been tucked inside our Bibles without our knowledge. We never knew who put it there.

One bitterly cold evening, we came home to find a huge pile of wood unloaded under our carport. We would later refer to this as our miracle load of wood. Our pastor, a man in his late sixties, had no doubt done this for us. He had no knowledge of the fact that our gas had been disconnected, and the three of us were trying to cook and stay warm by burning our last bit of wood in a small buck stove while huddling under every blanket and quilt we had available.

# FLAUNTING

The day Daniel made his unannounced exit, he had taken with him one of the two vehicles we had between us. I had paid for them both. Instinctively, I knew he must be involved in another of his multiple affairs, but I had no idea who this woman was. I soon learned from a nursing classmate that he was renting an apartment from her daughter.

One Sunday morning, we passed a fast-food restaurant near the turnoff to our church, and I spotted the car I paid for sitting in the parking lot. Seated near the window facing the road were Daniel and the other woman. My heart pounded with rage at the sight of them together. My taunter wasn't Daniel, it was Satan himself. He was using Daniel to inflict more pain, rob me of peace, and discourage us from attending church. Daniel had given so little yet had taken so much from us. I continued to church, unable to focus on anything else. My children went to their Sunday school classes, but I sat there on the pew alone, so overcome with anger that I heard nothing that was being said.

Salt was thrown in my open wounds Sunday after Sunday when I passed and saw him there, but I kept attending. Some weeks, I didn't see Daniel there as I passed, but even so, the pain became less and less. I still didn't know this woman's identity until the second semester of my second year in the nursing program.

My broken life was still actively bleeding, and I'm certain my classmates could see my pain. One day, I was approached by one of them, who told me she knew who this woman was. Apparently, she and Daniel had just rented an apartment together, and my classmate's daughter was their landlady. That's how I learned the woman's name. She was a waitress at that same fast-food restaurant where I had seen his car parked. Finally, I had confirmation of what I previously couldn't prove. I'm sure my eyes were gleaming as I responded, "I know where I'm eating lunch today!"

My classmate Maria quickly admonished me, "We've worked too hard to get through nursing school for you to throw it all away because you're angry. If you're going, I'm going with you." I agreed. Together, we made the drive over from campus. I parked my car in front of the restaurant, then walked through the door, having no clue of this woman's identity. I knew only her name and where she worked. I hadn't even thought about what I would say to her.

As soon as I entered, however, her body language indicated she recognized me. I caught her anxious stare from the doorway as she stood behind the front counter, serving a customer. Our eyes met, then locked in a fixed stare. She was what I'd call average in height and appearance, certainly not an exceptional beauty. She was dressed in the uniform of her fast-food chicken restaurant, with shoulder-length, medium brown, slightly curly hair and green eyes. I guesstimated her age to be mid-thirties and figured she was carrying about twenty-five spare pounds.

I calmly walked over to the counter and quietly asked, "Are you Sandra?" She nodded reluctantly. "I need to talk with you. I'm not here to cause you trouble, but I'm going over to the booth near the window to wait for you. I'm not leaving until you come talk to me." With that, I walked away. Maria and I took our seats in the booth. I watched Sandra walk up to her manager briefly, then come over to join us.

I began, "I'm not here to cause you trouble. I haven't come because I want Daniel back; I don't. The reason I came is to warn you of the mess you're walking into."

I continued, "You know he's been married before. I knew that when I met him also. He was able to explain away every one of those broken relationships and justify blame on the other person. I'd like to know how he has justified the breakup of our marriage."

Sandra replied, "He said you were okay, but he just couldn't tolerate your kids." If only she had known what a jerk Daniel had been to them, how he had bullied and picked at them, how he had incited them to anger!

I looked deeply into her eyes. "Sandra, someday, he will have an excuse for why things didn't work out with you as well. I came, hoping you might listen, and I could spare you that pain. Let me reinforce that I truly don't want Daniel back. That is not why I came. After today, you won't see me again. I will never bother or harass you in any way. That is not my style. I wish the best for you. If you listen to me, maybe I can save you some heartbreak. If you don't, remember I tried to warn you."

With that, I stood up and took a step toward the door. Sandra interrupted, "I like you. Under different circumstances, we could even be friends." She offered me her phone number and invited me to call her sometime. I declined.

## HINDSIGHT

Years later, when I was visiting my brother in that same town, I was riding with my sister-in-law when she pulled into the restaurant parking lot to get lunch for my niece. She parked away from the view of the drive-through and restaurant windows, left me in the car, and went inside. Sandra was still working there.

"Is that Beth I saw in your car as you drove by?" she inquired. My sister-in-law confirmed that I was with her.

"I wish she had come in. Please tell her I'm sorry. She was right. I should have listened. We had a baby, and now he has left us." Sometimes, people are destined to learn lessons the hard way. Many of my most valuable lessons were learned that way.

# Chapter Thirty-Two
## B.B.

### BATTLE STATIONS

I completed my associate degree in nursing (ADN) in 1988. This time, my dad came to my graduation. Finally, he was proud of me and I had earned his approval.

My first position as an RN was float nurse for seven counties, earning an incredibly pathetic wage of just over seven dollars per hour. To supplement that meager income, I picked up extra hours at a local hospital in the evenings, the conditions of which I liken to the intensity of being on a battlefield. As crazy progressed to horrendous, one night, I was the only RN for twenty-six patients on the medical/surgical floor. There were medications to give, intravenous fluids to hang, orders to take off as doctors made their rounds, and requested pain medications to administer for fresh postoperative patients. It was insane and dangerous, but I had to stick it out. To do otherwise would be considered abandonment.

I recall no easy shifts at that hospital. Mostly, I just laced up my running shoes and endured, doing the best I could. I prayed I made a positive difference and wasn't put in a position that would jeopardize my nursing license or cause a patient harm because I was overwhelmed and couldn't respond in a timely manner. But this night was the deal-breaker. It was my last shift. I would not allow them to put me on the schedule for more.

The silver lining in this baptism-by-fire work experience came when I was offered an opportunity to attend a national-level nursing conference in Boston, Massachusetts. At the age of almost forty, it would be my very first flight on an airplane and the farthest I had ever been away from home. From my years as a teen, I had longed to see what was on the other side of the mountaintops. Decades later, I was finally taking flight.

In Boston, I felt like I had stepped back into the pages of a history book. I was seeing with my own eyes where the earliest moments of our nation's history began. I saw such sites as the Old North Church, The Paul Revere House, Freedom Trail, and more. The architecture of the buildings was ornately grand, the oldest I had seen. We ventured out to Hyannis and Cape Cod, saw the fireworks at the waterfront of Boston Harbor, then wrapped up our visit to hear the Boston Pops perform. We found time to attend the nursing convention, the purpose of our trip, while there too.

## THE EDUCATION PLAN

"If you're going through hell, keep going." —Winston Churchill

My plan never deviated from the path of transferring to the university after both children had completed high school. I began to pick up prerequisites I would need to earn a baccalaureate (BSN) degree in nursing and spent hours upon hours in the college library, researching various books for available scholarships. I completed scholarship applications, wrote essays, and enlisted former instructors as references. I still didn't have the money, but I had the determination to go to college. I was awarded several small scholarships and one full scholarship covering tuition, books, and supplies, plus a monthly stipend. I accepted a Baylor twelve-hour weekend position at a hospital in an adjoining county while I was completing prerequisite courses for the baccalaureate degree program on the main campus in Lexington.

Seven months later, to bridge the transition for our relocation to Lexington, I accepted another Baylor weekend program at a large Lexington hospital. I worked every weekend plus an extra eight-hour evening shift every pay period, getting only two weekends off per year. I was considered a full-time employee and earned full-time benefits.

I set my alarm for 3 a.m. on Saturday mornings, got ready, loaded my car with clothes for the weekend, and made the 117-mile commute to Lexington before my shift started at 7 a.m. I made the commute back home on Sunday nights after my long, tiring shift ended. Fortunately, the hospital paid for my hotel accommodations on Saturday nights.

In July 1990, my children and I loaded a 24-foot rental van containing all our material possessions. Before we pulled out of the driveway heading for Lexington, we paused long enough to read the entire 139th Psalm (NIV), focusing on verses seven through ten.

Where can I go from your Spirit?
Where can I flee from your presence?
If I go up to the heavens, you are there;
if I make my bed in the depths, you are there.
If I rise on the wings of the dawn,
if I settle on the far side of the sea,
even there your hand will guide me,
your right hand will hold me fast.

We were excited and nervous as we embarked on that life-changing journey of higher education in a city filled with strangers. It was time to build bigger bridges. Before the move, I managed to find a small apartment within walking distance of the college campus. We waved goodbye to a handful of friends who helped us load the moving van. We left the protection of the mountains that day, exchanging the isolation for a maze of traffic and cultural diversity. We were totally exhausted once we finally unloaded everything into our apartment around 3 a.m.

I sold or gave away many of the material possessions to downsize to a much smaller space. We left behind friendships and familiarity in exchange for an opportunity to build a solid educational foundation. Unfortunately, I kept the old baggage of painful memories, guilt, and regrets.

Over the years, my children witnessed my sharp learning curve in terms of relationships with men and the scars they left. Sawyer often said he felt the anger I had toward the men who betrayed me being directed at him. I wasn't aware those old wounds still hadn't healed. The only insight I had was that something inside me was now dead. Although I felt deep compassion and empathy for others, I was emotionally numb on a personal level. I had erected a wall of granite around my heart. In the three days after Steve left and I mourned the loss of my friend, I emptied myself of tears and hadn't cried for years since. My hope of finding a companion to spend my life with was gone. Consequently, my desire for a relationship died with it. I became that person who just couldn't bring herself to ask others for help. I had been let down too many times by too many people.

## DIVERSITY CENTRAL

Transplanting from a small-town environment with little diversity to a larger multicultural city was not easy. We faced bias and ignorance, even from native Kentuckians who had never visited eastern Kentucky. I doubted that some of them had ever stepped off the asphalt. We were mocked because of our dialect and judged as ignorant because of our Appalachian roots. We endured ignorant, intolerant, and disparaging comments about our culture by those in the same higher echelons of academia who were to "educate" us on "inclusion" and a broader worldview. Thankfully, the three of us had a sense of humor and knew how to laugh at ourselves. What we wouldn't tolerate was disrespect.

I remember one particularly disparaging remark from an older male patient. There were no cognitive deficits to excuse him. Based on my dialect alone, he asked whether I lived in a trailer park. Here was a man, bedbound with open pressure wounds, depending on me for help, yet insulting me with a stereotype. As a nurse, you put aside personal comments and continue to be professional even when your patient, and sometimes their family, shows disrespect. Decades have passed, and that man has probably passed as well, yet I still remember his offensive words.

The transition from a small town with a population of approximately five thousand to a city with a population of over three hundred forty-eight thousand was not going to be easy. Each of us had to integrate, stretch, grow, adapt, and learn.

I was thirty-nine when I transferred to the university as a junior in the BSN program. I committed to two years of postgraduation service in exchange for a scholarship. Sara transferred as a sophomore and Sawyer enrolled as a freshman. During the week, I attended nursing classes full time and completed clinical hours. In the two years I worked on the Baylor weekend plan, I was never allowed to call off work for any reason.

## GRUELING WORK

I was assigned up to nine patients on a manically busy medical/surgical floor. Twelve-hour shifts generally extended to at least thirteen hours. I rarely had time to sit down except to chart on my patients. Some days, there was barely time to eat. Intravenous pumps infusing fluids, antibiotics, lipids, total parenteral nutrition, plus pumps with on-demand narcotic analgesia and apnea monitors alarmed endlessly. There were perpetual call lights to answer. The hospital had installed a call bell system that would revert to an emergency alarm if a patient pressed their call light for assistance and that call wasn't answered with a matter of minutes. If didn't matter that there were drainage tubes, trach care, dressing changes and other procedures to be done. In the midst of an already busy shift would inevitably come the dreaded announcement, "You're getting another admission." Doctors came in endless waves, writing still more orders for labs, procedures, preps, and new medications. The varicose veins in my legs and ankles were becoming as distinct as highways on a road map. The work was exhausting.

When I was off duty, I could still hear imaginary alarms going off. Even my hair dryer emitted high-pitched tones that sounded like the alarm of a distant infusion pump. Surely, this is a nurse's version of PTSS (post-traumatic stress syndrome), and there will be tormenting alarms going off in "nurse hell."

Monday morning classes were always brutal after those long weekend shifts at the hospital. My alarm was set for 4 a.m. so I could study and complete assignments before my 8 a.m. class. Copious amounts of coffee energized me.

Nursing academics at the college always frowned upon students working during the pursuit of a nursing degree. I gladly accepted my B instead of an A, knowing that I had a far greater obligation to the success and survival of my family than to care that they frowned. During the summer, I even signed up for extra shifts.

## THE NONTRADITIONAL STUDENT

Traditional college students are far freer to devote themselves to their coursework and to experience campus fun. I longed to know how it would have felt to experience some of those things I missed as a nontraditional student. Sometimes after classes, I would walk over to the student center, where I was surrounded by mostly traditional students. I ordered a cup of gourmet coffee and sat down with my books in whatever cozy chair I could find, soaking up the sun coming through a large picture window. I pretended to study, but actually I was people watching and soaking up the atmosphere like a sponge. I was surrounded by students in their late teens to mid-twenties, the age I would have been if I had gone to college straight out of high school. They sat huddled together at the tables, eating, chatting and laughing. Occasionally, I saw an older, nontraditional student such as myself. Most of those older students had the serious faces that come from carrying responsibility on their shoulders. None of them sat together, all loners like me. They were task oriented, there only to grab a quick snack or beverage, then quickly on their way.

There were a few times when my children's classmates spotted me at the student center, in seemingly casual repose. They would then mention in conversation to my children about the sighting. Surprised at the oddity of their mother in a student's world, my children then asked why I had ventured there. I always replied with a laugh and the comment that I was just "hanging out," and planned to continue to do so until I was sure I was getting it right.

# Chapter Thirty-Three
## B.B.

### MAXIMUM OCCUPANCY

Some of my very fondest college memories are those I made with my favorite adult college friends, my children. It was the end of summer, and fall semester was ready to begin. As a family, we decided to host a small group of college students who would be returning early to the campus area in the week prior to the start of classes. Since our apartment was small (1,100 square feet, two bedrooms and one bath), we would not wait until campus was bustling with students. I left it to Sara and Sawyer to get the word out because I was still working weekends. We planned the gathering for a Sunday night. We would grill outside, utilizing a small grill on the ground level of our second-story apartment. We anticipated that a small handful of students, perhaps ten, would show up. The party was due to begin about 7 p.m., just before I got home from work. Sara and Sawyer would be in charge of the guests. As was the case throughout our lives together, their friends became mine as well. Although I was viewed as the "mom" among the group, I was always pleased that they all seemed to genuinely enjoy my company as well.

As soon as I arrived home from work, I spotted the bustle in the parking lot of our apartment as a steady flow of students was coming to and from the outdoor grill. I smiled and greeted each one I saw, and I headed into our apartment. When I reached our apartment door in that nine-apartment complex, I found an already packed living room full of students, and more were still coming. As I glanced into our small kitchen, I saw that it was packed with students as well.

I smiled out of amusement, then headed toward my bedroom. There were students already sitting on the bed, eating and in conversation. The same was happening in Sawyer's bedroom. His bed was piled with students engaged in conversation and laughter. There was but one space left, our small bathroom. Sure enough, there were students in there, too, door open, lined up sitting on the side of the bathtub. Another was sitting on the toilet (lid down, of course). By this time, I was as giddy as the rest of them. This whole situation struck me as hilarious.

Eventually, students were lined up around the walls in every room, standing room only. The floor spaces were full of sitting students. If food, a drink, or a utensil was needed, there was a shout out, then whatever was needed was passed fire-bucket-brigade style to the requester.

We had seating space for a total of ten, but we had close to forty or more students that night with a steady stream up and down the steps, delivering food from the grill. That was one of the funniest and fondest memories I have of my college years. There was no alcohol and no drugs. There were no police complaints. There were, however, hours of laughter. Despite the crowd, nobody wanted to leave. Ours had become "the happening place" that evening. Reminiscent of the contests held on college campuses in the 1950s to see how many students could pack into a phone booth, it had even become a challenge to see how many students would fit inside our small apartment. Thankfully, the floor didn't collapse.

## GOALS ACHIEVED

O afflicted one, storm tossed, and not comforted,
behold, I will set your stones in antimony,
and lay your foundations with sapphires. —Isaiah 54:11 (ESV)

When the three of us entered college, the deck was stacked against us. Low-income and first-generation college students have consistently lower rates of college completion. Statistically, only about 24 percent of those in our situation were destined to earn a degree. Having family support readily available (e.g., each other) was critical as we went through a very difficult adjustment to college and city life. I had the added stressors of starting a new job in a demanding workplace. Sara and Sawyer received financial assistance and were awarded work-study jobs.

Completion of my baccalaureate degree in nursing finally came in August 1992. It was a milestone celebrated in relief rather than fanfare. I chose not to walk across a stage at a formal ceremony. I didn't need the extra expense of pomp and circumstance. The degree had cost enough of my life and time already. My diploma would be mailed to me later. I was exhausted and just wanted to move on with my life. There would be no proud parents or other relatives there to laud the moment, and my children were as relieved as I was that this ordeal was over. I had graduated three times before with associate degrees. The real celebration would come when Sara and Sawyer earned their degrees.

Sara changed her major three times before applying to the College of Education, intent on becoming a middle school teacher. Sawyer took his time declaring a major and finally found the right fit in the College of Agriculture. In 1996, Sara graduated with an undergraduate degree in education, with a focus on language arts and social studies. She began substitute teaching in middle school that fall.

## WEST COAST TOUR

Time was running out when I would still have Sara and Sawyer at home. The summer between Sara's graduation and Sawyer's last year at college, the three of us planned an epic three-week vacation out west. It would mark the first time we had flown together as a family. We began our journey by flying from Lexington into Salt Lake City, rented an SUV, the started our trek through Utah, Idaho and Yellowstone National Park. Snowbanks still towered higher than our heads along some of the roadways, and not all routes were fully open for the season. It was early summer, so seasonal tourist traffic was low, a wildlife lover's dream. We saw big-horned sheep, bear, elk, black-tailed deer, moose, bald eagles, and even a gray wolf. Park rangers quickly denied the possibility of a gray wolf sighting, but having seen coyotes in the wild and realizing the much larger size of this animal, we trusted our own eyes.

The Grand Tetons, Jackson Hole, and Mount Rainier were incredible. The hills and streams where I grew up seemed tiny by comparison. Clouds engulfed the majestic tops of the Tetons, all views that no camera could adequately capture.

From Wyoming, we flew to Oregon and made our way up the coastline into Washington state, camping one night near the border. As thoughtfully as we planned, we were totally unprepared for the low temperatures. I still remember our campsite being full of gopher holes. We laughed that it was a likely place for a game of Whack-a-Mole. To save us all from freezing, Sawyer built a roaring campfire. The three of us, the sole campers at the site, sat huddled around the fire until all the wood we scavenged was gone and the flames were down to glowing embers. Finally, we slid into our sleeping bags inside a tiny tent, huddling together for warmth until morning. After that one brave night, we vowed to nix our camping experience and check into hotels or bed-and-breakfast suites for the remainder of our journey.

In Seattle, Sara and Sawyer explored Pike Place Market, where they marveled as they watched fish being thrown overhead for waiting buyers. They explored an aquarium, the Space Needle, and the waterfront while I attended a nursing conference. Together, they scouted during the day, then in the evenings, took me back to the most fun places they discovered. This was a bonding adventure, rich with memories, worthy of the months of planning and every cent we spent.

By 1994, Sara had completed a study abroad program in education to Ireland, Scotland and Wales. Then in 1996, she completed her undergraduate degree and started her middle school teaching career.

Sawyer graduated in 1997 with an undergraduate degree in agriculture. For 150-plus years, our family had tilled the soil. His ancestors would surely have been proud that their legacy continued. The ink on Sawyer's diploma was hardly dry when he accepted a position with a university and moved back to his Letcher County roots. Ever the adventurer, he was so eager to spread his wings and leave the nest that it was impossible to be anything but happy for him as he waved goodbye and drove away.

Major bridges had finally been built, and both my children had a solid foundation for their futures. There were many times the three of us felt like those in academia wanted us to fail. How dare someone from our backgrounds think they could earn a degree from the hallowed halls of that revered university? Sara was told by her instructors that she should go back to eastern Kentucky to teach "because of her accent." I was told by nursing academia that I "lacked critical thinking skills." I doubt a single one of those professors could have survived the adversity of our journeys. While I certainly didn't fit their ideal model for a BSN nursing graduate, I doubt they had traveled my rugged, obstacle-laden path to college. Perhaps none of them had my dogged determination and sheer grit. Still, I was adamant all three of us would earn undergraduate degrees from this university. It was one of those moments similar to the day in 1979 when my dad told me I as "going to spend all my money and never amount to anything." We were determined to show this university a thing or two about the tenacity and fortitude of eastern Kentuckians.

# Chapter Thirty-Four

## B.B.

### TAKING FLIGHT

From 1992 to 1997, the borders of my world grew by leaps and bounds. I traveled twice to Brazil, once to Russia, and once to Ecuador on four separate medical mission teams, all requiring the use of translators. The beauty of Brazil, the Amazon, Rio de Janeiro, Mount Corcovado, and the Christ the Redeemer statue (one of the new Seven Wonders of the World) pale by comparison to the beauty of its people. Though there were many nurses and health professionals (a doctor, a dentist, and an ophthalmologist) who served, I was the only unpaid nurse volunteer, covering my own expenses, some through the support of various church donations. The others worked in a local hospital that sponsored each nurse and paid her salary while there.

I remember a boy, around age thirteen, who was living on the streets. One day, he was carried into our clinic when local hospitals refused to treat him. He had been "train surfing" and had come in contact with high-voltage power wires. Paulo had missed a public execution by death squads trying to eradicate Brazil's problem of poverty and homelessness one life at a time. It was a miracle that he survived either: the skin on one forearm and both legs were charred and covered with eschar, thick, black, nonviable tissue. He was unable to bend his knees or walk.

One doctor paused long enough to give me brief instruction in wound debridement, then quickly returned to his own task of treating the hundreds of people still lined up. Every day, Paulo returned to our clinic to see me for debridement and wound care. Every day, more and more of the eschar was softened and removed. It was a slow process in consideration of his pain tolerance. By the end of our time there, Paulo's wounds were all clean and pink, and he was able to walk again. We all witnessed the unfolding of a miracle. Paulo, his life considered a waste to some, was shown love and value.

Not all wounds heal. That fact was never made clearer than during our experience visiting a leper colony. Hansen's disease is endemic to the Amazon region, caused by the slow-growing bacteria *Mycobacterium leprae*, and curable if treated early. Many patients had missed early treatment and had lost fingers, toes, and even their noses to the disease.

I saw the futility of one lady's situation with diabetes. She was hoping for faith healing but had a gangrenous wound on her leg from chronic ischemia. She sought good news from American doctors, but it was obvious from the extensive wound size, pain level, and odor that she needed an amputation. After two days of her coming to our clinic, we were challenged to convey the seriousness of her condition with the help of a translator. Though she was in tears, we believed she finally understood that her life was in jeopardy without an amputation. She was referred to a local surgeon.

## RUSSIA

After the collapse of the Soviet Union, another opportunity came through a church partnership in 1994 to be a part of a medical mission team to Russia. Our team set up a temporary clinic and medication dispensary inside a church in Moscow. We were housed in a hotel and I shared accommodations with a team mate. One night I was having a particularly difficult time sleeping. My eyes were closed, but sometime around 2 A.M., I heard a quiet rustling of the newspapers I left on the floor at the foot of my bed. Immediately, I opened my eyes to see a man dressed in all-black clothing at the foot of my bed on his hands and knees going through my personal belongings. He was just over a shoulder length away.

I sat bolt upright in my bed in absolute terror. My response was an onslaught of deep, primal hara-like screams (like a karate "kiai" on steroids) so loud that they woke my teammates the floor above us. The intruder started to run for the door to escape and my adrenaline "fight" kicked in along with his "flight." I chased him out of our room and halfway down the corridor, still screaming, my heart pounding out of my chest. Just as suddenly, the question came to mind "what are you physically prepared to do if you catch him?" At this point I wasn't sure if he had taken any of my personal belongings. I stopped, retreated to my room, still shaking.

"Were you having a nightmare?" My roommate, also visibly shaken from the commotion asked.

"No, I just chased both our nightmares down the corridor!" I responded.

Only later in conversation did she admit that she had gone out of the room and forgot to lock our door when she returned. Thankfully, he had not taken anything, but the remainder of our time in Moscow, we pushed furniture against our door at night. Apart from losing my voice for a few days, I never felt safe the entire remainder of the 17 days we were there. When we ventured outside our hotel, we were cautioned to stay together in groups.

Older people were spotted on the streets, begging for food. In order to live on their meager pensions, Russians had to make do on the equivalent of $2.60 a day (2019) with no consideration for clothing. Even in 2016, the average salary of a doctor in Russia was only the equivalent of $320 per month.

Some of us managed to visit one of the largest hospitals in Moscow while there. The stock of medication for the entire hospital would easily have fit inside one of our suitcases. I understood there was one nurse on duty, but we never saw her. I saw no infusion pumps or monitors and heard no alarms or patient call bells. In our free clinic, the Russians were very selective about who they would allow to get care. If the person was not in some way connected to their church, they would not allow our medical staff to see them.

This guardedness comes from years of persecutions of Christians when they had to meet in secrecy. Little babushkas kept the faith and the underground churches alive, even when their husbands were killed or exiled to Siberia because they were Christians. Consequently, we only provided care to a fraction of the people we could have seen otherwise.

# ECUADOR

Two years later, through a partnership with my church, I volunteered with a team providing free medical and dental care to indigenous people living high up in the mountains of Ecuador. Our flight landed in Quito, Ecuador, at over 9,000 feet elevation, amidst towering volcanos. Lodging for our team was a basic shelter high up in the Andes Mountains, where it was warm during the day (July) until the sun went down, then quickly became cold and windy. I donned every article of clothing I brought with me and it was still too cold to sleep at night. While there, we provided healthcare and medications to hundreds.

The women of Ecuador impressed me with their strength and talent. Daily we saw them carrying huge filled baskets on their heads and carrying heavy packs on their backs. In the open marketplace, I saw beautiful handwoven alpaca blankets (one I brought home for Sawyer) and an array of beautiful handmade items such as clothing, shawls, sweaters, belts and shoes from local artisans. There were no food booths as we were accustomed to seeing at an outdoor fair. Instead, there were whole pigs and ears of corn being roasted in the open air.

I'll never forget being offered a live guinea pig, a local delicacy, that they would prepare to order. Knowing they are used as pets and even research animals, I quickly declined, offering the lady her asking price of five U.S. dollars just to let it live.

Innocently beautiful children dressed in colorful native dress with their shy unassuming smiles were always present, innocently peering at us around doorways. Others with chubby, chafed and smudged cheeks seemed more interested in vying for a drink from a single bottle of soda.

I was asked to go on home visits to see shut-ins while I was there, seeing firsthand the sharp contrast between their level of poverty compared to what I had seen in America. My contributions weren't a speck compared to the need I saw but I was part of a bigger purpose.

When I was a teenager, hearing those far away train whistles from my bedroom, I never imagined traveling beyond the borders of my own country. Those medical mission opportunities reinforced that I was not a failure. I was born on purpose, to make a positive difference in the world around me.

## PIVOTAL DECISION

In 1993, I accepted a position in community health, working in an immunization and international travel clinic in Lexington. Soon after, I had an opportunity to pick up hours working in their home health program. I loved the freedom of being away from the office and interacting with people in their own environments. It taught me a great deal about the reality of discharge teaching when a person leaves the hospital after an acute stay. I saw firsthand the environments and resources patients had available to them.

To further my education, I attended a specialized nursing program in Atlanta, Georgia, where I spent nine incredible weeks obtaining new skills that qualified me to sit for the exams to become board certified in wound, ostomy, and continence care. It was a pivotal decision in my nursing career, one that opened doors and built new opportunities I would never have had otherwise. I would spend the next twenty-one years of my nursing career focusing on patients who benefited from those skills. Education truly was the key.

I remember the early morning in late October 1994, when I loaded up the new vehicle I had just bought, waved goodbye to my adult children, and headed on that six-hour journey to Atlanta. At the age of forty-three, I was a student on my own for the very first time. My host home belonged to a nurse who accepted students taking the same course. Directly across the hall was a Cuban nurse from Florida. She and I were polar opposites. This was as close as I came to a college dormitory hall experience.

There were weeks of evenings spent alone in my room. I filled my time studying, missing my children and wondering about their activities. I had no television for entertainment and no mobile phone to call and hear their voices. I remembered my college career adviser's encouragement. His words "You can do this" carried me through the lonely evenings. I finally believed if I didn't quit on myself, I could succeed. It was seven days before Christmas when I completed the course and returned home. Another critical milestone in my career was completed.

By 1996 and 1997, Sara and Sawyer had both earned their baccalaureate degrees. Sara had already begun her teaching career by the time Sawyer graduated in 1997. I will never forget his joy and excitement the day he accepted his first job, back in Letcher County. For Sawyer, it meant going back to his roots. He was my youngest, but ever the adventurer, the first to spread his wings. I watched him drive away in his first truck, loaded with all his personal possessions, including items I contributed to help supply his first apartment.

## HONORING MY DAD (EXODUS 20:12)

Eventually, age and black lung disease (coal worker's pneumoconiosis) from forty-two years of work in an underground coal mine caught up with my dad. By 1997, my stepmother's health and mental status were declining, resulting in multiple falls and broken bones. Both were eighty-five, and neither of them was able to care for the other. Her children made the decision to place her in a nursing home, and Dad, unable to care for himself, came to live with me and Sara.

It was a heartbreaking discovery when I learned that Dad was going down to the snack machines and buying cold sandwiches to eat. The only hot meals he had were the ones they served at a senior citizens center nearby. Before his wife went to the nursing home, he walked, using his cane, about a mile away to carry meals back for both of them. I never knew this until he came to live with me.

Dad had only ever lived in small towns with two-way streets and few traffic lights. Multiple lanes of traffic all headed in the same direction were amazing to him. Dad had so many small but significant experiences after he came to live with us. He had never seen a plane take off or land. He had only seen the small single-engine planes flying overhead in the mountains.

One day, Sara took him to the airport, and together, they spent the afternoon watching jets take off and land. He was amazed as he watched the landing gear come down. He hadn't spent a lot of time thinking about *how* those big jets land. I would have loved to have taken him up for a flight, even a short one, but he was afraid. At least he got to see jets up close. It expanded his world just having the experience with Sara. This is when you realize just how drastically the world has changed in the course of nearly a century and how much we take for granted as technology changes.

I enrolled for further specialty training in diabetic foot care at a university in Charleston, South Carolina. Sara and I decided we would turn this trip into a memorable adventure for the three of us. Dad had spent a lot of time confined to his tiny apartment in the senior living facility before he came to Lexington, and I could tell he missed his friends from the senior living apartments. Consequently, he always loved going out for a long ride. He didn't even notice the day Sara and I were packing suitcases into the car before we departed. By the time we crossed the Tennessee state line, he was really curious about where we were headed. Next, we crossed into North Carolina, and he remarked, "That's it. I'll never live to get back home to Kentucky again!" Sara and I both laughed.

"You're going to have a great time. You're going to see something you've never seen before." We crossed over into South Carolina, and he was wondering when we were ever going to stop driving (despite our numerous rest stops along the way). This was the memory of a lifetime for the three of us. "This is the farthest I've ever been from home," Dad remarked.

Finally arriving at Folly Beach, South Carolina, Sara and I parked the car and rolled Dad out on a long fishing pier in his wheelchair. It was a lazy evening, and dozens of people were lined up fishing off the pier, while instrumental jazz music played softly on the upper level of a two-story gazebo at the ocean end of the pier. The sound of the waves lapping the sides of the pier was mesmerizing. It was a perfect, clear, sunny day with a gorgeous blue sky and gentle, warm breezes. At the tender age of eighty-five, having spent his life in the tree-covered hills of Kentucky, this was Dad's very first view of the ocean.

"What do you think about the ocean, Papaw?" Sara asked.

Dad paused a few moments, then replied, "This is the furthest I've ever seen without trees."

That was it. Certainly, it wasn't the response we might have predicted, but it was nevertheless his first and lasting impression of the Atlantic Ocean.

He had a great time at my training course while he was there. I got special permission to bring Dad to class, and he was treated like a VIP for the three days of the course. His feet were, of course, the center of attention and a great learning experience for our entire class. Who needs a textbook when you have the living examples present? His feet were pampered more than in any expensive spa pedicure as my classmates and I lavished attention on my dad.

A few short weeks thereafter, I heard Dad coughing constantly throughout the night. Soon, I started finding large spots of fresh blood on his pillowcases in the mornings. I got him to an internal medicine doctor for evaluation. After a series of tests, the doctor concluded that Dad had lung cancer. His prognosis was not good. All we could do was to provide supportive care and comfort measures. Because of his age, I refused to allow him to be made even more uncomfortable with invasive testing that wouldn't change his prognosis. I remembered in vivid detail my mother's painful ordeal and was determined to protect Dad from tests that would cause him needless discomfort. His appetite was diminishing, and despite my preparing his favorite foods, he ate very little.

He was mobile throughout the day at home, enjoying his favorite pastime of whittling cedar sticks. He enjoyed watching birds from our balcony feeders and feeding the squirrels shelled corn. He took short walks in the neighborhood with his cane. When it was sunny, he sat out in the yard under a large shade tree. Urban living was a huge adjustment for him. He was dependent on me for supportive care. From the moment my feet hit the floor in the morning, Dad needed me. He needed me to help him dress, prepare his food, lay out his medication, put on his compression stockings, set up his nebulizer treatment, and even make sure his oxygen tubing wasn't tangled. Countless times, I heard him say he didn't ever want to be in a nursing home like his wife, Edith. Each time, without fail, I promised him I would take care of him at home no matter what. I tried my very best to put his mind at ease.

Probably my most challenging role was to be a nurse/daughter caregiver. I was never off duty. I was still working, and Sara was now teaching. Between the two of us, we tag-teamed to give Dad the support he needed. I needed desperately to just be his daughter. Still, I am immensely grateful for the time I was given to help my dad. When he needed care, his own private duty nurse was always there. I needed to hear somebody tell me I was doing a good job for my dad. I needed to hear that it was okay to cry. I needed those things, but I was never afforded that luxury.

Palliative care was called, and when their nurse came to do the admission, she questioned Dad about the severity of his pain, using a pain scale rating of zero to ten. Dad said he couldn't rate it that way.

"All I know is it's a death pain," he said. I felt like I had just been punched. Reflecting on his behavior and irritability, it all made sense to me now. Some people try to hide their pain, especially the elderly. I interrupted, "Dad, I'm so sorry you have been in pain. I wish I had known so I could have helped you. Now that I know, I promise you I will do everything I can to make sure you are not in this kind of pain ever again." I kept my promise. One day, he remarked to me, "I always wanted my daughter to be a nurse." He had never told me that, but it explained a lot. He never wanted me to work in the coal mines, but he wanted me to be able to help people.

Palliative care stepped up to fill the gaps, caring for Dad and giving him some companionship during the day when Sara and I were both at work. I made sure Dad had breakfast available, even though his appetite was so diminished that he ate very little. I laid out his clean clothes and prepared a lunch for him that only needed to be reheated. The palliative care assistant came while I was at work to help him get washed and dressed. Before leaving, she heated and served him lunch. Some days, the nurse would come. The chaplain visited too. If a problem arose, I could call them for help.

Dad managed to navigate through the house to the bathroom, despite an endless trail of oxygen tubing. One day, he innocently said, "I've never died before. I don't know what this is supposed to be like."

It was hard to choke back the tears. "I haven't either, Dad, but I'll be here to help you. I won't let you be in pain." He was getting even more frail, though he was not bedbound. At the conclusion of a particularly rough weekend, Sara and I desperately needed respite. I arranged to admit him to the inpatient palliative care unit for what we thought would be only a few days.

One afternoon, I was at work, doing a home care visit over one hundred miles away, when Sara called. She had gotten a call at work from the palliative care unit. Dad had taken a rapid turn for the worse. She had been encouraged to come to the hospital quickly and to contact me. I believe the words were "If you want to see him before he passes, you need to come now." I broke every speed limit on the way to the hospital. I never got pulled over for speeding, even when a police car passed me on my way. I was there, and Dad didn't even know I was present. I was encouraged to talk to him because the sense of hearing is the last thing to go. How fitting. My dad had always been able to hear a pin drop.

I encouraged Sara and Sawyer to each take turns alone, talking to their papaw and telling him what he meant to them. Their papaw had stepped up twenty years ago when their own dad abandoned them. He had been like a dad to them as well as to me. Each emerged from his room with tears in their eyes. Still, he lingered. On and on, he lay for hours, somewhere on his departure journey. It was torturous to watch. What was he waiting for? Why was he lingering? I had already reached the point where I just wanted him to be free of all his burdens. I loved him enough to let him go. I had known from losing my mother that true love is desiring what is best for the other person rather than wanting to selfishly keep them here. I wanted Dad to be free too. It was Friday the thirteenth. Dad had been injured at work twice, both on Friday the thirteenth.

Everybody had said their goodbyes to Dad, except me. I promised him I would be by his side through it all. I realized I was the only one who hadn't yet said goodbye. At this point, I sent Sara and Sawyer out of the room so I could have my own final moments with him. I held his hand and whispered in his ear, "Dad, I love you. You know how much I love you. I know you can hear me even if you can't answer back. Don't worry about me now. I'm going to be okay. It's alright for you to go. I don't know where you are right now, and I don't know what it looks like there. I've never been where you are either.

But if you see a bright light somewhere, just go toward it. That will be Jesus guiding you home. You're safe now."

Within ten minutes, my dad had finally arrived safely home. Through his final months, he had become dependent on me for care, decisions, and guidance. He had waited for me to tell him what to do and to "give him permission" to go. This was not another Friday the thirteenth for Dad. It was now 12:01 a.m. on Valentine's Day, Saturday the fourteenth. On a day that is all about love, I loved my dad enough to let him go. He was finally free. Inside, my heart was still broken. He had been the only man in my entire life who I knew without question really loved me. Today, I was an orphan.

"You keep track of all my sorrows. You have collected all my tears in your bottle. You have recorded each one in your book." —Psalm 56:8 (NLT)

Eventually, we went back to church, but I couldn't sit still on the pew. I don't remember a single sermon. I sat there in tears, just waiting for the service to end. What I really wanted to do was get up and run out the back door. There were a few times I left before the service ended.

About six months after the loss of my dad, I was standing in front of my bathroom mirror getting ready for work one morning when the full impact of the loss suddenly hit me. I had had no grief counseling after he passed. I was strong. I had kept myself busy and had allowed myself to believe I was doing fine without it. I was the one who usually helped others.

Sara had gone to work, and I was completely alone. Sadness engulfed me. What was the point in living? I hadn't felt real joy in so long that I no longer remembered how joy felt. I couldn't see anything positive in my future. All I felt was a huge void.

In my moments of despair, I caught myself considering the possibility of taking my own life and ending this pain. Of course, I would have to make it look like an accident so it wouldn't hurt my children. They would be devastated otherwise. Immediately, my nurse's brain kicked in with red alerts, and I recognized that I desperately needed help.

As I recounted the events of the past several months, I realized that I was angry at God. That was why I always wanted to run out the back door of the church. There was no sense in denying it; God knew anyway. I just finally admitted it to myself. At this point, I was like a child throwing a temper tantrum. I didn't care if I was struck dead on the spot; I felt dead inside anyway. At least I would be free of the emotional pain I was feeling. I decided I would "unpack" my emotional baggage directly on to my Heavenly daddy. In my opinion, He had allowed bad things to happen to my earthly dad. How dare He take away the only man whose love I never doubted? I was now fatherless, an orphan.

As I looked up toward Heaven and shook my fist at Him, the tears started to stream down my cheeks. I started screaming the words "I hate you!" I screamed over and over, as loud as I could scream, as though God were hard of hearing. I hadn't felt that He had heard my prayers for a very long time anyway. Tears now flooded down my cheeks as though a dam had broken. I screamed at God until there was nothing left unsaid. I poured out the rage, bitterness, and venom that had festered inside me to the God of the Universe. I emptied myself that day. I was broken again, but God knew it. He was now holding those broken pieces I had flung at Him. The burden had once again become too heavy to bear. I had carried it as long as I could, and it had become destructive to me. I wondered if this was how God felt at the moment when He turned His face away when Jesus was crucified. Was it too painful to look at? Was that the reason Jesus cried out, "My God, my God, why have you forsaken me?" (Matthew 27:46).

That day, the air was cleared between me and God. What He spoke back to my heart were these words: "I will not leave you as orphans; I will come to you" (John 14:18). I received the assurance that I will always have a Heavenly Father who will be there for me. He will advocate for me. He will carry the burdens I cannot bear. He has always wanted the very best for me, even when I had to wait to receive it. I am His daughter, and He will always be my dad. What I received in return that day was a deep sense of peace.

In 1998, months after I lost my dad, Sawyer married a quiet beauty named Marcy from our hometown. She had long, straight dark brown hair with a classic Mona Lisa-type smile. I have never heard her laugh aloud, but frequently catch her looks of amusement at some of our family antics when we all get together. She has a wonderful, compassionate heart, perfect for her calling to the field of social work. I don't deny that we had struggles at first because I was still grieving the loss of my dad. We saw each other infrequently because of distance, so it took a few years for us to get acquainted. Now she feels like a daughter and is a blessing to our whole family. Sawyer certainly chose well.

# Chapter Thirty-Five
## B.B.

## IT'S NOT ABOUT THE POUNDS

I was never an athlete, but I was never a couch potato either. Crooked knees, asthma, and the burden of carrying around too many pounds were huge hindrances to athletic success. Sara was the one who initiated a visit to the gym we later decided to join. That decision was pivotal in my life and hers. It caused me to view myself differently despite those hindrances. I was astounded to discover that the very people I viewed as thin with perfect figures had just as many body-image misperceptions as Sara and I did. Consequently, I am convinced that all mirrors lie. When I gazed into a mirror, I saw a distorted image of the truth. I saw the image of a person who was never good enough. Perhaps mirrors should be labeled with a disclaimer: "Images in this mirror are far more beautiful than they appear."

We made it a point to work out early in the morning before our brains were awake enough to start coming up with excuses. We weren't there to impress; we were there to be healthier and to get fit. For us, it wasn't about the pounds. Our dedication paid off in many ways. Our circle of friends grew inside the confines of a women's locker room while waiting in line for showers and getting dressed after a workout. New bonds of trust were formed. We laughed together, and we were sounding boards for all sorts of ideas, workout tips, personal training advice, relationship advice, workplace issues, and more. We were a team of encouragers doing life together, starting each day by taking some time to help our bodies grow stronger. I accepted challenges and achieved physical successes I never dreamed I could.

Sara and I completed a 10K and multiple 5K races. The handicaps of carrying about eighty extra pounds, asthma, and knees that were 23 degrees out of alignment did not make me a loser. It's not about finishing first. Everybody who completes the race is a winner. No marathon runner could have been prouder than I was of myself that day! This experience taught me to push myself beyond my perceived abilities of physical endurance. It laid the foundation for another challenge I hadn't yet seen coming and taught me I was stronger than I ever realized.

## MOVING ON

I spent the next two years working in a near-four-hundred-bed acute care hospital as a wound, ostomy, and continence coordinator. Those were hard years, as I was still recovering from the loss of my dad. The patient care demands and expectations of the administration were high, as I was the only nurse working in my specialty. In the midst of all that, I accepted a weekend on-call position in palliative care. I had always been good at consoling others, yet I found little consolation for my own loss. In retrospect, I desperately needed grief support, including a grief support group. That was not really discussed, and I didn't reach out and advocate for myself.

## IT'S ABOUT INTEGRITY

In August 2000, I was on the elevator at the hospital where I worked, getting ready to head home. The doors opened, and the liaison for a local home health agency stepped on. We greeted each other, she eyed my name badge, and we struck up a conversation. "Our agency has been trying to recruit someone with your qualifications. I am so excited to meet you! Would you consider giving the owner of our agency a call just to see what he might have to offer you?"

I was forty-nine years old at the time, and the hustle and bustle of acute care was really wearing on me. My knees were beginning to hurt all the time as I spent a good bit of the day on my feet and traipsing up and down the halls of the hospital. My stress level was tremendous, and my hair was starting to fall out. All the signals were there that I'd better look after my own health.

I negotiated a nice raise for myself with the new privately owned agency, knowing that it is wise to negotiate going in the door as a new employee while you still have options. There are never guarantees of raises or bonuses afterward. Usually, a new job comes with a honeymoon period. For me, there has never been a honeymoon, at work or otherwise.

There would be loud, abrupt announcements over an intercom throughout the day while I was in the office. The agency owner, a power monger, was forever calling for specific staff members to "report to my office immediately." Like a student being called to the Principal's office for discipline, staff members not summoned usually had looks of relief on their faces. There was a culture of incivility among the staff.

I would often be questioned about my physical assessments by those in administration who had never seen or evaluated the patient. I discovered that my documentation was being altered after I turned it in. I began making copies of my notes before I turned them in, keeping my own private records. My notes were being changed to make it appear that patients qualified for more services (especially physical therapy) than they actually needed. After only a year on staff, I was alerted to this blatant fraud by another nurse. Immediately, to protect myself and my nursing license, I began searching for another job. The timing couldn't have been worse. The 9/11 event had caused the economy to take a downturn, and even nurses were losing their jobs to layoffs.

I could almost hear my dad advising me, "You never quit one job until you have another one to go to." While this is normally excellent advice, when your nursing license and your reputation are in jeopardy, you do what you have to do. I was tormented by the need to quit and unable to sleep at night. Once again, I got down on painful knees, cushioned by pillows, and begged the Lord to show me, without question, what I needed to do. All I could hear as he inaudibly spoke to me was, "You have to go. Trust me. I'll take care of you." The next day, I turned in my two weeks' notice. Personal integrity should never be compromised to keep a job.

Within a few months after I left, the agency was cited for multiple counts of fraudulent billing. None of my nursing notes were ever questioned in their audit. Sometimes, you really do have to burn bridges.

# Chapter Thirty-Six
## J.D.

SALCO MOBILE PHONES, 1996-2002

After the induction, I was directed to my workstation and was met by Derek Stanton, my interviewing engineer. I was assigned a temporary position on the team and informed I would be flying out that evening for a prototype build in Finland. Derek handed me two folders containing the company policies and procedures and a manual for the software I would be using to test the prototype once it was built. This was the orientation fast track that some might call "baptism by fire."

The build went as expected, and I was shown around the building as well as the manufacturing process and introduced to other engineers. Two, I was told, would be working with me on my project. The return to the UK went easily, and I went back to my lodgings.

The next day, I was informed I would be relocated to the main company building on Monday. That evening, after arriving back home, I began to tell Mary some of the details about the trip. She gave the impression of being vaguely interested, but her constant going on about being alone whilst I was "galivanting" and "enjoying" myself proved otherwise. I had brought local papers over so we could see the prices of houses in the area and were very surprised at the high cost. Now we began wondering whether we could actually afford the move. Sunday evening soon came, and I headed off back to my lodgings.

Mary and I eventually found a house to rent, which made her a lot happier, although she was still not happy with the amount of traveling I had to do. Eventually, our flat sold, and we were able to buy our own house. It was right at the top end of what we could afford, but it was the right size, with good, sociable neighbours, and very close to where we could walk the dog.

Soon, that project ended, and I was assigned to another project. Thankfully, there was a lot less traveling with this project. While Mary appreciated that I was home more, it did not improve my home life. She had been constantly and badly let down by her aunt Molly. They would arrange to go somewhere, and then at the last minute, Molly would cancel when her daughter visited her from London. Mary would get a phone call from Molly, saying, "I can't come out to play today. Sandy is coming, and we're all going out shopping and for a meal." This left Mary feeling hurt, let down, and lonelier whilst I was away. She, too, would have loved to be with her cousin as well as her aunty Molly, but Mary was kept well away from them. These letdowns when she depended upon her aunt whilst I was away occurred more and more frequently. There was always something from which Mary would be excluded. She had depended upon her aunt, who did not reciprocate Mary's need. She had also been let down by the relatives who we had purposely come to live nearby. It was their presence in the area that induced me to apply for that particular job.

Once we moved, their attitudes toward Mary caused her major anxiety. It soon became apparent they were not as thrilled to have Mary close to them as she had been to move there. Perhaps her constant presence was disruptive to their own daily routines. Perhaps her emotional neediness caused them to withdraw. Since I was traveling, I didn't witness their interactions firsthand. I only knew what Mary was like around me. Unfortunately, I bore the brunt of this. There had been many upheavals during our marriage due to traveling. It affected her to such an extent that she would either go and stay with somebody or have somebody stay with her whilst I was away. She could not tolerate being alone, although she never expressed any specific fears. She could no longer rely on her aunty Molly. After Mary's mother died, she stayed with her father whilst I was out on builds. That improved the situation quite a lot, but not completely.

Meanwhile, I bought a PC, as I felt the need for some form of relief and escape from my oppressive home life. I ventured into some online chat rooms. I was very careful which ones I visited, and what I wrote. In the end, I stayed with one, as it was such good fun. The chats were always light and funny. One time, Mary and I met up with some of the members for a weekend. Unfortunately, I was the only man there, and Mary was getting the distinct impression (and rightly so) that one of the ladies had a "thing" for me. Soon after that weekend, I stopped going into the chat rooms. At first, I missed them, but I soon realised they weren't doing me any real good and only supported my dissatisfaction regarding my real life.

One evening whilst browsing the Internet, I found a site about Malta. It was just as I remembered it, and I wrote a comment saying when I had been there and talking about a waitress I had met in a bar/restaurant in Pretty Bay. A few days later, I received an email from somebody saying my description of the waitress fitted one of her cousins. It turned out to be Francesca's cousin. She gave me Francesca's email, and we began corresponding. It was just like old times. We had a lot of catching up to do!

Later, to try and earn a bit more money, I began to learn how to design websites. This turned out to be good for bringing in a bit more money. In a more practical effort to appease Mary, I needed to find a job where I didn't have to travel. I kept looking and getting in touch with recruiting agencies. It seemed the only way would be to move again. Mary wasn't too keen on another move. "I feel like I'm just a 'camp follower,'" she whinged. My home life was now further deteriorating.

One day, I read of an identical job advertised by Virtus, a subsidiary of Salco. I called a couple of company contacts I knew for information. They were very tight-lipped about the position, except that it did not involve traveling. This suited me, so I applied. The subsequent interview went well, and I was later offered the position as a test design engineer. Sadly, a short time before I was due to start, Mary's father, who she dearly loved, died. This put a black cloud over the good news of the job.

# Chapter Thirty-Seven
## B.B.

After leaving the home health agency, I started my own nurse consulting business in the specialty of wound and ostomy care. Eventually, I established my own legal nurse consultant business. Over the next several years, I was retained by a number of law firms as far away as Arizona to serve as an expert witness in legal cases involving wounds. Out of necessity, I challenged myself in ways I never before imagined.

In 2002, my contract work led to full-time employment as a telehealth nurse consultant to nursing homes across the US. My world expanded exponentially as I now began to travel coast to coast within the US, to visit different long-term care facilities and to conduct continuing education programs and onsite patient rounds with facility staff. This was quite amazing for the girl who once only daydreamed of travel. I had never been on a plane until age thirty-nine. By 2006, sixteen years later, I had either flown or driven to thirty-four states and visited ten foreign countries. I had come to realize that the mountains hadn't trapped me at all. What trapped me was my own fear. The sounds of train whistles in the distance had once mesmerized me. I had now exchanged train whistles for the roar of jet engines. The world was finally open to the girl who once only fantasized about what was on the other side of the mountains that encircled her.

After four years, traveling for work finally ceased to be fun. There was little time to explore or enjoy each new destination. I would be in a health facility to evaluate wound patients or conduct educational programs during the day only to be in a different motel in a different city that night. I ate alone, sometimes not arriving at my destination until the local restaurants were closed. Often, I filled my stomach with junk food I found at a service station. There was always the hassle of rental cars and lugging equipment and luggage. I decided that the loneliest place in the world must surely be inside a busy airport, surrounded by a sea of strangers.

I was not in charge of my travel accommodations because I was unfamiliar with the locality. I occasionally stayed in remote areas where accommodations were limited and I didn't feel safe. The noise of window-unit air conditioners, dripping faucets and running toilet tanks tormented me. Some of the rooms smelled moldy, felt icky and didn't look like they had been cleaned. Carpets were stained, dirty and I dared not go barefoot. Mattresses were lumpy and I was forever checking for evidence of bed bugs. I considered sleeping in my vehicle one night, but the dark, secluded area outside my room looked straight out of a crime movie scene. I never felt so alone or abandoned.

My work-travel destinations no longer held an illusion of glamour. At the age of fifty-five, I no longer wondered what was on the other side of the mountains or where a far-away train was headed. I just wanted to be home, where I could sleep in my own bed, where things were familiar and I had a network of friends and family.

## FLO'S FINAL FRONTIER

Once I reached the point of burnout with work travel, I began to explore nursing opportunities closer to home. During a job search, I ran across an ad for a correctional nurse position and applied. Florence Nightingale, the founder of the nursing profession as we know it, was famous for providing nursing care on the frontlines during the Crimean War. I was considering a battle zone where even "Flo" had not practiced. Correctional nursing, a battlefield all its own, was surely the final nursing frontier.

I was done with acute care. My knees could no longer handle the brutal twelve-hour shifts. Having done home care in twenty-six of Kentucky's 120 counties, I was done racking up mile after mile, wearing out my personal vehicles. Months passed, and I had forgotten about my job application, convinced they weren't interested in hiring me.

One day, I received a call from Jim Korn, the human resources director for the local correctional institution posting the vacancy. He told me what the agency could offer. It was substantially less than my current salary. I replied that I wasn't willing to accept a pay cut with my years of experience and was ready to politely end the call. He responded that he could offer me 15 percent more than my current salary if I would send a letter verifying that salary. I agreed, then asked for a tour and a meeting with the director of nursing.

I didn't even tell my children because I knew there would be objections, especially from Sara. She was very protective of me and would be concerned for my safety, much like she was when I worked in an underground coal mine.

The prison was a historic old building built in 1935 on the outskirts of Lexington, secured like a fortress with chain link fencing surrounding its perimeter. The long, winding drive off the main road was flanked on either side by warning signage that gave an air of foreboding. Once I parked my car, I glanced up at sun reflecting on the gleaming rows of spiral razor wire and began mentally questioning my decision to be there. Once I reached the entrance gate and electronic sallyport, I pressed the intercom button and a masculine voice responded, inquiring the purpose of my visit.

My heart was racing as I responded that I was there to meet their Director of Nursing about a nursing position. I heard a loud electronic lock click, allowing me entrance and was told to close each gate behind me. The same electronic lock clicks were heard as I cleared each of the sallyport gates and finally the front entrance door.

I was met in the front lobby by a no-nonsense female officer who, without facial expression, initiated an exhaustive onslaught of security questions. With barely a breath between, all were recited from memory. I was directed through the electronic screener, where I promptly set off an alarm. After being scanned with a handheld metal detector and receiving a thorough pat down search, I was eventually cleared.

Finally, I was met in the lobby by the director of nursing, a fiery redhead who I soon learned was respected by nursing staff, revered by medical staff, and feared by her administrative foes. She was a true visionary in patient care and immediately had plans for how she would eventually utilize my skills in wound care. As we walked through the corridors together and onto the inpatient unit, I was struck by the tiny rooms, drab gray paint and spartan hospital furnishings. I had toured hospitals in third world countries, and this was comparable. Inmates not ill enough to be on the hospital unit were not secured behind metal bars in single or double cells. They were housed dormitory-style on housing units with freedom of movement among the correctional officers and prison staff.

I felt the stares of male inmates, dressed in khaki pants and shirts, as we walked past. This was far different than I had seen on television and in the movies. Only when under disciplinary restriction for rules infractions were they locked in single unit cells. The correctional staff were unarmed, equipped only with radios.

Maximum age at initial hiring is thirty-six. I was already fifty-five.

Where shortages existed in certain job titles (as they did for registered nurses), hiring waivers could be granted. Unfortunately, there were no special age allowances made for the required physical ability test. I would be expected to complete the same physical requirements as those in their twenties. I would be required to run, climb a ladder and stairs, drag a seventy-five-pound dummy for a specific distance/time and complete an obstacle course. These were tests of speed, strength, agility and physical endurance. If I failed the initial test, I would have the opportunity for one retake. If I failed the retake, I would be terminated. Included were self-defense classes as well as training on a variety of firearms, including a 12-gauge pump action shotgun. I began work in August 2006, but it was February 2007 when there was an open slot at the training academy in Georgia. Lastly, there would be extensive background checks in order to gain security clearance.

Just three days after I began my new position at the prison, Marcy and Sawyer blessed us with the gift of Allie, my first grandchild. Throughout an excruciating seventeen hours of labor, Marcy grimaced, but never uttered a single complaint. Finally, her obstetrician decided to do a C-section.

I remember the emotion in our packed waiting room that evening when we finally heard a lullaby player over the hospital intercom, signaling Allie's birth. Soon after, Sawyer emerged from the delivery room to share the good news in person. His face was still wet with tears with the joy of witnessing his daughter's birth. We could also see the concern on his face for Marcy, still in the operating room. None of us knew until after the birth that Marcy's epidural was not properly placed and therefore not controlling her pain. She had endured that whole ordeal with minimal analgesia. Marcy was one very tough new mother and Allie was one very loved baby.

## THE TEST

Six months after I began work at the prison, I was scheduled for mandatory training at the law enforcement training center including the dreaded physical ability test (PAT). Had I not spent six years at the gym, worked with a personal trainer and already run multiple 5K races, I would never have considered the challenge. I struggled through the quarter-mile/400-meter run on that cold February morning. My asthmatic lungs screamed with every breath. Average time for a female beginner in my age bracket was approximately 2:20 but my time was 3:00.

The obstacle course was next, where I hoped my time would improve. The course required climbing, crawling and running, all while maneuvering around obstacles like desks and tables. On the return portion of the course, I slipped on sand on the tile floor, then immediately when down on my outstretched right arm. My instructors immediately began yelling, urging me to get up and keep running. I managed to get up and complete the course, but knew I was injured.

I moved on with our group to the next test, the stair run, but when I continued to favor my injured shoulder, I was pulled out and sent to a medical officer for evaluation. While the rest of my classmates went on to successfully finish, I was sent home. It was Valentine's Day, a day once again marked with tragedy.

I was told I'd get another chance to pass the PAT once my shoulder was rehabilitated. Regardless, I felt like a failure and was received back to my institution as such when I returned to work. Most staff were younger and had passed the PAT on their first attempt. Following rotator cuff surgery in July, I returned to work on restricted duty status six weeks later. In the event a situation arose with an inmate that required the use of force, I couldn't be left alone on the unit because of my physical limitations. I was a "lame duck" correctional nurse in an environment where inmates delighted in "drowning the duck." This is a phrase describing what happens after an inmate compromises a staff member into doing "favors." I didn't accept or give favors.

Surprisingly, the director of nursing took this as an opportunity to implement her vision and utilize my skills and expertise in wound care. She pulled me away from the inpatient unit to establish an outpatient wound clinic. I would be a few rooms away from the other staff nurses in an area that used to adjoin on old operating room. I began stocking the wound supplies I needed, searching the health records for inmates with open wounds, then began scheduling appointments for them to be seen in my clinic. I was so thrilled to finally be returning to my passion of wound care that I never once considered myself vulnerable. I was mature and I was there to apply my skills to make a positive difference in a not-so-positive environment. I carried a radio in the event there was a problem with an inmate and immediate assistance was needed.

As news of the wound clinic spread throughout the agency, many inmates with wounds were either transferred to our institution or designated there. I found most inmates genuinely appreciative. It was rare that an inmate failed to thank me at the end of a clinic visit. Considering how inmates outnumber staff at every institution, it is critical that respect is earned.

Determined not to allow my knees to interfere with my repeat PAT success, I scheduled an appointment with my orthopedic doctor right before I made the return to Georgia the following January. He did steroid injections to both knees to reduce the inflammation and pain. With his assurance that the injections usually help for several months, I felt as ready as I would ever be to face this challenge a second time.

Just before I left Lexington for the academy, I was approached by a more senior male nurse who asked "Why are you doing this to yourself? Not everybody is cut out to work in a correctional setting. Maybe it's too much for you. You're in your fifties. If I were you, I would just get a job somewhere else." I thought about how his words rang in my ears. Regardless of his actual words, they equated to "You're too old. You shouldn't be here. You're not good enough." His words felt too much like those my dad once said, just like the words some male coal miners had said to me. Instead of the discouragement he intended, for me, it resulted in dogged determination.

When I arrived back in Georgia for my second PAT attempt, I was assigned to room with a girl from West Virginia. We bonded immediately. At age thirty-four, Whitney as just two years younger than Sawyer. I loved her positive attitude and bubby personality.

It was about 6:30 a.m. on a crisp, cold January morning. Still anxious about my first attempt at the PAT, I prayed I would be successful this time. My first attempt and subsequent injury wasn't actually considered a failure. For this reason, I was allowed to return and retest. If I failed (uninjured) I would be given one final chance on a different day to retest. If I failed the final attempt, I would be terminated.

The inhalation of cold air and strenuous exercise are my two biggest triggers for an asthma attack. I took several puffs from my albuterol ("rescue") inhaler upon arrival to the track for the quarter-mile run.

So many things were racing through my mind that morning. "This is it, regardless. I hate this but I must do it," I thought. This was far different from all the 5K runs I had done when I was competing with my own best time and not against a required time. My livelihood and future retirement hinged on successfully passing the PAT. I was apprehensive, but in terms of my rehabilitated shoulder, I was confident. I had given my physical therapist a description of the PAT requirements, and she had taken the initiative to construct a mock simulation inside the physical therapy department that included an obstacle course, i.e. crawling under and climbing over objects, even simulating the dummy drag portion of the test. The timed run and handcuffing of a non-combative person were the portions of the test I dreaded most. I had little opportunity to train outdoors in the cold. Running inside a heated gym on a shock-absorbent indoor track was just not the same. My completion time for this segment, once again was about the same as before.

Following completion of the PAT, I was called into a private office the next day and informed that I had failed. My times and distances were not good enough. Those were not the words my instructor used, but nonetheless, "not good enough" were the words I heard. I would be given one final chance the next morning.

My employer was notified by phone that I had failed and would be doing a retake. The HR director who had been instrumental in hiring me, Jim Korn, had taken the call. I would learn later that Jim, a believer, had immediately closed his office door and started to pray. "Lord, you know we need this one here." Back home, prayer warriors recruited by Sara & Sawyer were praying for me.

My roommate, Whitney, twenty-one years my junior, had already passed her test. Still, she wanted to help me succeed. She grabbed a stopwatch, and that evening the two of us headed back to the academy gym in our free time. We found the ladder used for the ladder climb portion of the test. Stopwatch in hand, over and over, she timed me as I climbed the ladder. We stayed until I was doing the ladder climb in well under the required time for a passing score. By excelling in one area of the test, I could compensate for the areas where I struggled. The weighted average would determine my pass/fail score.

To achieve the same mood and excitement of my original first attempt, our instructors asked for volunteers to join us at the track that morning to simulate the audience of the day before. My roommate, Whitney, was among the volunteers there to support me and encourage me. As twice before, I was admonished not to stop. It was clear that I would immediately fail if I did. Forever in my memory was the story our instructors recounted about the doctor who collapsed and died while running this same track. His classmates, like ours, had been told not to stop. Instead, our instructors would aid the "man down." It was hard to fathom running past someone having a medical emergency.

As the dreaded whistle sounded, my first challenge began. By the time I made it from the starting point to the first curve of the track, I was already becoming short of breath. I headed down the straight stretch beyond. With each step, I was struggling more to breathe. The crisp air was causing airway constriction. I was almost to the second curve in the track and every step was torture. All this agony would be over if only I would stop.

Like a whisper, this verse came to me: "But those who hope in the LORD will renew their strength. They will soar on wings like eagles; they will run and not grow weary, they will walk and not be faint." (Isaiah 40:31, NIV)

For the entire rest of that day, I coughed up bright red blood but I said nothing. I didn't want to be sent home again. By evening, I was fine, and the symptoms were gone. I could handle the self-defense and firearms portions of the training. I could pass the written tests. The worst was past. God had answered many prayers. I had refused to quit and allow failure to define me.

Why did I put myself through that ordeal? I remembered the "tests" I passed from my earlier years as a female in the male-dominated coal industry. This day was another defining moment in my life. It was a day I look back on as the day I built a bridge. That bridge didn't just impact my own life, it spanned the tide. It impacted all those I would help, amputations would be avoided, wounds would be healed because I refused to quit. I ran the race for those patients too.

# Chapter Thirty-Eight
## B.B.

### EMPTY NEST

From a sixteen-year-old bride to a nineteen-year-old mom, to a twenty-seven-year-old single parent, I had never been truly alone. When I was a young mother, people remarked that it was great that I had my children so close in age. They reasoned that when my children were grown, I could do all the things I'd ever wanted to do. Somewhere along the way, I got so consumed by being a parent that I forgot to figure out exactly what I was missing. The almost insurmountable task of providing for my children without support from their dad had hit me full in the face. I never looked at a future beyond being the responsible parent. Their lives were my life. They were my identity.

### THE BOND

Sara and I were inseparable after Sawyer left. From my perspective, it was a comfortable arrangement. We ate together, shopped together, went to movies together, went to the gym together, even shared many common friends. When I went attended nursing conferences, she usually accompanied me. From Nashville, Seattle, Toronto and more, she was my traveling companion.

She was bubbly and full of life, a middle school teacher by profession, and now age thirty-seven. We shared common interests and struggles. She was my confidante, my companion and my best friend. She had a sparkle for life and a flair for fun and adventure. She had a beautiful soprano voice and was gifted with rhythm. Although she never went to dances, she could pick up whatever new dance moves were in style with little effort. Like me, Sara had always struggled with her weight, even when she was on the flag squad in high school band. She never allowed her weight to hold her back. We kayaked together, biked together, and even volunteered on several disaster relief missions in Louisiana and West Liberty, KY. The mundane life I had back in the 70's was anything but mundane now.

Although we were living and traveling companions, Sara and I each longed for more. When I discovered Sara was telling her friends that she lived in the basement of our home while I lived upstairs, it hurt me deeply. It was as though she was embarrassed that she was living with me instead of being on her own, like most of her friends. Every nook and cranny of our house was filled with items Sara was continually adding to her "hope chest." I knew the day would come when she would eventually leave home, but I didn't want to think about it. I didn't want her to feel trapped either.

Sara watched as friend after friend married, some more than once. They had their own homes and began their families. She shed many tears wondering why it hadn't yet been her turn. I was inept as her comforter, because deep inside, I felt the same. It was also an awkward situation. What if one of us found that special person and the other didn't? Wouldn't it be crushing to the other? Wouldn't it feel like the ultimate rejection?

Sara's friends at work encouraged her to check out a Christian dating site. Through this site, Sara met Ed in December 2007. Neither of them had been in a serious relationship before. Their relationship began around the time I was totally focused on rehabilitating my shoulder from the injury at the law enforcement training academy. I was preparing to return to retake the physical ability test in January 2008 when they first met.

Sara and Ed began to alternate weekends, driving nearly one hundred miles to spend time together. As their relationship grew, Sara was rapidly severing our mother-daughter bond in favor of a relationship with Ed. While I realized this was the natural course of events, I had to face my own codependency. I felt abandoned and rejected. Letting go was hard.

Ed was a reporter/writer. When I met him, it was awkward and at a very challenging time in my life. His personality was totally opposite to anybody in our family. We tried to break the ice with each other through some teasing at first. Unfortunately, some people struggle to tease without crossing the line of disrespect. Ed is an introvert, and despite our efforts to engage him in conversation, he retreats to a book or old reruns of NASCAR races. He is, in most every way, our opposites in opinions, politics, and interests. It is often awkward to be diplomatic and avoid drama at family get-togethers. It is a constant effort to find common ground, but most important to me is that he shows continual love, respect and support for Sara.

While I was away in Georgia in January, retaking the physical ability test and completing my training, Sara moved into her own apartment. I knew beforehand she planned to move out while I was gone. That would actually be easier than watching her pack up her belongings and drive away. I had given her permission to take a number of major furniture items to furnish her new apartment.

When I returned home from Georgia, the joy I felt from passing the course was tainted by the emptiness of a nine-room, two-story home and a life without Sara. I walked from room to room, staring at the bare space with a heavy heart. Her bedroom was empty, but the unbearable void was the sound of her laughter, the warmth of her smile, and her readily available hugs. I was faced with a house filled with cold January emptiness.

That same January, I did an enormous downsizing of personal possessions. I sold much of what I didn't need. I donated or discarded much of what I owned or couldn't quickly sell. I moved from a 2,900-square-foot home to a tiny two-bedroom, second-floor apartment approximately a mile from Sara. Although small, it was just as cold and empty as the large house I left behind.

I still hoped that Sara and I would do things together as we always had when she wasn't with Ed. Sara, however, was enjoying her new independence and new relationship. She didn't call or come by for almost a month. The loneliness was crushing. It was like having a child ripped away, even though it is perfectly natural for children to leave the nest and start their own families. When the last child leaves home, it is radically different for a single parent. In thirty-seven years, I had never allowed myself to develop my own identity apart from my children. In a city of over two hundred eighty-four thousand, I was never more alone. Apart from my work, I felt completely lost.

I was the odd person out in a couples' world. I didn't take vacations. Going on vacation alone was worse than being home alone. Sawyer took his family on vacations. In 2009, Sara and Ed married, so the two of them went on their own. I had become pathetically insignificant. Right or wrong, it is how I felt.

As a nurse, long hours and sometimes chaotic schedules made it hard to connect with old friends or make new ones. Connecting with people is easy enough via phone from the comfort of home. Most of the people I knew were from work, and by the end of the workday, the last thing we wanted to do was be with each other socially. The conversations we had would only be about work anyway.

When dining at a restaurant, the server called out seating as "party of one." When it's a party of one, is it truly a party? It wasn't in my opinion. I was keenly aware of the couples and families seated around me. I buried my nose in my mobile phone and pretended not to notice. I began choosing to dine at home where the hot meal waiting for me was the meal I had put in the slow cooker before going to work. When I got home, I plated up and served my own food. I closed the blinds and retreated to isolation mode. The only way to escape the loneliness was to watch TV until I started to doze off. At that point, I got up and went to bed.

About 5 a.m., the new day would repeat the same routine. What a contrast to how men came home from their workdays in the early 1960s when a stay-at-home wife had a hot meal cooked and waiting for them. Days passed when I heard from no one outside of my workday. When my phone rang, it was usually a telemarketer. People were busy with their own lives.

Somewhere in the midst of all that, I was determined to redefine my identity. It was time to spread my wings of independence. I had survived so many things, I was confident I could survive this too. Maybe I had never really grown up and become my own person. I had become the person I had to become to survive.

## (LITERALLY) BACK TO MY KNEES 2009

Day after day, my knee pain grew worse. The steroid injections I received just prior to my return to the academy usually bring relief for months. Mine had lasted only two weeks, but it was enough to get me through the physical ability test. MRIs revealed that my knees were both so deteriorated with arthritis they were literally bone-on-bone. All the cushioning cartilage was gone. I was in pain before I even stepped out of my bed in the morning, and the pain was never really gone. Non-narcotic analgesics made it just bearable enough to work. My knees had once locked up when I tried to do a seventeen-mile bike ride with Sawyer and his family, but I took ibuprofen and kept on going. I dared not take narcotic analgesics. As a correctional employee, I was subject to random drug screening. I had worked too hard for this job to risk losing it. I was adamant about avoiding any drug that could cause dependency.

As a nurse, I often use analogies and mental imagery when I teach my patients. Something relatable is easier to understand. I considered the analogy between my own human joints and the mechanics of automotive alignment. Most automobile owners know that proper alignment is essential when it comes to even tread wear and the overall tread life of tires. When the front end of your vehicle is out of alignment, it can shake and shimmy all over the road, in addition to wearing out your tires. Applying deductive reasoning, it made sense to utilize computer technology to align human joints.

My search for a doctor using this technology led me to the hospital where the very first joint replacement surgery was performed. This hospital also had the lowest infection rate and was located in New York City. Sara thought I had legitimately lost my mind. I would have no family or support network there. I hadn't even been to NYC. She reasoned that if I had complications, nobody would be there to advocate for me. In her eyes, I was vulnerable because of my knees and therefore an easy victim.

Over and over, I reassured her that I was going to a place that I trusted to do the best for me. I had done my homework. This was my version of stacking the deck in favor of my full recovery. A possible poor outcome would make me dependent on others to take care of me. I wanted both knees replaced, not just one. No doctor in Lexington would agree to do both in the same surgery. I was determined I would be fine. The morning Sara drove me to the airport, she was in tears, but this transplanted small-town girl was no longer afraid, not even in a city of nearly nine million strangers.

I arrived in NYC several days before my surgery date to meet my surgeon and to be cleared by a cardiologist. After that was completed, I explored NYC unaccompanied, spending the week of my fifty-eighth birthday exploring Times Square, Ellis Island, Liberty Island and the Statue of Liberty, the United Nations building, Ground Zero, Wall Street, and more. Before I exchanged my arthritic knees for titanium, I was determined to eke out every last remaining mile. I explored quaint little shops and dined at ethnic restaurants. I rode subways and buses and experienced the absolute madness of riding with New York cab drivers. I was treated with both kindness and curiosity wherever I went. People offered me their seats on the subways and buses. My pain must have been obvious to them. They helped me with directions. They played games guessing where I was from based on the way I enunciated my words. They never laughed or mocked me like the coworker from Kentucky once had. They showed respect. They guessed I was from Texas, Louisiana, Tennessee, North Carolina, Alabama, or even Mississippi, but never Kentucky. I always smiled. I was always polite. We are all ambassadors when we travel just as we are ambassadors when we welcome others.

On September 25, 2009, I had bilateral total knee replacements. My surgery was the last case of the day, starting at 9 p.m. at night. Before my surgery, I thought Dr. Mays already looked tired. I remember my glimpse of the OR right before anesthesia began. I have never seen anything quite like it. There were tables set up everywhere, left and right, with row after row of instruments lined up on sterile green drapes. I have the deepest respect for those who work behind the scenes in operating rooms. It certainly has impacted my life in a positive way. I was blessed to have no complications after four hours of surgery.

I called Sara once awake, though still sedated. I was trying to assure her I was okay, but I was still groggy from anesthesia and not coherent. Dr. Mays had called her once I was out of surgery to reassure her that everything had gone well, and I was fine. My phone call had quite the opposite effect. She was frantic because I was still not fully coherent, and she wasn't there to see for herself that I was okay.

The first day I stood on my feet was the absolute hardest. I was not delusional enough to think it would be easy. Mentally, I had prepared myself to work through whatever pain I felt and to give physical therapy my 100 percent best effort. I did not whine, but tears streamed down my cheeks. Every day after that got better. When I rang my call light, I was usually asking for fresh ice packs. I quickly discovered that ice helped me far more than pain medication.

I depended on my mobile phone for contact with family and friends. At this point, I was in a hospital in NYC, and all my friends were long-distance friends. At night, I would gaze out the window of my hospital room to see the multicolored lights illuminating the Empire State Building. Ironically, the rehabilitation hospital was located on Thirty-Fourth Street, and for me, two new knee joints truly was a miracle. When I had trouble sleeping, I chatted via messaging app with a family friend who was traveling to China for work. Nobody I knew in the US would still be awake. He teased that since I had new titanium knee joints, I must be bionic.

I made some wonderful friends among the hospital staff while getting rehabilitation. I have maintained friendships with two of them eleven years later. The care I received was multicultural and multiracial. All of it was excellent. I reunited with a dear friend from NYC who had gone to the nursing course in Georgia with me. She proved to be a special blessing. She and her young son were my only visitors for the three weeks I was hospitalized there.

# Chapter Thirty-Nine
## J.D.

### VIRTUS, 2002–2013

Virtus, a subsidiary of Salco, was a new company focused on the luxury mobile phone market. These were phones for the incredibly wealthy. The role was the same as with Salco, so there was no real change other than the fact that all the builds were carried out on-site rather than traveling to Finland.

After Mary's father died, she offered to buy me a new car in respect of all I had done to help her and her parents. I declined, as I knew how much she would be losing buying a new car. So, we decided on a nearly new car.

I was still writing websites at home. Most nights, I would be at the computer, sometimes until 1 a.m. to 1:30 a.m. I found I was getting extremely tired, and I found myself suffering from lack of sleep, plus being under pressure to get the projects ready on time. All this stress began to take its toll on me, and realising what was happening, I dropped the website design work and began to get more rest.

After a few months assisting the customer service department in designing and building a special-to-purpose test rack for the company service centres, I was offered the position on a permanent basis. My new job title would be test and devices manager. As the job progressed, I began to make the job content more varied with a wider scope.

My marriage was still deteriorating slowly. Mary would find ways to verbally attack me for the slightest reason. She would be upset at any time for the most puerile reason. At times, I dreaded my drives home from work, never knowing what would face me as soon as I entered the door. Mary hadn't looked for work in at least ten years. We had no children, and she had all day to think. The only other distractions that filled her days were going to her clubs on Tuesdays and Fridays. These were groups who mainly played bingo and cards (usually Haymarket). It was also a time for the group to catch up and chat.

Often when I arrived home from work, I was met with the dreaded words "We need to talk." This usually translated to Mary talking and me agreeing with everything she said in an effort to ensure a quiet, peaceful life. Otherwise, she became even more volatile, her words more vicious. I felt I was walking on eggshells around her.

If we were invited to a party, she insisted I sit right by her side the entire evening. It didn't matter that the men in the group had gone off into another area to talk about topics of interest to men. If I left her side during the evening, the siege of venomous words would come later. I avoided attending company parties and social gatherings because it always resulted in the same controlling, suffocating behaviour. After many invitations were declined, they eventually quit coming. In order for me to have any degree of peace, Mary had to be in control. I felt trapped and isolated.

I took an interest in watching genealogy programs on TV, which inspired me to search out my family's history. I often stayed up late at night to do this after Mary had gone to bed. There had never been a real marital relationship between us anyway (apart from a brief period at Harlow when she felt she would like to have babies), and the genealogy research passed the time. I stayed in the marriage because I had made a commitment and was trying my best to honour it.

When Mary had insomnia, she would call out to me, "Why are you looking for dead Aubreys when there is a live one here waiting for you? You know I can't settle down without you!" This wasn't exactly true, as many times, I'd go to bed, and she would be fast asleep and snoring away. Then woe betide me if I disturbed her and woke her up accidentally, even though she was spread out, taking up the space I would occupy in an English king-sized bed. Then she would have a whiskey to settle her down. When she didn't fall asleep after one drink, she would have another, and then another. If somebody upset her, she "medicated" with whiskey or gin. Her drinking had got to the point that I started hiding the alcohol from her.

It was soon after I started my new job when my mother passed away. I spoke to Mary about attending the funeral and helping my brother sort out the details. Mary's response was unbelievable. "I'm not going! How are you getting up there? Not in one of *my* cars, you're not! You take one of those cars, I'll report you to the police for taking without the owner's consent!" She had bought the car for me some years earlier after her father passed away, but as it was paid for from her family's inheritance, she insisted the car be in her name.

After that outburst came the next interrogation that just went on and on and on. "How do you think you're going to get up there? Where will you stay? How long do you expect to be away? What am I supposed to be doing whilst you're galivanting around?" I tried to explain where I would stay, but nothing I said pacified her. The endless questioning went on and on, just mentally wearing me down. By this time, I had enough of arguing. I swore inwardly and nonchalantly walked away, totally disgusted with her attitude.

The day of the funeral, I took the day off and went for a walk, alone with the dog. Then, at the time of the funeral service, I sat in silent respect in remembrance of my mother. I had never felt that amount of anger or hatred for somebody in my whole life as I now felt for Mary. I could never forget or totally forgive. Mary was never sorry, and she never apologised. I took refuge in my work and building up my family tree. On occasion, I would take a break to try to locate old friends. This provided a welcome diversion to the personal prison my life had become.

# Chapter Forty

## J.D.

### RENEWED CONTACT WITH BETH, 2010

One night, whilst working on my family tree, I opened the drawer of my desk to get something, and there at the top was the Irish blessing bookmark Beth had sent to me all those years ago when we were pen pals. I had carried that bookmark with me since she first sent it to me as a gift, even throughout my various postings in the RAF. It was now well worn. The plastic wrapping had all but gone, and the original emerald-green cotton tag had been lost somewhere over the years.

I held the bookmark in my hand, wondering what had happened to Beth. I decided to open the web browser and do a search to see if I could locate her. An identical name immediately came up, right at the top of the list. I couldn't believe I'd found her so quickly. I closed the browser, then tried again. There she was again. I closed it all down again, deleted the history cache, then tried again. The result was the same. I opened the link. This took me to her old high school alumni website. The page with information she had posted to the site came up.

According to the details she posted, she had two children, a boy and a girl, and was now divorced. I was saddened to read that, but I didn't know the circumstances. I looked across the page and saw a message area. I filled in the sender details and began writing in the message area. "I am not sure if you remember me, but I believe we used to be pen pals." I continued giving snippets of information, such as I was going in the Merchant Navy, being in the Marine Cadets. Enough to trigger a memory without giving away too much personal information. When I finished, I clicked the "send" button. I wondered if I would ever get a reply, or whether she had totally forgotten about me.

A couple of hours later, I received an email from an unknown address, but with a reference to the message I sent to Beth. I opened the email, and it was from her. It began, "Of course I remember you!" Her email continued as she shared more details of her past life. I was surprised and saddened about the divorce but happy that she had children.

I quickly replied and gave a bit more information. As each of us began to reveal the gaps in our lives since 1968, it wasn't long before the previous forty-two years melted away. I confessed I reconciled the sudden end to our pen pal relationship by surmising that she must have been pregnant. I learned this was not the case. As I read her email and learned the background story, I began to understand. Once again, we were pen pals, but this time, there was no waiting three weeks to receive the replies! Our emails kept communication going, and our friendship as adults began to grow.

My job was still going well. My home life, however, wasn't quite so good. Sometimes, I would arrive home mentally drained or exhausted. Mary seemed to pick up on this vulnerability and begin her verbal attacks. By this time, I was past caring. I agreed with her because that seemed the easiest way to make her stop the verbal siege. It didn't necessarily mean I was sincere with that agreement, but it was just an appeasement to keep her from hounding me incessantly on the same subject.

One of my colleagues, Steve, a divorced dad, lived a couple of houses away. He had had a major heart attack and was subsequently fitted with a pacemaker. He was hospitalised for quite a while, and once he was able to return to work, I gave him a lift to and from work. I also helped him when he needed to go shopping and often dropped in for a chat. Inevitably, we ended up discussing projects at work.

As a result, Mary made false and mentally twisted accusations regarding the nature of our relationship. Most of the other engineers were male, and we spoke the same "language." Mary could not grasp the concept of the nature of the work, despite the many times I tried to explain to her. She wanted me to be available to her at all times and resented any time I was away. It did no good to try and reason with her. Over the years, she had grown progressively worse. If I didn't immediately agree with her, all hell would break loose, and she would fly into a rage.

One weekend whilst we were away, I didn't feel well. The day after our return, I visited the doctor. When he checked my vitals, he was unable to read my blood pressure. I looked at the doctor and joked, "I knew it. I'm dead!" He looked back at me and said, "Not yet. It looks like I'm going to have to do this the old-fashioned way." With that, he took out a sphygmomanometer. As he checked my blood pressure, he looked a bit concerned. When he finished, he told me he was going to book an urgent electrocardiogram (ECG) for me. He suspected atrial fibrillation. That same afternoon, when I had completed the ECG, I saw the printed graph: it looked just like my heart was swearing at me in Morse code! I was immediately put on warfarin and other medications to prevent blood clots and a stroke.

When I got home and told Mary, she was shocked. Her mother had passed away due to a stroke, so this brought back a lot of memories. "What's going to happen to me if you croak? What will I do? Who will look after me?" There was no genuine concern for how I was feeling. Her concern was purely for herself. I had reached the point in our marriage that I didn't particularly care about who would look after her.

Our marital relationship, such as it was, had eroded to the point where I would just be happy to be out of it. It wasn't one major thing, but the little things, then the bigger things, the vicious words that left scars that grew deeper as the years passed. I didn't have a life, or freedom. I was merely existing in a well-entrenched day-to-day routine, until the next verbal tirade came out of nowhere. There were times I would look at camping equipment to see what I would need to run off and live a wandering life. Then I realized I wouldn't be able to carry it all plus the food I would need. It was escapist theory, but it made me feel happier for a short time.

A few months later, I received an appointment letter from the hospital scheduling me for a cardioversion procedure. I had been expecting it for a long time, as the doctor had mentioned this to me. I hadn't told Mary because this would have initiated yet another "sackcloth and ashes" session due to the procedure having to stop my heart and restart it using a defibrillator. She had seen TV shows in which the patients jumped up off the table when one was used. However, during a visit to the doctor together, she asked the doctor about the procedure. No matter how much he tried to calm her down with facts and tell her it wouldn't be like she saw it on TV, nothing would keep her mind off what she perceived as my death during the procedure.

I would need to be driven to and later picked up from the hospital. I would not be allowed to drive. Mary's reaction? "I'm not going to take you.

Can't you catch a bus or take a taxi? Maybe somebody could take you and pick you up." I ended up telling her I would arrange something. Somehow, I refrained from reminding her of the time I left work early to comfort her when she got a letter regarding an abnormality on one of her mammograms. I took her to the hospital some twenty miles away so she could have the abnormality thoroughly checked out. Thankfully, it was only a cyst. She said many times how grateful she had been for me that day, and the previous days when she wanted to get familiar with the route. When it came my turn for help from her, her sympathy was sadly lacking.

I was just disgusted at her attitude, but it was not surprising to me. It was, however, surprising to the people I worked with. I hadn't shared information about our marital relationship. Work was the one place I could be myself. Telling my colleagues my private business would be pointless. Steve was the only person I could ask, especially as he only lived a couple of houses away from me.

Steve said he would take me for my procedure. The cardioversion procedure worked for only a few minutes when my heart reverted to atrial fib. When it was time for me to return home that evening, I called Mary, but she refused to come pick me up. Instead, I called Steve, and he came to bring me back home. When I arrived at home, Mary was sitting in a chair, watching some TV program. She showed little concern about what I had been through. I had to serve my own dinner. So much for "in sickness and in health."

During the winter, we had a fairly heavy snowfall. I went out with the dog and checked the state of the roads. The main roads had been well-treated and were clear of the snow. I decided to travel to work. I had to carry out a task in person, a task that no one else could do. Mary, of course, wasn't happy with it. She pointed at the snow coming down. "Look at it! Just look at it! You're not driving out in *this*!" I explained to her I had to as I was the only person who could do this particular job, and it had to be done that day. Mary replied, "Well, don't expect *me* to visit you if you end up in hospital!"

"I don't expect you to," I replied forlornly, as I walked out of the front door. I knew she would be mulling this over all day and then blowing it all out of proportion by the time I got home. I wasn't surprised when it happened. I just shrugged it off and ignored or just agreed with her, as usual. A few minutes of verbal bombardment was all it took; then all went quiet. She was expecting an argument, but I refused her that chance, which must have hurt her more.

Two years later, my older brother and only sibling passed away. The response from Mary was much the same as she gave about my mother. "How do you think you're going to get up there? If you try to use my car to make the trip, I'll call the police and report you for taking it without the owner's consent! Where will you stay? How long do you expect to be away? How much will that lot cost? What am I supposed to be doing whilst you're galivanting around?" More rants and more complaining ensued. "Here we go again," I thought. My ears picked up the sound, but I didn't let my brain absorb it all, just the same old whining I had heard so many times before.

Again, I took the day off. At the time of the scheduled cremation, I lit a bonfire in the garden incinerator, then poured myself a very large whiskey. I raised the glass and toasted my departed brother. Mary stayed indoors and didn't come out. To be honest, I really didn't want her there. This was just between me and Terry. I didn't care or worry about what Mary would say or not say. This was my only sibling, and I would say my farewell to him my way. He taught me a lot and helped me so much when I was younger. He deserved a good send-off. I poured myself another large Scotch as I sat there watching the flames die down. I raised my glass again. "Ta-ra, Terry. Bon voyage!"

For some months, Mary had been complaining about how we never got out enough in the caravan. She used a retired friend as a reminder of how she would be happy if I was retired, and we could go away at any time and for as long as we wanted. This was her latest dig at me because I was working and only had a set number of days of leave allocation.

At work one day, I was at a group project meeting, and the group project manager was showing timescales for future projects. It was then I realised I didn't want to do this anymore. I was done with work, and it was time to retire. Besides, Mary had been going on about my retirement. We lived in an expensive area in a three-bedroom terraced home. We had managed to live primarily on my income for most of our marriage. Mary didn't deny herself nice things, regardless of our income. I dared not protest her spending habits. If I said anything, she would snap back at me and say, "Don't I deserve nice things?" Arguing was useless. I had heavy debts hanging over my head that I hoped retirement would actually pay off.

I began thinking about how I would finance an early retirement and what I would do. "Are you with us, Jim?" the project manager eventually asked. I snapped out of my thoughts. Looking at the screen, I replied, "I am now, but I won't be then!" We all laughed. They knew my normal retirement would be before a number of those projects were due to begin. Little did they know that it would be a lot sooner, provided the pensions were sufficient.

The letters from my pension companies arrived, and I did a number of calculations. There would be sufficient funds to wipe out all my debts, including my mortgage, leaving plenty in hand to live on each month. I wrote out my letter of resignation and the next day handed it to my group manager. He was shocked as he had no idea I was even considering taking early retirement.

Mary's attitude was also a factor in my decision to retire. It was exhausting, hearing her constant complaining about how others were living a lovely life in their retirement. She went on and on about how they were able to get away whenever they wanted, whilst we were stuck, limited to a set number of leave days. I was sick of hearing about how she was stuck at home "skivvy" washing, drying, and cooking all day, every day. Her expectations of my position and duties in the workplace were very unrealistic. She was forever asking why I couldn't work from home permanently. I was fortunate because at times, I could actually work from home. Still, those were special and specific times and not the norm. My last day at work was November 29, 2013.

# Chapter Forty-One
## B.B.

### THE INTERNET ERA

Once I returned home from the rehabilitation hospital in NYC, I had about two and a half months until I would return to work. I applied myself to several days of intense physical therapy for my knees every week. One weekend, I made the journey to visit Sawyer, Marcy and my granddaughter Allie, now age three. For the first time in months, I was able to get down on the floor and play with her dolls and dollhouse. We ever had pretend tea parties together with a miniature teapot and cups, substituting diluted apple juice for tea.

One day, in general conversation, Sawyer mentioned that my old high school now had an alumni link on its website to reconnect former classmates. Although I didn't realize it, this would prove to be a pivotal turning point in my life.

Memories flooded back as I visited the alumni link and posted my contact information. Our class had only held one reunion, our tenth. My classmates were still hanging out with their same high school best friends at the reunion while others were trying to impress. Many still lacked the maturity to shed false pretenses and just be real.

I wondered whether the thirty years that followed our first reunion had been kind to my classmates. I entered my contact information and gave a brief summary of what I had done since graduation. By this time, I had been divorced from Daniel for twenty-one years. I posted photos of myself, my senior photo versus a current photo. I also posted photos of Sawyer and Sara. It had been forty years since my graduation, and some of my classmates had already died. Others had simply disappeared, and nobody knew where they were. I hoped to reconnect and rekindle old friendships. Apart from that, I had no expectations.

# A MESSAGE FROM THE PAST

Time passed, and I forgot all about entering information on the alumni link. One day, totally out of the blue, I received a random email. The content was odd, I thought, yet it definitely wasn't spam. That name was strangely familiar. My mind switched into full retrieval mode, like flipping through the names and addresses in an old Rolodex file.

"I think we might have been pen pals at one time," he said. That would have been back in the late '60s, over forty years ago. What? It couldn't be! Jim Aubrey! I shook my head in disbelief. He asked in his email whether I remembered him. Of course, I remembered! As if I were refocusing the lens on an old camera for clarity, I tried to retrieve a mental image of this young boy who had been so important to me so long ago.

I went to my closet in search of those carefully stored bins of old photographs. Seated on the sofa with the bins on either side of me, I went through the photographs one by one, pausing as a particular memory was triggered. Finally, there they were, retrieved like recovered treasure, the same two photographs Jim had sent me forty-two years earlier. One photo was of Jim standing alone in the doorway of his home. He was squinting slightly from the sun, the shadowed silhouette of his photographer visible from the side. The other was a group photo of Jim as a Marine Cadet. How had he found me, and what had inspired him to look? There were so many memories, and so many more unanswered questions. I wondered what he must look like now, all these years later. I wondered about his life, his family. Had he married? Did he have children? Was he at sea, and what kind of work did he do? I had searched the random selection sequence of the draft lottery in 1970. If Jim had been here in the US, based on his birth date, he would most certainly have been among the first of those "unfortunate sons" drafted into the Vietnam War. Many times, I thought and even verbalized to my friends that the person I was supposed to be married to must surely have been a casualty of that war.

Jim later told me he had been researching his genealogy and happened to run across the bookmark I sent him in an envelope one Christmas. He had carried it with him everywhere he had gone, even when he was stationed with the Royal Air Force in Northern Ireland. That simple bookmark had prompted him to search for me. Sadly, I had none of Jim's old letters to reread. I had discarded them all after I had written him a final letter, explaining why we could no longer write to each other. I discarded his letters, but I could never bring myself to discard his photographs.

Jim had none of my old letters and no longer had the photo I had sent him. His mother had burned them all while he was away in the RAF. My first email reply to Jim was a long one. Not only did I remember him, but I felt I owed him far more than just a simple response. I owed him the truth, with details, and an apology. I poured out the painful details from the sincere depths of my heart. In true Jim fashion, he understood.

## A FRIENDSHIP REBORN

In our email exchanges, even though I was now fifty-nine and Jim was now sixty, our hearts and minds were as though we were in the late 1960s. When I received an email from him, my heart leapt just as when I had received one of his letters from the post office all those years ago. I felt the same excitement as when I was a teenager, thrilled to receive a letter from a pen pal in another country. Just as when I was fifteen and Jim was sixteen, I quickly sat down to send him a reply. Only now, because of the era of the Internet, it would no longer take two weeks or more for him to receive it. The content of our communication had significantly "grown up" to real-life subjects as we slowly filled the gaps of time lost over a span of forty-two years.

After our last exchange of letters, Jim joined the RAF. He had eventually married in 1977 but had no children. I knew little more about his wife than her name. If he mentioned her at all, it was in one innocuous sentence. We had always been able to talk about anything together, but she was the one exception. I was grateful to have his friendship, so I didn't pry.

Since I also had a social media account, I suggested we reconnect there as well. It was March 16, 2010, when Jim and I became social media friends. Although there were multiple people with the same name, Jim said he easily recognized me because my smile hadn't changed from all those years ago when I first sent him my photograph. My profile photo was one of me standing beside my son's blooming lilac bush on Easter Sunday. Our social media and email interactions soon evolved to real-time messages.

Our communication continued from this point forward, about three to four times a week, as we shared events from our day-to-day lives. All the while, we filled in the blank spaces for each other, as best we could, about our years apart. My abrupt departure in 1968 certainly wasn't because of an unplanned pregnancy. He deserved to know, even though he never questioned. Just as when we were teens, there was nothing I couldn't discuss with him freely.

# Chapter Forty-Two

## B.B.

C onversations with Jim expounded on a variety of topics, from my work at the prison to the demands of his job. We talked about local weather conditions. For Brits, that usually includes rain, predictably coinciding with bank holidays. We talked about our pets, political leaders, the structures of our governments, and the novelties of British politics. Our opinions of each of those leaders were decidedly skewed, as influenced by media perception in our respective countries. I was amused to learn about Great Britain's Monster Raving Loony Party. At least one political party was honestly named!

We compared our respective countries' healthcare systems. He explained how the National Health System works in the United Kingdom as I explained out-of-pocket copays and deductibles for doctors, procedures, anesthesiology, prescription medications, labs, and the like in the US. Each system has its own challenges, and neither is actually free.

Humor exuded in our email exchanges as we took turns catching each other up with an exchange of puns. I was no match for the "master of punny." All his puns were clean and incredibly corny. While we both enjoyed photography, Jim had a natural talent for artistic composition. Often, he shared his nature photography with me. He was naturally artistic and devoted himself to developing his talent by joining art groups. Painting on his break at work or in a cramped, unheated garage at home, he created amazing pastel seascapes and acrylic landscapes. His art had been in an exhibition in London. Many pieces had been sold to art collectors in different countries.

## APPLES AND WINE

On a rare occasion when I was feeling especially lonely, our conversation turned personal. I mentioned the "lack of a decent fella," and he responded with a story called "Apples and Wine" by Pete Wentz. The story starts:

Girls are like apples…the best ones are at the top of the trees. The boys don't want to reach for the good ones because they are afraid of falling and getting hurt. Instead, they just get the rotten apples that are on the ground that aren't so good, but easy. So the apples at the top think something is wrong with them, when, in reality, they are amazing. They just have to wait for the right boy to come along, the one who is brave enough to climb all the way to the top of the tree.

He followed that quote with one by Jill Shalvis: "I've heard that men are like fine wine. They begin as grapes, and it's up to women to stomp the sh*t out of them until they turn into something acceptable to have dinner with."

He went on to say, "I'd definitely put you at the top of the tree." No matter how down I was, Jim always left me smiling from the inside out. Our conversations had certainly changed from those two teenagers' whose discussions usually focused on music, rugby, and school. We could make conversation about the serious to the most trivial subjects. It seems strange to say that we were long-distance companions, yet that was exactly what we were. We even exchanged recipes. In all our communication, we were equals, and Jim was always positive, respectful, and encouraging.

I wrote about my children and their activities. I wrote about work challenges, sometimes high-stress situations at work. I wrote about being an independent thinker and refusing to be whittled on like a piece of a jigsaw puzzle that doesn't fit. I wrote about refusing to become part of the establishment and my ability to make changes, even if it meant working elsewhere. I wrote about the beauty of the countryside on day drives to the Amish community to visit one of their furniture stores. I wrote about their local restaurant near Russell Springs, Kentucky, serving such homemade foods as banana pudding, blueberry cobbler, and real fried chicken, all foods Jim had never tasted.

I wrote about the joy of the sound made by walking through a pile of dry, crunchy leaves in the fall, and the childish fun of popping the ripe seed pods of speckled jewel weed. On bleak, empty evenings, I wrote blog posts about such things as my travel experiences, my family, my childhood, and especially funny experiences, like getting locked in the backseat of my car in the hospital parking lot at work one cold winter night. I blogged about causing an airport terminal to get shut down by security because I inadvertently left an unattended cardboard box of Dungeness crab behind while rushing to change gates.

Jim always commented that he felt like I had taken him along on my journeys, and he could "see" my experiences as though he were there with me. He was my dear friend and confidant, and I poured out my heart to him in my letters. His responses were genuinely sincere. No matter how down I was, he always managed to cheer me up, sometimes with a joke, sometimes by remembering a special holiday. I also wrote about my loneliness. It was then that Jim would respond, "Put your left arm around your right waist. Next, put your right arm around your left waist. Now squeeze. I am sending you a hug." That always put a smile on my face, even if he never saw it. He often closed his email with that same virtual "b-i-g hug." It was amazing how much that simple gesture meant to me, yet my heart ached with loneliness for real companionship and human touch. I wrote often about the value of his friendship and what it meant to have a friend "to share life with, if only long-distance."

When our discussion turned to family, I could sense his sadness as he wrote volumes in only a few words about the lack of contact with his family. Again, I didn't pry. Sometimes, he would drop a brief sentence about his wife, and on those rare occasions, I looked for words that would tell me more about what his life was really like with her. I looked for any hint of what their marriage was like or phrases revealing true affection between them. It was never there. Again, I didn't pry.

I fantasized about making a trip to England. Then I imagined a what-if scenario. I would go to the city where Jim lived and surprise him with a message that I was there. I was never sure what his reaction would be. Would he come to see me, or would he refuse because of Mary? I could not bear the possibility of rejection. Consequently, I kept these thoughts in my head and never shared them with anybody, especially not Jim. I didn't want to lose or put at risk the timeless friendship we already had.

## DUAL ROLE

I was a caring, empathetic, compassionate nurse but was expected to be firm, fair, and consistent with inmates. I was taught that inmates would try to "drown the duck" who was trying to help them. Twenty years of nursing experience and over a half-century of life experiences had still not prepared me for the variety of games inmates play.

The bigger surprise was that the very coworkers I relied on to "have my back" in the event of trouble inside the prison walls were often the ones at the root of the problem. They had all passed a rigorous background check, yet that didn't mean they could all be trusted as people of integrity when nobody was looking. I learned, in time, that the symbolic "sharp object in my back" didn't necessarily come from the homemade shank of an inmate. Far too often, it was the "knife in the back" from a coworker.

Shortly after I arrived, someone started a rumor that I didn't like LPNs. That rumor finally made it back to me one evening. Amy, an LPN with grit, approached and questioned me about it. My response was laughter and the explanation that surely the person who started this false rumor wasn't aware that I was once an LPN. I had gone back to school twice, progressing from an associate degree to a baccalaureate degree in nursing.

I was the only RN at the institution with a board certification, which required a baccalaureate degree in nursing. I was well qualified for my role in wound care, yet nurses with more seniority at the institution felt they were entitled to the role based on their seniority alone. Those nurses complained to the union that my position should be posted to a roster so that all the other nurses, including LPNs could bid for it, regardless of qualifications.

Battles like this never ended for me among the nursing staff. Despite the fact that the other nurses preferred a compressed work week with twelve-hour shifts, there was still resentment because I worked eight-hour shifts, five-days per week with weekends and holidays off. I was not being reimbursed for my board recertification fees, and the institution had not paid for my initial nine weeks of specialty training.

I never came to terms with why these petty battles continued, but I learned that I needed to protect myself from weapons of every sort. I held fast to Isaiah 54:1: "No weapon forged against you will prevail, and you will refute every tongue that accuses you. This is the heritage of the servants of the Lord, and this is their vindication from me," declares the Lord.

Promises made by directors of nursing were made to me and broken time and again regarding raises and pay scales for special roles like mine. I was to receive special pay as the result of taking on a specialty nursing role requiring three separate board certifications. It never came. There were huge gaps in my annual salary compared to nurses in my specialty practicing in the private sector. Time and again, I submitted formal requests for raises, essentially asking that the promises made to me be honored. They never were. I applied for other jobs outside my agency.

Each time I shared info about a new job search, Jim was supportive, recalling his own post-military/RAF job search disappointments. He ended his emails on a positive note, telling me not to get "bogged down with bad vibes" and closing with "always your dear friend."

Eventually, I was selected to fill a position at another agency. The position would require me to move 135 miles from home and to another state. It offered a better salary and benefits and more vacation time, and it was in my nursing specialty. I thought that was exactly what I wanted until the night I had an unusual dream.

In my dream, I died. The first people to greet me when I arrived in Heaven weren't friends or family: they were inmates. I got a very clear message in that dream. Regardless of salary, I was exactly where the Lord wanted me to be. Everything is not about money. As a result of the dream, I didn't accept the job, and I ceased further job searches after that. I was finally at peace with the fact that ministering to inmates in the prison setting was part of God's plan for my life.

I was surrounded by inmates convicted of drug dealing, murder, money laundering, embezzling, sex offenses, pedophilia, and the like. They spanned every walk of life and profession. Many were gang affiliated. One inmate had fifty-seven different aliases, while others had terrorism connections. Some learned from their mistakes, others never did. The crimes they committed and the mistakes they made didn't have to define who they were. There was a common thread. They had all made mistakes, like me. Maybe not the same mistakes, but mistakes, nevertheless.

One of my patients was an inmate from New York who loved to play "tough guy" with the other inmates. He was the "shot caller" or kingpin on his unit. He even dictated to other inmates in his housing unit what time they had to turn the lights out. When a new inmate was transferred in, he made sure they knew he ran that unit. Of course, from a correctional standpoint, he didn't, but he could probably make life miserable for the inmates who challenged him. He habitually missed call outs (appointments) to wound clinic. Missed call outs are a huge security issue in a prison. If an inmate isn't where he or she is supposed to be, then where are they? Have they escaped? When there is an internal movement (such as changing classes in school), the intercom announces the beginning and end of the period in which inmates can move in an orderly manner from one location to another within the prison. They have ten minutes to complete the move. At the end of this movement period, a call out list shows which inmates should be at a particular location. If inmates are not where they're supposed to be, they are "out of bounds."

This inmate wanted staff to acquiesce to his whims as well. He had missed call outs several times when I wasn't at work, yet had not been written up. Consequently, his wounds were getting bigger because they had not been properly cared for. In this regard, he was his own worst enemy. Patients who are not incarcerated can come and go as they please and miss treatments. In prison, it's a security and accountability issue. He could refuse care by signing a written refusal once he arrived at the wound clinic, but he still had to show up for his call out. Those who don't show up, exhibiting disregard for the rules, should be written up for the infraction. If this is repeated behavior and there is insubordination, they can actually lose "good time," thereby extending their period of incarceration.

This inmate had missed his call out on the day I was working. I wrote him an infraction ("shot"), and it was served to him by a lieutenant later that day. The inmate was livid. The next day, he was on my call out again. This time, he showed up insisting he wanted to refuse care, saying that I might as well stop putting him on call out because he was going to refuse care every time I was working. I bluntly told him I was still going to place him on call out regardless, and he would still have to either show up or get another write-up. I reminded him that his wounds had measured larger the last time because of his multiple refusals of care. Every day, I was going to do the right thing by giving him an opportunity to get wound care. It would be up to him to do the right thing for his body by accepting treatment.

He became angry, shouting and making aggressive gestures as he started coming toward me. I keyed my portable radio and called out, "Wound clinic to control. I'm having an issue with an inmate." Within seconds, I heard the thunder of feet in the corridor as a herd of at least fifteen staff members from all departments arrived on the scene in a show of force. More correctional officers were still coming, including lieutenants. The inmate was still shouting and belligerent as he was escorted to the lieutenant's office. He was eventually placed in solitary confinement in the Special Housing Unit, where he spent six months for an array of charges that day.

"Armed" only with a radio, I sometimes found myself alone with inmates, but was never afraid. At the end of the day, it comes down to respect. I gave respect and expected respect in return. I dealt swiftly with those who didn't give respect, and the word soon got out to the rest of them. I was fair. I didn't play favorites. I liked some of them more than others because of their behavior, but still I gave no preferential treatment. I met only one inmate who openly admitted he was guilty of the charges against him. Others said the only mistake they made was getting caught. I had no judgment for any of them. The court system had already done that. God is the only judge that gets it right 100 percent of the time.

I know beyond a shadow of a doubt that this prison was exactly where I was supposed to be. I know beyond a shadow of a doubt that I made a huge difference in many of those inmates' lives. Most were appreciative and rarely failed to thank me for the care I provided.

Years later, one of my long-term diabetic patients (now a free man) told me he was able to walk out of prison at the end of his sentence on both his legs because of what I had done for him. I invested my best efforts to try to get every wound to heal, just as though they were members of my own family. I genuinely cared, and they knew I cared.

Unfortunately, not all wounds heal. I was once asked, "What are the hardest wounds to heal?" Without hesitation, I replied, "The wounds that are on the inside." If you have a deep thorn inside, it will continue to fester and cause pain over and over again until it's removed. Once it's removed, healing can occur. Time, the right treatment, and a lot of patience can bring about healing. Even scars can be sensitive. Scars fade and mature with time but will always be a visual reminder of the wound. We can't change the past events of a person's life, but at the very least, we can show some compassion and be kind.

# Chapter Forty-Three
## J.D.

### RETIREMENT, DECEMBER 2013

The first Monday morning of my retirement felt like any other day, except I knew I didn't have to get up so early. I took the dog for a walk along the river. As I passed some office buildings, I looked at the people inside and was so glad to be free of all that. No longer would I be sitting in front of a computer screen all day. I was out in the fresh air, having a pleasant walk with the dog.

The euphoria didn't last long. When I got home, Mary was already up, drinking her usual morning pot of tea and watching TV. I fed the dog, got my breakfast, and began reading through the Sunday papers again. Then I was told that I would be going with her to her clubs. She enjoyed them, and the company, even though at times she said they infuriated her. I decided not to argue as this would not have been a good start. She would go on and on about how I needed to get out and about, rather than lazing around. She insisted I needed to meet new people. Again, I opted for the quiet life, so I reluctantly agreed. She was oblivious to my lack of enthusiasm.

When I finally went to my first club gathering with her, she introduced me to her friends. The first bit of recreation was bingo. "Oh God! Spare me this!" The numbers were called out in a slow monotone. The women (they were all women there, except for one other man) called back the appropriate response when certain numbers were called. "Two little ducks, twenty-two."

"Quack-quack!" they responded. It went on, boring game after boring game. Then I had a win. Anybody would have thought I'd won the lottery the way they carried on! "Pick your prize!" I had to get up in front of everybody and enthusiastically pick a prize. Nothing really appealed, so I chose a notebook. At least that could be used to write down phone messages. "Why didn't you pick the biscuits? We could have shared them," Mary said.

After a tea break, it was time for cards. The arguments ensued because one half of the table couldn't hear or see clearly what the other half was doing. It wasn't their fault they were hard of hearing, and with all the background noise, even I was having problems trying to follow what was happening. How anybody won, I don't know! Players were playing out of turn or playing the wrong suit. The combinations of errors were endless. At the end of the afternoon, it was time to put the chairs and tables away. As "the man," I had the main job of doing that. Then it was home and time to take the dog for a walk. Friday was much the same, with the same people, doing much the same, except they did have better games to play. Some were a bit more taxing, but there was always bingo. The next week, I had the same clubs to look forward to.

The club members were good and kindly people, and most were widowed, so this was really their only source of real social interaction. After a couple of months of this, I would take a crossword in with me to complete whilst they were playing bingo; I couldn't stand that boring game anymore. It was a hint that I didn't really want to be there, but Mary was totally oblivious to that.

Other afternoons were spent taking the dog for a walk and then going on a trip to a garden centre. I had seen more than my share of them. In the winter, there wasn't much to see anyway, but I still had to go. This was my retirement, but it was still all about appeasing Mary. Walking the dog, cooking, women's clubs, garden centres, and watching TV. It was only after Mary went to bed that I could get to watch anything I wanted to watch on TV.

Sometimes after she had gone to bed, she would lay awake mulling, twisting and distorting some trivial comment or detail that had occurred that day. On those occasions, she would come back downstairs, put her hands on her hips, and say, "You're not engrossed in this, are you?" The way she said it, it wasn't so much a question, but more of an order. I sighed as I sarcastically replied, "Obviously not" and switched it off. Then she would begin the accusations or whatever notion I might need to defuse. Most of the time, it was something outrageously ridiculous. I wondered how much more of this mental torture I could take. I thought of Beth's emails and how much more pleasant and fun-filled her life was than mine. I wasn't living; I was merely existing.

One day, Mary surprised me. "Why don't you join an art club or something?" She had noticed an art group advertised at the local hall where we went to her clubs and pointed it out to me. I took the leaflet and called the organiser when I got home. We had a discussion and agreed I could join them at their next meeting on Monday. I called up to Mary, who was ironing upstairs, about the news. "How long will it last? What am I supposed to do whilst you are away? Why are you so keen to abandon me?" So, it went on. I turned and called back dejectedly, "I'll not go then!" I don't think she ever expected me to actually make enquiries or actually join an art group, or anything that didn't include her, even though it was her suggestion.

This was how it went on, time and time again. I knew how to calm her down, but I had grown weary of the constant need to do that. She was getting progressively worse. Sometimes she would have a screaming childlike temper tantrum. I had taken her mental abuse far too long already.

Throughout all this mental stress, the emails from Beth kept me going. It was lovely to email her. She was a piece of tranquility in my life. Whilst out with the dog, I would think of her, and any anxiety I was feeling would soon evaporate. All the while Mary would be tearing me apart, I would just ignore her and think of Beth. I felt at peace when I thought of her.

For many months now whilst out with the dog, I had looked towards the west and silently said, "Beth, oh Beth! My lovely Beth, how I long to be with you!" I said this to the wind in the hope that it would reach her. If I wasn't whispering it, I was thinking it. It reminded me of seeing a group of Nepalese women wading in the river, giving offerings to the water. Their religion stated that those offerings and prayers would in time reach the sea, which would eventually carry their prayer back to their homeland. My cries were much the same. I did this just about every day, more often when Mary was acting up, which she did more and more.

# Chapter Forty-Four

## B.B.

### AGE AND EXPERIENCE

I had the rare distinction of being the oldest nurse at the prison. Verbal jabs about my age were not uncommon. One of the younger nurses, half my age, once made a snide comment about my "bionic parts." I responded that I "had shoes older than him." I had long since learned never to let them know their comments bothered me.

Once faced with gender discrimination in the male-dominated coal industry, I was now determined to hold my ground regarding age. I dared not allow my brunette hair to go gray. It would only give my younger coworkers more opportunity to exclude me from their conversations and discredit me as obsolete and outdated. I was in a much different place personally and professionally than any of them. I was grateful that my nursing specialty provided autonomy, allowing less opportunity for exclusion.

On a personal level, while my younger coworkers were dealing with young children and their tireless extracurricular activities, I already had a granddaughter. I made an effort to show an interest and contribute to their conversations, but they seldom showed interest in what I had to say. While most of my colleagues were interested in acquiring more impressive houses, I was downsizing mine. While my colleagues were planning their next big family vacation, I was painfully aware that I had no vacation companion.

I was not intimidated by the fact that my supervisors were younger and didn't discredit them for having less experience. Differences in private interests had no bearing on my ability to contribute as a professional. I wanted to mentor newly hired and less-experienced nurses, yet my supervisors were so shortsighted they never made it a priority.

Jim responded that he got similar teasing from his younger colleagues, but he gave back as good as they dished out. He would ask them when they were born. When they replied, he told them he was alive before they were even a twinkle in their father's eye. He would then go on to ask them how many more years they had left to work. When they replied, he would say, "No one's got that long to go!" As the oldest in his group, he would then tell his colleagues he had a mere four and a half years left until retirement. He would tell them that in a few years, he would drive by their workplace one day and think of them slaving away whilst he'd be out enjoying his life. I wished I had the quick-witted responses he had!

Most of my friends were married. By contrast, I came home to an empty townhome. Twelve-hour shifts and irregular work schedules are not conducive to a social life. At the end of a long day, the last thing I wanted was to go to a restaurant at 8 p.m. (or later) where I would be dining alone. I was a misfit in a world of couples. My (now ex) husband had come home at the end of his workday in the early 1970s to an already prepared hot meal. Most of my hot meals came from a slow cooker.

My reality was different. I was under no delusion that a knight on a white horse would come and rescue me. For this reason, romance novels had no appeal. I recognized the stark contrast between romantic fantasy and reality. Still, there was no escape from the emptiness I felt.

## SEEKING

The holidays, especially Christmas, had changed. I had to "share" holidays with my adult children's in-laws. Very often, I didn't see my family on Christmas at all. 2014 was the year Christmas passed me by. I didn't put up a single bit of decoration or send a single card. This was quite a switch from the same person who had so lovingly decorated a 7 1/2-foot Christmas tree with a cherished collection of unique ornaments, many handmade or hand carved. Contrasting memories of happier Christmases when Sara and Sawyer were children and still at home felt like a crater in my heart now. Our closely knit family of three had memorable Christmases filled with excitement and laughter.

Jim surprised me with a large Christmas card that year. Sometime in the past, I had mentioned that I love jazz and blues music. Inside the lovely card was a hand-sketched charcoal-and-white-pastel picture he had drawn of Jim Lee Hooker, a famous blues artist. The envelope bore no return address. I deduced this was a subtle way of letting me know I wasn't to reciprocate with a card. Perhaps receiving a card from me would only add to the drama he

263

already had in his marriage. Instead, I simply thanked him for remembering me and praised his artistic talent via email.

The winter of 2014 felt like it was never going to end, and spring was never going to come. The bitter cold and snow were relentless, the worst winter we'd had in over a decade. I was living in a townhome about a mile from my daughter. Closing the blinds felt cozier than staring out the window on those cold, gray winter evenings. Even when there was no snow on the ground, it was frigid. I came home to that same gloomy environment every single day. There was little warmth either in my home or my life. My gray tabby cat, Button, was my only companion. As I stepped out of my car in the driveway, I could hear him meow a greeting as he waited inside the front door.

I spent evenings watching TV with Button curled up on my lap or by my side. Mindful of the electric bill increases in the winter I lowered my thermostat during the coldest winter in recent years. To compensate, I donned thick wool socks, PJs, a heavy housecoat, covered myself with a thick blanket, then sat down on my sofa with a bowl of whatever I had simmering in the slow cooker. My treat was a piping hot cup of dark cocoa. Before long, I began to doze. I was painfully aware of the sharp contrast between living and merely existing as I climbed the steep stairs to my bedroom. Soon I cradled myself between pillows and fell asleep. Such was my life.

Many evenings passed without a single phone call (other than a telemarketer). Visitors were rare except when my daughter briefly dropped by, maybe once or twice a week. Between her school commitments of lesson grading, chaperoning after-school events, and professional development requirements and my work schedule, we were both too tired and too busy to see each other more often.

Months sometimes passed without seeing my son. He has always been an avid outdoorsman and returned home to his mountain roots as soon as he graduated from college. The two-and-a-half-hour driving distance has kept us from seeing each other more often. Helping those in local agriculture and hiking trail development to promote tourism commands his professional time. Hiking and backpacking are the activities he loves to do most. He began section-hiking the Appalachian Trail with friends during the summer when he was still in college. There are always evening workshops he needs to do, meetings to attend, a garden to tend, church events, and family time. The city traffic where his sister and I live, combined with the absence of trees and hills, has no lure for him. On the occasions when he does visit, he can't wait to get back home to the mountains. Having him here for more than a night or two is as unlikely as putting a horse inside a house. My crazy schedule of twelve-hour shifts, working every other weekend, made it hard to travel or have any kind of social life.

One evening, I sat on my sofa, overwhelmed with a deep sense of loneliness. As I took mental inventory of my pathetic existence, the tears began to flow, and I began to pray.

"Lord, I've always heard there was somebody for everyone. I have waited my entire life for somebody to love me as I have witnessed the love in other couples who have been married for decades. I'm a good person. I'm not perfect. You of all people know I'm not perfect. You know every single mistake I have ever made. You know every single fault I have, and you love me in spite of them. I've been hurt by broken relationships in my past, and the things those people did left scars. It has taken me twenty-eight years to get over it. For the longest time, I didn't even think I cared anymore, but now I realize I do. I had completely given up hope that anybody would ever love me. But after all this time, I am finally over it. I am finally ready to move on. Lord, if you truly have someone for me, would you please send him? I'm ready, Lord. If he's not ready, would you please get him ready?"

I vowed that night that I was going to start making the effort and check out the Christian online dating sites. I had been waiting on the Lord for what felt like a lifetime. At the age of sixty-three, I was asking that the wait finally be over.

Sawyer, now an adult, once told me that I had held him emotionally responsible for all the hurt inflicted by other men in my life. He said it was evident by the way I treated him. Those words hit hard, but I needed to hear them. I love my son dearly, and I know he loves me. I have had to ask him to forgive me because I didn't even recognize that my behavior was hurting him. I had to look at myself through the eyes of someone who knew me well. That someone was Sawyer. I had to own the bitterness that blinded me and heal from it. I needed to start over fresh, with an unpainted canvas. I needed to forgive and let go of the hurt inflicted by others before I could start over and build a healthy relationship with any other man.

For me, emotional healing took longer than most. The scars were many and deep. I reckoned that God had put me on a lengthy, God-sized relationship "time-out." I didn't need to enter a new relationship as a wounded, damaged, bitter woman who could only remember broken promises, lies, emotional abuse, and disappointment.

## ONLINE DATING

Many who are divorced already have issues with broken trust. I considered online dating sites with much trepidation. I had been warned against online dating altogether by some older married friends. I quickly disregarded this because of the number of couples I know that have met and married from online matches and who are very happy.

I tried a couple of dating sites, eventually chatting back and forth with two different men. I had had time now to deduce what I didn't want. It also taught me to look for subtle cues. If you listen closely, people will tell you who they really are. If you give the relationship some time without jumping in with both feet, that person will eventually show their true colors I was learning to guard my own heart.

## THE SCAMMER

A Christian dating site disaster came from a man whose online persona was that of a widower, living in Michigan. He claimed to be an electrical contractor who often worked out of state. He described himself as a Christian with really old-fashioned Christian values. I wasn't sure what he meant by that, so I just "listened" to what he wrote. He knew I worked in law enforcement. That should have been a hint that whatever he told me, I would seek to verify.

After several weeks of communication, he told me he had landed a huge contract to build a large hotel in Istanbul, Turkey. My eyebrows rose when I read those words. In an attempt to prove the legitimacy of his story, he sent me a photo of himself along with a photo of the "contract" he "landed," showing the amount of money he would be awarded at the completion of the contract. The wording of the contract was amateurish and certainly not the detailed legal language I expected to see. He emailed me an obviously bogus flight itinerary of his anticipated journey, so I would know where he was and "be able to remember him in prayer on his journey." He claimed to have obtained a special cell phone plan "at great expense," that would enable him to text and call me while he was in Turkey. On his return flight back to

Michigan, he would make a stopover at my local airport, and we would finally get to meet face-to-face.

My discerning "BS antennae" was on red alert. I ran every background check available, and nothing was adding up. My instincts kept telling me, "Wait for it. Eventually, he is going to ask you for money, and you'll know he is nothing more than a scammer."

I happened to be sitting in an annual refresher training class at the prison one afternoon when a text message came. Supposedly, a large piece of equipment he needed to complete the building contract had broken. Predictably, he needed me to wire him $3,000 to repair it. The money would be repaid to me at 25 percent interest when the "issue" he had with his local bank account in Istanbul was resolved. This was the immediate confirmation of what my gut feeling had already told me. I had wanted proof that he was a scammer, and this was it.

I replied that I would definitely not be sending him any amount of money. I went on to say that he had misjudged my intellect and had chosen to scam the wrong person. He wasn't ready to admit defeat, responding that he was "crushed" that I would accuse him and mistrust him in such a way. I deleted and blocked his phone number after that, but at the very least, I had a few weeks of free "entertainment" with a scam artist that cost me nothing but my time.

Until this happened, I hadn't mentioned anything about joining online dating websites to Jim. I had talked to him about many things, but my dating life was an awkward subject to discuss with a married male friend. I had mentioned the lack of good men, but I wasn't sure he ever realized just how lonely I really was.

## EXPOSING THE SCAMMER

I chose to blog about my online dating experiences, focusing on the scammer. I shared his photo and a copy of his phony contract. Jim was an avid reader of my blogs. The fact that I exposed a scammer on the Internet gave me a great deal of personal satisfaction. Sharing my story along with the scammer's photo on my personal website caught the attention of a detective at Scotland Yard in London. I received an inquiry in a private comment on my blog, asking me to provide more information and the IP address from which his emails originated. I was initially cautious about responding to that inquiry. After my bad experience, I had a hard time believing this detective was even real.

## A LEAP OF FAITH

How could I possibly do a background check on somebody in the United Kingdom? Hmm…who did I know that I could trust enough to do that? Jim was the only person I could think of who was savvy and trustworthy enough to do such a search. It was a huge imposition to ask this of someone. It was also very embarrassing. His initial reaction to my request was an unhesitating "yes." He would do it. At the same time, he was relieved that the scammer had not succeeded in his attempts to scam me. He was also deeply saddened to discover the degree of loneliness I had never before confided in him. He was angry that someone would try and take advantage of another person in this way, especially someone he considered a dear friend.

Within the next day or so, Jim personally emailed the detective at Scotland Yard. He was able to verify that this detective worked in their Cyber Crimes Division. After concluding that the detective's request for information was legitimate, I exchanged several messages with him, giving him details, including the sender's IP address. I learned that the scammer was likely part of a Nigerian ring and that he had managed to scam a large sum of money from a woman in the UK. Unfortunately, there was little hope of recovering any of it for the victim. Since I had not actually lost money to this scammer, I was not considered a "victim" by the US Department of Homeland Security.

I had never been in a situation where I needed to ask Jim to do anything for me. I had never had to place my trust and confidence in him. Amazingly, I felt completely secure. Even four thousand miles away, sight unseen, Jim was someone I could trust.

# Chapter Forty-Five
## J.D.

### BETH'S SCAMMER

One day, I received an email from Beth telling me about a scammer she had managed to get away from. I knew she had lived alone for years. Until then, I had no idea she was lonely enough to visit a dating website. I felt sad and sorry for her. I wished that we lived closer so I could help and comfort her. On a number of occasions, I had written to her and told her to place her right hand round her left side. Then place her left hand around to her right side. Then squeeze long and hard. This was my way of giving her a long- distance hug. I wanted her to know that even though I was not with her physically, I was with her in thought and spirit.

I had often included pictures of the meals I had cooked. They would include some dishes such as spicy sweet potato soup, leek and potato soup, beef casseroles, roast lamb or beef with roasted potatoes and parsnips, and a medley of fresh vegetables. The Christmas dinner table with a starter of crab and prawns wrapped in smoked salmon, garnished with a light salad. The roast turkey with all the trimmings of homemade cranberry sauce, sage and onion stuffing, sausage meat and chestnut stuffing, roasted and fresh vegetables. Beth really enjoyed seeing them and learning how I had cooked the dishes. I am sure she drooled over these pictures.

It was after the incident with this scammer that I wrote and told her how I would love to cook, care for, and look after her. I could hardly bear the thought of her being so lonely she needed a dating website to find happiness. Even more distressing was the fact that somebody would try to use her to steal hard-earned money from her. I was saddened at this thought.

She had written a personal blog, which was more of a warning to other women, sharing the scammer's photo and details of the scam. In response, she had received a private comment from somebody who alleged he was from Scotland Yard and said he was investigating the same scammer. Apparently, the scammer had taken a lady in the United Kingdom for a large sum of money. Beth asked me if I could do anything to verify this other email. I did a few searches to trace the IP address of the email. I found the server was in a location close to New Scotland Yard, the headquarters of the Metropolitan Police in London. This checked out as well as I could ascertain. I also checked on the identity of the detective sergeant who wrote the email. During this search, I found a newspaper article from when he had received an award. From this information, I concluded the email from New Scotland Yard was genuine. I wrote her an email to this effect. That came as a relief to Beth, and I was happy to help.

# Chapter Forty-Six

## B.B.

## THE CONFIDANTE

Of the handful of female friends I made from eight years of working at the prison, there was one I trusted to share my most guarded secrets. Amy, that LPN with "grit," who was married to a correctional officer. It was Independence Day weekend 2014, and my adult children were both on vacations elsewhere. Once again, I would be spending a holiday weekend alone. She invited me to join her and her husband at the local cinema. My desire for companionship outweighed my objection to feeling like a misfit who was intruding on a date night. I don't remember the movie, but I'll never forget her kindness in inviting me to join them. Soon after, she invited me over to her home.

I confided that online dating attempts had been disappointing. I was lonely and tired of not having a companion to share my life with. She really listened. In a city so large, I had never felt more alone. I had seen many couples meet, marry, divorce, and remarry. I had seen beautiful people with much to offer remain alone, while those with average (or unfortunate) looks were happily married. From my perspective, it was an easy choice. I would rather spend the rest of my life alone than be with someone who didn't truly love me. As I talked, the emotion poured out, and my eyes filled with tears. She had seen the vulnerable side of me, rather than the guarded facade of our prison environment.

"What about that 'JD' fellow you're friends with on social media?" she asked. I laughed nervously. "You mean my pen pal, Jim?" I asked. The surprise was evident in my response.

She replied, "He is crazy about you. I can tell by how he responds to you in your social media posts." Her words caught me totally off guard. Still stunned, I quickly replied, "He's just my friend. We have been friends for years. That's not the kind of relationship we have. He doesn't even think of me any other way than as a friend."

"Are you really that blind?" she replied.

Suddenly, her words illuminated Jim's subtle messages. Until now, I had disregarded Jim's prompt responses to my messages, even challenged by a five-hour time zone difference. He was totally in tune with my life and work schedule. As soon as my alarm clock went off at 4 a.m. and I was out of bed, my phone pinged with a message from Jim. It was already five hours later, 9 a.m. in England.

In my aloneness, he had been undeniably present, despite the distance. We communicated in real time. My day started with a smile, knowing Jim was thinking of me and wanted to include me in his life. We exchanged messages until it was time for me to head out the door to work. We chatted, hands-free on speaker, as I drove to work. He had become my long-distance but real-time companion. As soon as I got off work around 7:30 p.m. and was in my car, I found a message waiting for me on my mobile phone. He was in my thoughts throughout the day. Sometimes, his messages were simple, just a cute emoticon followed by a greeting. They usually led to a nice, long conversation on instant chat. Few people at work knew about Jim. My smiles were evidence of my mental escape from the prison environment. My "pen pal" relationship with Jim remained a secret.

My bad experience with the online dating scammer and Jim's supportive response were pivotal in building a solid foundation of trust between us. Broken trust is not easily restored. Until then, I had no foundation of trust whatsoever in any of my previous relationships. Coming from that background, I had a very difficult time learning how to trust someone I could see, much less someone so distant. I waited for evidence that Jim was like all the other men in past relationships. I waited for the cracks to show. They never did. He had been consistent, solid, and unwavering, from the teenager I first came to know, to the mature adult he was now. He was, and still is, the most positive person I have ever met.

One day, we were having an instant chat. Jim's artistry didn't end with photography or paint on a canvas. While we were chatting, he told me what he had prepared for dinner. Clearly, he was as artistic with food presentation as he was with photography or his painted art and pastels. I remarked that he was a gourmet chef, since I had just reheated a meal of slow cooker leftovers.

Suddenly, Jim commented, "I'd love to cook, care for and look after you." I remember being puzzled by his comment. That was the most directly personal thing Jim had ever said to me. I remember feeling awkward and thinking this was an odd thing to say. I dared not ask what he meant by that. I chose to think his words stemmed from a cultural background very different from mine, and that he was simply being a polite British gentleman. I wouldn't allow myself to read anything more into his words, and I didn't ask for clarification. No person had looked after me since I was still a child living with my parents. I had always done the cooking for, caring for, and looking after others. I had always been the giver.

I couldn't get Amy's words out of my mind. The cryptic meaning of some of Jim's subtle messages and emails were now as clear as if a beacon had been shined. It had taken the lightning bolt of her words to make me realize how little geography meant when two people have a deep connection. This polite, reserved British gentleman had been expressing his affection for me, and I had been too blind to realize it.

My mind had been switched off for so long to the possibility of having somebody share my life. Finally, my mind and my eyes had been opened to Jim's true feelings for me. But how and when did this happen? In the two years we wrote as teenagers and the five years since we reconnected in 2010, we had never talked about personal, romantic things. Neither of us had crossed over personal boundaries. We hadn't as much as flirted in our letters. All we had ever been was friends who were real with each other from the beginning. We were an ocean apart, so there had never been a need to pretend to be something we weren't. All we had ever done was share our thoughts, interests, hopes, dreams, struggles, and even disappointments. Somewhere along our forty-eight-year journey, our friendship relationship had grown and deepened, even in the absence of visual or physical contact.

Never considering a long-distance relationship a remote possibility, I had been in denial about any deeper feelings I had for Jim. All I ever allowed myself to do was daydream about making a trip to England to meet him face-to-face. If I never shared my true feelings, then I would never feel possible rejection and bitter disappointment. After all, as far as I knew, he was in a solid, committed, happy marriage. I would not want to cause problems for him or make him feel awkward towards me.

I concluded that I needed to guard my heart, knowing I wouldn't be able to handle the rejection after all these years of knowing him. I couldn't risk spoiling a friendship for a selfish personal desire to meet him face-to-face. I always quickly dismissed my daydreams as needless self-torture.

# Chapter Forty-Seven
## J.D.

## THE END AND THE NEW BEGINNING, 2015

It was heading towards the caravan season once again, and I knew we needed a better car to pull the caravan. Mary agreed to trade in one of the cars I had paid for (but she currently had registered in her name) for one more suited to towing the caravan. The agreement was that this vehicle would be registered solely in my name. I found and purchased an all-wheel drive diesel SUV. Finally, I had my own transportation. There would be no more arguments about me driving her vehicle or threats of calling the police if I drove her car without her permission.

The days were gloomy, routine, and boring. The clubs were our primary social function. It was even hard to complete a crossword there at the clubs because of the constant interruptions and noise. I felt like an intruder in another world. This must be how people become stagnant and dull in retirement, through sheer boredom! This mundane existence was a far cry from the club and pub experiences I had in my early years in the RAF. I began to wonder if it was truly possible to die of boredom.

The depths of winter finally gave way to spring. Mary heard some sad family news: one of her cousins had died. She recounted the events of their childhood, and I felt really sad for her. A while later, she heard that her cousin's brother would not be attending the funeral. I never heard the last of it. "How can somebody not go to his only brother's funeral?" Mary said repeatedly. Every time she made that remark, it was like rubbing salt in an old and open wound, as I remembered how she prevented me from going to *my* only brother's and my mother's funerals. "You hypocrite!" I thought. I was inwardly seething at her double standards. Any remaining love I felt for her was rapidly draining away.

Later, there was yet another visit to a garden centre, almost a daily pilgrimage for her. Mary chose some spring flowers for the garden. There were about a dozen pots of them, but they really brightened the area where I planted them. She came out of the garden, took a look back at them, and remarked, "They've really brightened up the garden, haven't they?"

I replied, "It didn't take much."

Mary exploded: "Do you realise how much I spent on those flowers? You say it doesn't take much?" Her arms were flailing around with her outburst. She was so unpredictably volatile, I never knew what would set her off, and the repercussions could continue for hours, even days afterwards. I was tired of tiptoeing around in my own home.

I thought, "That's it! I cannot take any more of this!" I let her rant whilst my thoughts turned to leaving her and filing for divorce. I had finally taken all the hypocrisy, rants, and verbal abuse I intended to take. Retirement was supposed to be fun, not hell. At least at work, I could escape for a few hours. Each hurtful incident separately may seem petty, but once added up over a period of decades, they become a huge entity, equaling the straw that broke the camel's back.

I couldn't concentrate on anything else except how I would get away from her. All the while, my mind was in turmoil. I thought of the fun times we had together. The walks on the beach, drives in the country, the parties with Andrew and Jean Zahra and their family, the caravan holidays, the family get-togethers with her family at her aunty Molly's (before we moved closer, that is). Yes, they were fun times, but sadly overshadowed by the bad times that came frequently. We had been partners, but we never had a full marital relationship. I finally got tired of the continual rejection and gave up trying. I stayed because I had taken vows, and I had every intention of keeping them. I remembered the times we supported each other. Then the memories flooded back of all the hateful and unforgivable things she had said and done. She made it clear on multiple occasions that she would not be there for me in times of sickness. I never knew what would set her off again or what her reactions would be. I was forced to go where I had no interest in going. I was manipulated with the words, "Husbands and wives do things together." Whenever I wanted to do something by myself, Mary would rant on and on and on that I was being selfish and inconsiderate of her. "What about me? What am I supposed to do?" It is accurate to say that she was her own top priority, and to keep peace with her, she had to be in control.

After a few days' thought, I made the decision to leave her. It wasn't easy after thirty-eight years of marriage, but the constant mental and verbal abuse had taken a huge toll. I looked at the dog lying comfortably on my lap. Then I directed my gaze to the back of Mary's head as she sat in her chair a few feet away from the TV. I stroked the dog, knowing I wouldn't be stroking him for much longer. I dreaded the morning when I would be walking him for the very last time. It would be hard leaving him. Every moment with him became more and more precious and special. It was sad, really, that I would miss my dog far more than Mary. My dog loved me, whereas Mary loved herself and what I could do for her.

All the while, I was making a mental list of everything I needed to do. What would I pack? Where would I stay? I finally decided to go back to the Blackpool area. Hotels were plentiful, and property was cheaper. I decided on a hotel for a week, while searching for a flat to rent.

# Chapter Forty-Eight

## B.B.

### NEW BEGINNINGS

As that cold winter turned toward spring, I continued to explore my feelings for Jim. I paid closer attention to his words, looking for incongruencies and the cracks I had always found in past relationships. I was finally catching Jim's sincere subtleties. Amy was right. I finally recognized that Jim had deep feelings for me but was as afraid of rejection as I was. We had long ago passed the stage of liking each other as friends. Our friendship had grown into so much more. For me, it was a journey to that realization that friendship had evolved to love. Until now, I never believed any man other than my own dad, and of course my son, ever loved me. Even my dad had disappointed me and let me down. Jim spoke volumes about his feelings for me, without ever actually saying those three essential words I needed to hear.

It was Saturday, February 21, 2015, and we were communicating via instant chat. Our relationship had already endured separation, time, and distance. We had grown from teenagers to adults, developing respect, admiration, and trust for each other. Our friendship was solid. I finally felt safe enough to take the risk of telling Jim what he meant to me. The reserved British gentleman had only been giving ambiguous, subtle messages. If Amy was right and if I interpreted those messages correctly, taking the risk would be safe. That day, on instant chat, I poured out all the reasons that made Jim special to me, then added the words "Yes, I love you, my dearest friend."

I wish I could have seen the expression on Jim's face the day I was courageous enough to write those words to him. His response was a dam-burst of emotion.

"I love you, my dearest darling, Beth! How long I have waited to hear those words! I never want to be without you in my life, even if it is only via computer."

"Why, Jim, did you never tell me how you felt about me?" I implored. "I was afraid to say these words to you for so long, but finally decided to take the risk because of some of your subtle comments. I thought I might be reading more into your words than you intended. My friend Amy has seen your comments to me on social media and asked if I have really been so blind that I couldn't see the love you obviously have for me. I suppose I have been, but why didn't you say something before now?"

"I lost you once forty-two years ago, Beth. I didn't realize how much I loved you until you wrote that letter telling me you wouldn't be writing to me again," Jim replied. "I never wanted to risk losing you again, not ever. Even if we could never have more than a long-distance friendship, I want to keep you in my life. I had no right to say anything more to you because I am the one who is currently married, and I have remained true to my vows. I didn't know how you felt about me because you never told me either. I imagined all kinds of scenarios of what your reaction might be if I told you. The most frightening scenario was the reaction where you never wanted to hear from me ever again. I just can't let you go out of my life again."

Admitting my true feelings for Jim was like flipping a switch. The tone of our conversations changed and became more deeply personal. All fear of rejection was gone. Usually when the words "I love you" are first shared between a couple, there is a kiss and an embrace. The distance between us now became torturous. We had to find a way to change that, but I was not the one in charge.

Jim said he was making the long flight to America to see me. He wanted to know when I had planned a vacation, and that was when he would come. Finding it all still hard to imagine, I told him my vacation was in June and the number of days I had available. I confided in a nurse colleague who traded one of her vacation weeks so I could extend my time with Jim. She was one of only four people at work who knew about him.

From this point onward, the next moves were up to Jim. Meanwhile, all we could do was video chat with each other and screen share information about places of interest I would take him to when he arrived. I would give him a sampling of my small corner of America while he was here. He could choose those places I'd take him à la carte style. I was pleased that one of the top places he wanted to visit was my hometown, including the small-town post office in Jenkins, Kentucky, where I received and mailed his letters. He even remembered my old post office box number by heart after all those years.

None of this felt real until the day Jim emailed me his flight itinerary. He was really coming, and I remember telling him he would have to pinch me when he arrived so I would realize I wasn't dreaming.

# Chapter Forty-Nine
## J.D.

I thought back to the email from Beth when she told me that she loved me. I remember how elated I felt. I had wanted to tell her the same before this, but I had already lost her once, and I did not want to risk this happening again. I was married, and Beth knew that. Had I told her, she could easily have rejected me and said I had no right to feel that way, being married. It was hard for me not to tell her, so I just gave her hints of my feelings towards her.

Meanwhile, I booked my hotel near Blackpool and packed some bags to take. Thankfully, Mary didn't see me doing this, because it would have incited the verbal siege from hell. I had planned many projects throughout my career, and this plan was finally coming together. I was like a prisoner plotting my escape. The day of the move arrived. I watched Bailey run around as he always did, knowing this would be my very last walk with him. I kept watching him and his antics. I whistled his "call" whistle, and he ran back to me, as usual. He stood, tail wagging expectantly for a gravy bone treat. Back at the house, with a heavy heart, I fed him a generous meal. It would be the last meal I would ever get to feed him. I prepared myself something to eat, then put my last bit of baggage in the car while Mary was occupied having a bath. Once done, I grabbed my coat, gave the dog one last hug, then placed my goodbye letter on the mantelpiece.

I walked out, got into the car, and drove off. Mary was quite unaware I was leaving. I thought over and over about what would be the least dramatic way to leave. This was it. I had no idea what she might do if I confronted her and told her I was leaving. There was no question there would be drama, maybe violence. I had seen too many times what she was capable of, and I had had a lifetime of venom spewed on me when things didn't go her way. As I drove off, rounding the corner of the street, I yelled out loud, "Freedom!" Solicitors could eventually sort out the financial details, but at last, I was physically free.

I drove towards the hotel, a four-to-five-hour drive away. My emotions were all over the place during that drive. I had the ringer to my phone turned off, but Mary kept calling me and leaving messages. There was no turning back. To return would mean a return to even greater fury from Mary. The unknown future was less fearful than the foreseeable future with her. Since Beth had declared her love for me all those weeks ago, I couldn't keep her out of my mind. I admit that had my marriage been stronger and better, I would have told Beth that any relationship would be futile; I might even have ceased writing. As it was, I looked forward to writing to her when I got to the hotel. Beth's declaration had no influence on my decision to leave Mary.

The drive seemed endless, and I was very relieved to see the signs for Blackpool. I knew it wouldn't be long before I would arrive at my hotel. At last, I could rest.

# Chapter Fifty

## B.B.

### HEARING HIS VOICE

One day, I was preparing to send Jim a message on instant chat. Instead, I accidentally hit the phone icon on the instant chat screen. I heard the unusual sound of a phone ringing, then a beautiful, deep bass, delightfully masculine British voice answered, "Hello? Hello?"

Surely, my heart did a triple somersault when I heard him. This was the first time I had heard his voice to actually engage in conversation. My heart raced with excitement as I stumbled over the next few sentences, realizing Jim was actually talking with me in real time. Instantly, I reverted to that giddy teenager from 1967 as we did a rapid-fire exchange of conversation. I can't even remember what we talked about. I was too excited to finally be speaking with him.

I was aware of the huge smile on my face. We continued to talk, both marveling at how far technology had come since the years when we wrote each other letters, then waited for weeks for a response. I recall thinking, "Oh my goodness, my phone bill will be over $300!" Still, I couldn't bring myself to hang up. We must have talked for an hour before I finally relented and we agreed to end our voice call, opting to return to instant chat instead.

The next day, I was relieved to learn that our call was free on Wi-Fi. From that point onward, we talked daily. His voice was music to my soul. We were still separated by time zone differences. While Jim was accustomed to Greenwich Mean Time (GMT) and British Summer Time (BST), my daily life followed Eastern Standard Time (EST) or daylight savings time (DST). For most of our communication, it was five hours later in Great Britain than in Kentucky.

At long last, I got to hear Jim say the words "I love you." What's more,

I knew he meant it. We had never been on a date, never held hands, never even spoken about anything romantic. There had been no touching and no physical contact, yet each of us felt a deep connection and affection for the other.

That evening, Jim followed up the words "I love you" with a question that caught me by surprise. "Will you be my wife? I can't wait to finally hold you in my arms and spend the rest of my life with you."

At that moment, I felt a mixture of peace, calm, and joy come over me, unlike anything I had ever experienced. Despite physical separation, each of us on different continents, I could feel and hear the sincerity and love in his voice as though we were standing face-to-face. This was the closest I ever felt to the experience of his full embrace.

Good things like this don't generally happen to me; I'm usually the one sitting in a cinema, eating popcorn, hearing those words directed from actor to actress. I had secretly prayed that someday, somebody would really love me like that. I prayed that somebody would love me for exactly who I am, imperfections and all. Unlike in the cinema, this moment was real, and this time, after a lifetime of waiting, those words were being spoken to me.

With a smile he couldn't see and eyes filled with tears, my response was "Yes! I would love to be your wife. However, we have a couple of problems with that."

"What's that?" Jim inquired.

"First your divorce needs to be finalized and then you need to come over here and ask me that question again, face-to-face."

"I certainly shall." Jim replied. "I'm making arrangements on both those things even now."

## COINCIDENCES

Often, Jim remarked that a series of coincidences had brought us together. About the day he first heard my name called out over the pirate radio station, Radio Avaline, near the Isle of Man, he remarked, "Wasn't it a coincidence that I had just gone upstairs and switched on my radio to listen to Radio Avaline," the day he heard my name called out on the radio for a pen pal? "Wasn't it a coincidence" that I had just entered my contact information on my high school alumni's contact page? And "wasn't it a coincidence" that he just randomly opened a drawer and rediscovered the bookmark I had sent him forty-two years earlier, prompting him to do an Internet search for me?

Each time, my response had been, "No, I don't believe in coincidences like that. I believe it has all been part of God's Master Plan."

Each time we had had these conversations, these non-coincidences had opened a much bigger door with Jim. I could clearly see God's hands at work in even minor details, but Jim couldn't. He hadn't been to church since he was twelve years old, when he was in choir and attended with the Cub Scouts, fifty-three years ago. He had completely dismissed church at a young age, having experienced churches focused more on ritual, rules, and judgment and less on discipleship, relationships, and grace. When he had asked questions at church about things he didn't understand, he had been scolded for "questioning the word of God."

Consequently, Jim had become embittered by churches due to their unwillingness to respond to the legitimate questions he asked as an inquiring young man. At that time, I don't think he even owned a Bible. In every interaction, for as long as I had known him, Jim had always been sincere and positive. But his opinion in matters of faith was cause for real concern.

The nature of our conversations changed in many ways after that. I discovered that church is extremely different in the United Kingdom than it is in America. Jim explained to me his own perceptions of "high church," which was focused on rigid rituals and rules. Not once did I hear him mention the words "relationship," "discipleship," "grace," or "love" as they pertained to church.

My children and I had experienced a loving church, focused on discipleship and on helping us mature in our faith and develop a personal relationship with God. We no longer viewed God as distant, sitting on his throne, high up in Heaven. Instead, He is right here with us, out of personal sight and touch, but just as present.

My children and I learned that God loves each of us unconditionally. He also loves with a far deeper love than our Earthly father or mother is capable of. We learned that He is the Father who will always be with us, even when our own parents have either abandoned us or come to the end of their lives. We learned that we don't have to worship God only in an ornate sanctuary, in a constructed building on a Sabbath. He is always with us, and the lines of communication are always open. He is the very representation of love. It doesn't matter how many times we have screwed up our lives or how many mistakes we've made. God can still take those broken pieces of the mess we've made and create the perfect plan for each of us (Jeremiah 29:11).

I will always remember one morning when I was standing in my bathroom, getting ready for work. I was overwhelmed with grief about six months after losing my dad. I finally admitted I was angry at God and that I had blamed Him for taking my daddy away. It didn't matter that morning that I had yelled and screamed at God. It didn't matter that I had raised my fists and shook them at God in anger. He had big shoulders. He knew my heart was broken over my dad, and I was having a hard time dealing with that loss. Just like a loving parent, He listened, and He forgave me. He is a God of love and forgiveness. But first, I had to confess that anger and get it out. I had to communicate with Him, even in that anger.

If you're happy or thankful, or even angry, God wants to hear it. If you're sad or lonely, sick, troubled, or broken in spirit, He wants you to talk with Him about it, no matter if you're in the shower, at work, in your car or on a plane. Location simply doesn't matter. God is always ready to listen.

God's timetable is different, just like His plans are different from ours. I have created plans for my life, hoping God would give them his rubber stamp of approval. It doesn't work that way. I had to learn about the heart of God by getting to know Him through prayer…through the many times He took me onto His lap and comforted me when I was brokenhearted. God doesn't operate or communicate at the warp speed we'd often like. Who wants to wait for something they want until the timing is right? God doesn't operate on our schedule, and he doesn't change despite the changes in the society around us. He is constant, stable, unwavering, and steadfast.

In the busyness of my life, and the "noise" of my chaotic daily schedule, I had been the one who had shut Him out. Like a child who just fell and cut their knee, I cried out to God when I was in pain, and the rest of the time, I tried to handle things on my own. It was my equivalent of telling God, "I've got this. I don't need your help. I'll call you when I need you." God ended up too many times being my last resort instead of my first one. If we are still, we will hear His gentle whisper to our hearts (1 Kings 19:12 NIV). Being still is something I struggle with every day.

There were times I didn't go to church because I didn't have what I believed were nice-enough clothes. I had to learn that God is far more interested in what is in my heart. God pulled me out of the absolute wreckage I made of my life so many times.

I began to share my own spiritual journey with Jim. I asked him to set aside what he had experienced in the past while I told Him what God had done for me. As he had always done, Jim listened. I told him about the little church I currently attended with Sara and her family. The members came in the clothes they usually wore, usually jeans.

Once a month, for their worship music, they featured "banjo Sunday." Remembering my dad, I can never resist the opportunity to see and hear the banjo being played. One Sunday, one of their worship team members played a banjo rather than the usual guitar. Another member of the worship team played either a harmonica or the hilarious homemade instrument given to him by his grandfather called a "thangamajagger." It was completely homemade from a sawed-off hoe handle with a rubber cane base. Mounted on the sides were a bike horn, bicycle bell, a wooden game call box, two round cake pans clamped together, and a string of canning lids. The instrument was bounced up and down while being struck in various locations by the drumstick. During one particularly vigorous and lively tune, the canning lids went flying across the stage and landed in a corner. This resulted in much laughter, but the musicians were undeterred and finished their song.

Jim listened in disbelief. "You would never see anything like that here in England!" he exclaimed. I asked if he had heard of J-Love radio station. He hadn't. I invited him to listen to the station via live streaming online. I had found such encouragement when I listened, that I hoped he would as well. I was pleasantly surprised when he reported in subsequent conversations that he had not only listened, but he really liked the music.

Little by little, I conversed with him in analogies. (Jesus often taught through parables.) In a well-known, very popular adventure movie, a famous actor was looking for clues to find the Holy Grail. In one scene, he was in a library, standing right on top of the clue he needed, hidden in plain sight on the vast floor. It wasn't until he climbed the steps to the upper floor of the library and looked down over the rails at the same spot that he realized he recognized the clue on the floor below. It took looking at the puzzle from a different vantage point.

"Our lives can be like that as well," I told Jim. "Like a gigantic jigsaw puzzle, jumbled and strewn. We try as hard as we can to see the big picture, but we can't. God, however, has the master plan. He is able to see where the intricate pieces and details fit." He is at a Heavenly vantage point. "Jim, I don't believe in coincidences," I explained. "There are simply not that many coincidences. It was no coincidence that my life was spared from the roof fall, and your life was spared from accidental hanging or from being struck by the automobile when you wrecked your bike and felt the whoosh of the car's tire narrowly missing your head. I do believe that God has been at work in both our lives even when we didn't know it. All these series of events that connected us when we were teenagers, then reconnected us all these years later, were not coincidences. They were part of a bigger plan for both our lives!"

My mother died of hereditary polycystic kidney disease when she was only fifty-two. As the laws of heredity go, my brother and I had a fifty-fifty chance of inheriting the same disease. If we had, there would be no cure. Dialysis or kidney transplantation would be our only treatment options, and our lifespans would've been, at best, fifty to fifty-five years of age. Neither of us inherited that disease. Do you know how many times I have come to a crossroads trying to find directions, and a decision had to be made to either turn left or right? Almost without fail, I end up turning the wrong way when it is entirely my decision to make. This is a God thing, totally out of my control.

Over a period of several weeks, Jim and I had several conversations about spiritual things. Jim had repeatedly referred to how many "coincidences" it had taken to get the two of us together. First, it was the timing of the reading of my letter over Radio Avaline at the very moment he decided to go to his room and turn on his radio. Next, it was about me, learning about my high school's new alumni link and posting updated personal contact information while visiting my son. It was shortly thereafter, when Jim was doing genealogy research, that he pulled out his desk drawer, rediscovering the bookmark I'd sent him forty-two years earlier. His curiosity had prompted him to do an Internet search for me, leading to finding my contact information on my high school alumni link. There just aren't this many coincidences. This was part of a bigger plan neither of us could possibly have orchestrated.

I didn't press the issue, but at each open door in our conversation, I took the opportunity to share bits and pieces about my own faith. I was pleased to learn that Jim had recently bought himself a Bible. One evening, I asked Jim whether he had ever accepted the gift that God had given us by sending His son Jesus to bear the burden and consequences for all our past mistakes. He acknowledged that he had. I asked whether he had ever asked God to forgive him for all his past mistakes. He wasn't sure he knew how.

That night, right there in my living room here in America and Jim in his, in England, separated by an ocean, I prayed with Jim. That night, he began his life as a brand-new creation in God's eyes at the tender age of sixty-five. I'm certain there were tears of joy, and I was overwhelmed with emotion that I had gotten the privilege to be present when the man I love came out of past darkness, from death to life. His past mistakes were wiped completely away, just as God had done for me. The slate was clean. When the weight of a burden that huge is lifted off your shoulders, you feel immediate relief. I know the angels in Heaven rejoiced, because I certainly did!

Mistakes are made daily, but God helps us not to keep making the same ones over and over. There are times I look at myself and think I must surely be God's slow learner, yet He is always patient and ready to forgive me every time I ask. I make no claims to perfection, and I made sure Jim knew that. And his reply to me? "Who is? I'm certainly not!"

# Chapter Fifty-One
## J.D.

Arriving at the hotel, I removed the only bag I would need to get settled in. I checked in, not needing anything fancy or a sea view, just somewhere to sleep. I found my room, then dropped my bag on the floor and collapsed onto the bed. My phone rang. Without releasing it, I answered it. It was Mary, very angry and disparaging. I simply told her I had had enough, and our marriage was over. I hung up and switched the phone off.

After dinner, I walked for a while towards the shopping area. I came across a solicitor's office and made a note to see them in the morning to begin the process of the divorce. Later, I checked my voice messages. Amongst all the ones from Mary was one from my sister-in-law, Natalie, who lived nearby. I called her back, and we talked for a while. She was very concerned about me and was asking about the circumstances of my leaving. She told me Mary had called her to see if I was with her. Of course, she told her I wasn't. Natalie then offered me a room if I needed one. I hoped that it wouldn't come to that, as I would be looking for a flat. I was very grateful for the offer and her concern.

Upon returning to my room, I lay down and began to do a search on my tablet for available flats. I found a few that looked good and within the price range I had set for myself, so I decided to visit the agencies the next morning. It was going to be a busy morning. I made a trip to the bar for a quiet drink, whilst looking at other agencies and conducting a search for solicitors.

The next morning, I headed towards one of the main letting agencies in Cleveleys. I had seen a couple of suitable flats from that agency in the Thornton-Cleveleys area. I would be looking for a solicitor there anyway.

Finding the location of the letting agency, I entered and discussed my requirements and was shown some available flats. I was then asked for two photo IDs. I had neither. My driver's licence was the old paper style with no photo. My passport was out of date. I had no other forms of identification. The agent left and spoke to a manager; she returned and was very helpful. I told her I could pay six months' rent up front plus the deposit (thankfully, I had considered this when I transferred half the money from the joint bank account into my personal bank account). She told me this was a legal requirement when renting property, so their hands were tied. As I had given them plenty of background information, she did say she would contact the landlord.

Afterwards, I visited Natalie. After explaining the situation with the photo IDs, I asked if I could take her up on the offer of the room. The offer was still open, so I gratefully accepted. She also agreed for me to use her address as my address so I could get my new driver's licence and passport.

On my way back to the hotel, I went to the post office to pick up the required forms for the passport and driver's licence. Both forms required a birth certificate. In my haste, I had inadvertently forgotten my birth certificate. Back in my room, I opened my tablet once again and found the site to apply for a replacement certificate. I also purchased a replacement marriage certificate. I was now able to list Natalie's address as my address. I completed the forms to be returned to the post office. Now it was just a waiting game.

I went for a walk on the seafront for some fresh air to clear my head. Mentally, I began listing all the items I would need to furnish the flat and thinking about where I would buy them. These items had to be secondhand to keep costs down because eventually, I would be donating them back to charity anyway. I returned to my room to make a shopping list, then calculated a budget. I had more expenses to consider in the future.

The next day, I traveled to Blackpool to search for the furniture and to estimate costs. Eventually, I found a large charity shop full of furniture. I was told that stock was changing daily, but at least I was getting a feel for prices. Once back at the hotel, I began putting approximate prices on the shopping list.

I scheduled an appointment with a solicitor. I was able to keep in contact with Beth via email and messaging applications, sharing my progress. Beth was pleased I had finally got the courage to leave what she described as a toxic relationship. She had become not only a good friend, but also one with whom I could discuss my problems. She always encouraged me to take the right action to ensure my own peace and happiness, whether that benefited her or not. She always had my best interests at heart. I just wish I could say the same for Mary, especially in the later years of our marriage.

The five-hour time zone difference made it well past midnight when we were able to connect, and we usually talked for a few hours at a time. That five-hour time difference was very tiring for both of us, as she had to be up to get ready for work by 4 a.m. It was just general talking, as good friends do. What we had been doing in the day, the progress of the flat, furnishing, etc.

Soon, my time at the hotel was finished, and I moved into Natalie's spare room. She was an incredible hostess and a wonderful listener. Finally, through a crisis in my personal life, I was able to reconnect with the family I had been kept from all those years. Mary had always discouraged any contact I made with Natalie, my brother, and my mother. For some reason, she had taken a strong dislike to them. It was in part, I believe, because Mary never got the credit for the efforts and money she spent to choose, pick, and mail presents to my mum. When Mum received the parcel, she would thank me and not Mary. Obviously, Mary resented this. Even when I told Mum it was Mary who did it all, she would just pass it off with, "Weeeeeell, I meant it for both of you." I, too, did not like this attitude and empathised with Mary on this point. It became rare to talk to my family, yet the family ties had not been totally severed.

After a week, I received a call from the letting agency, requesting I come to their office. On arrival, I was informed the landlord would accept me as a tenant, provided I could obtain references from two people who could vouch for me. Neither reference could be related to me. I emailed two good friends who agreed to serve as references. All they were required to do was to email the agency on my behalf.

The letting agency called me a week or so later, telling me the flat would be ready to move in on May 1. I arranged for the furniture delivery. Natalie contributed linens, which was a big help. I was very grateful to Natalie and Margaret, and on my last night at their home, I treated them to dinner.

The next day, I packed up the car with my belongings and drove to the agency to sign the lease contract. Then I headed to the flat to prepare for the delivery of my furniture.

Being on my own came hard. I walked a lot, but felt odd, just walking around alone. In the end, I decided to bring my camera with me and take photographs. I photographed just about anything, as this made me feel less conspicuous. I was on my own, but at least with a purpose. The camera became a shield. Back in the flat, there were times when the walls seemed to be closing in on me. At these times, I walked across the road to the pub for an hour or so.

Beth and I talked in real time via chat messenger each evening. We would share how our days had gone and what we had been doing, and I updated her on where I had been. Beth told me what she could, as most of her work was covered by patient confidentiality.

There was always something that needed to be bought, but I soon found out that cooking for one didn't use as much food, especially fresh vegetables, and soon found I was throwing away vegetables that had gone bad. In the end, it got to the point that I didn't want to cook just for myself. I began to eat from takeouts.

One time, I invited Natalie, Simon, and Margaret over for dinner. Unfortunately, Simon, my nephew, couldn't make it, so it was just the three of us. We had a good evening talking. It made such a difference to being here on my own. It turned out this was the only time they came as the stairs had proven difficult for Natalie to climb.

Until this time, I had enjoyed walking, particularly with the dog. Now I had no dog, and I began to understand how Beth felt being on her own for all those years. I found it quite disheartening to come home to emptiness.

For me, the days began to drag. Natalie told me her brother-in-law was involved in the restoration of an old diesel railway engine and reopening a local railway line that had been closed for many years. She asked if I would be interested in assisting for two mornings a week as a volunteer, and I agreed. The following Saturday morning, Geoff, Natalie's brother-in-law, picked me up and took me to where the renovation was being carried out. The area was close to where I used to live, but it now looked desolate and a bit dilapidated.

I was introduced to the group and set to work wiring up the engine's control panel. There was a lot of friendly banter going around, and they were all enjoying the work and each other's company. Some were working on the line, and there was an audible buzz of chain saws cutting bushes. Soon, there was a call of "tea up!" As soon as the sound of a ringing handbell was heard, the chain saws stopped. I continued as a volunteer for the rest of the time I was living in the UK. My job allocations varied from wiring the engine control panel, to cleaning, painting, and assisting fitting of parts, to some track work and bush clearing. It was a great group of volunteers, and I would be sorry to leave them behind.

When I told Beth I had booked a flight from Manchester to Lexington to see her, she found it hard to believe. It wasn't until I emailed her my actual flight itinerary that she finally believed I was coming to see her. What she didn't know was that I also checked out various hotels in the area just in case things didn't work out as well as I hoped between the two of us. However, since Beth had offered me her guest bedroom, I did not need to actually book a hotel room.

When the departure day finally came, I was packed, ready, and up at 4 a.m. to begin the sixty-mile trip via taxi to Manchester Airport. It would be my first trip to America. Security procedures had changed quite a bit since the last time I had flown. Once through security, I headed toward my gate, passing first through the duty-free shop. This was the only route to the gates.

Throughout the flight, I played over possible scenarios in my head. What if Beth and I didn't hit it off right away? Was I crazy for taking a chance like this? My return flight was seventeen days away. That could feel like an eternity if things didn't work out between us, and I found myself checking into a hotel in a country where I wouldn't even feel safe to drive myself. The road signs would be different, the cars had steering wheels located on the left instead of the right, and they all drive on the "wrong" side of the road! Nevertheless, I was now committed to the journey, and I had to see this through.

Beth told me Atlanta was a large airport, but nothing prepared me for the enormity. Once we disembarked, I, with the others, headed towards Immigration. The officer took my passport, asked a few questions, took my photograph, and then had me place my fingers on a pad to obtain my fingerprints. My passport was stamped as he issued the cursory greeting, "Welcome to the United States." I claimed my luggage from the carousel, then dropped it off on a conveyor for the transfer flight to Lexington. Next came the security check. I dropped my shoulder bag onto the belt and entered a scanner. "Ashoomth'pushishn!" a voice said. I turned around, unable to understand what I was being told to do. The voice repeated, "Ashoomth' pushishn!" Again, I looked round and said, "Pardon?" The voice came from a security officer as he again repeated, "Ashoomth'pushishn!" This time, I noticed somebody else in the next scanner standing with his arms raised. I followed his example, and the scanner whirled, and a part revolved around me. Once I completed this part, the security officer must have given up on giving me verbal instructions (he probably thought I couldn't speak English) as he then gestured for me to stand on a mat with two foot outlines for a further scan.

The rest of the transit through the airport was straightforward. Once I located my flight, terminal, and departure gate on the huge departures board, I headed to my terminal via the transit train. I was feeling hungry, so I walked around to find something to eat. I had never seen so many food options in an airport, and I had never heard of any of them. Instead, I settled for a cold beer.

Eventually, I was on my flight to Lexington, and in less than an hour, I arrived at my final destination. I knew Beth had arranged for a couple of friends to accompany her and capture the memory of our first meeting in photographs. Now that it was all becoming a reality, I was unbelievably nervous. After all these years of writing and waiting nearly fifty years from our first exchange of letters, I would walk through the double doors and towards the escalator where Beth would be waiting at the bottom.

As I approached the top of the escalator, I took a deep breath, stepped on, and began my descent. My eyes were continuously scanning my view, waiting for a first glimpse of her. Then as my gaze passed below the overhang of the ceiling, I saw her. Her face glowed beneath her lovely auburn hair as she beamed one of her big, warm smiles. She was wearing a knitted black cardigan over a light turquoise shirt with black capris. As soon as I reached the bottom of the escalator, I ran towards her, and she ran to meet me. Her arms were already outstretched in a warm welcome as I continued to descend. From that point, I was oblivious to anyone else. All my eyes could see was Beth. As soon as we met, our arms closed in a tight embrace. Time stood still. After a few moments, we looked up into each other's face as though in disbelief that this was really happening. Now sure this wasn't just a dream, our lips met in our very first kiss, all captured in photographs. There was an audible click, click, click, click as Beth's friends took pictures, surrounded by a puzzled group of arriving passengers. They must have wondered who this VIP was and why the "paparazzi" were there.

Beth paused briefly to introduce me to the photographers, as they continued taking photos. They were friends of Beth's who had offered their photograph services as a silent auction fundraiser. Beth's daughter, Sara, and her husband, now married just over six years, were raising money to adopt a child. After some time, Beth presented me with a blue T-shirt with a "UK" logo and the outline of the state of Kentucky in white, which she spread across my chest from shoulder to shoulder. We both laughed as she said, "From the UK to UK." What an appropriate welcome gift!

"Thank you, Beth," I replied, now regretting that I hadn't brought her anything.

"How was your flight?" Beth asked.

"Alright until I got to Atlanta." I then recalled the problems I had encountered. Beth laughed at my not understanding the accent. I then thanked her for the information on the train.

By this time, an announcement came over the PA system that the baggage from my flight was being offloaded onto the carousel. I found my shoulder bag, but when the carousel finally stopped, my main piece of baggage was missing. Beth then intervened, and we headed to the lost baggage desk to report the situation. After a phone call, we were informed the bag had been located and would be delivered to Beth's address the next day.

Soon, we exited the terminal to continue the conversation and photos outside. As we were posing for another photograph, Beth said, "Show me your proud British face." Immediately, I stood ramrod straight and held my head high. We laughed about this pose, also captured in a photograph, for a long while.

After some chatting and laughter, the photographers took their final photos and departed. We headed towards Beth's car. "What's happened to your number plate?" I asked Beth as we approached her car.

"What do you mean?" Beth asked.

"It's missing."

"Here in Kentucky, we only have one number plate. It's on the back."

This seemed very odd to me. I then placed my bag in the back of the car, and we headed to get some dinner. It wasn't long before I noticed Beth turning right when the traffic light was still on red. "What are you doing?" I exclaimed. "The light's on red!"

"We can turn right on red if the road is clear." I had never done this before. Back home, red meant stop in all directions. I had a lot to learn.

By now, I was famished as we headed to a restaurant. It was to be my very first meal not only in the US, but also in Kentucky.

"As you are now in Kentucky, you need to try a Kentucky Hot Brown," said Beth. We ordered the food and drinks. We talked as we ate. Somehow, for a first meeting and meal together, we felt very comfortable in each other's company.

When we finished, it was time to pay the bill. The server came by our table, and Beth had to explain that we pay the server directly. Beth asked the server to take our photo and explained why: this was our first meal together. The server was only too pleased to do it. I was amazed at the friendly chitchat inside the restaurant between servers and their customers. In the UK, there is very little interaction with the waiting staff. They bring the meal, then go. Occasionally, they will ask how it is, but that is about all. I was also surprised by how the diners addressed the waitresses as "Ma'am." That is never done in the UK. It is usually a very curt "Miss?" to get her attention. The diners are so much more respectful of the staff than in the UK.

As I was about to fill out the check, Beth told me in a low voice, "Don't forget to add the tip."

"What?" I asked. She then explained how giving a tip to the server is common and accepted practice. They rely on customers' tips to make up their wages. In the UK, they are paid a salary, and any additional gratuity is left up to the customer's discretion. Something else I would need to get used to. We thanked her, finished our drinks, and made our way to Beth's house.

The house was a terraced town house, which had a drive that could fit a couple of cars at best, with a small front garden. We got out of the car and entered the house. It was much bigger inside than I had imagined from the frontage. The kitchen was a good size, as was the living area. I dropped my shoulder bag, and Beth and I hugged and kissed. We were giddy with excitement. It was like having the joy of all the best Christmas mornings of our lives rolled into one evening. Beth made me feel so welcome that I felt completely at home. There was no need to be concerned about looking for a hotel room. She even placed a small box of Bourbon Balls on the bed in the guest room for me, a symbol of hospitality.

It all seemed so natural for me to be here with her. Beth made us a coffee, and we sat talking and laughing until well past 11 p.m. I had been up almost twenty-four hours without sleep and was running on adrenaline. I didn't want to take things too fast or assume too much, but I was now exhausted from the journey. It was just natural that we fell asleep in each other's arms that night. Beth had quite a schedule laid out for us for the next seventeen days.

## CULTURAL ADVENTURES

The next day was a "banjo Sunday" church service, so we went to Winchester to Beth's daughter Sara's church. As we approached, I could not see a church, as we seemed to be heading towards a shopping centre. We pulled up, and I saw a number of people heading into what appeared to be a store in a shopping centre, but it turned out to be space rented to the church congregation. It was not how I envisioned any sort of church, nor was it like anything I had seen in the UK. We were welcomed by Sara's husband, Ed, who was greeting people as they entered. The interior contained rows of seats and a platform where musicians were getting ready to perform. One had a banjo, another a guitar, plus there were a couple of singers and a drummer at the back. The music started, and everybody stood. Some in the congregation sang along, as others just swayed in time to the music.

I had never experienced this sort of worship before, only the very staid Church of England and the fire and brimstone of a Wesleyan chapel. After a few songs, the pastor delivered his sermon. After the service, Beth, Sara, Fraser, and I left to have lunch in a small restaurant out in the country. I cannot recall what I ate, but I do recall my first taste of beer cheese. It was certainly something I had never experienced before. It was the smoothness and spicy aftertaste that I found interesting.

After lunch, we went to the local baseball park to watch my first minor league baseball game. I had a basic idea of the game, having played softball when I was at RAF Neatishead. What surprised me were the crazy games played in between the innings. For example, two "bouncy horses" with a kid on the back of each riding, or rather bouncing, in a race to the winning line a short distance away. The crowd were eagerly cheering them on. Again, I had never experienced this in a sporting event.

The next day, it was a near three-hour drive to Beth's hometown, to see the house where she grew up and further up the road where she raised her two children. This was followed by her showing me the post office and the PO box where I had addressed my letters all those years ago. This I found to be quite emotional. Even though the boxes themselves had been renewed, it was the memory and seeing the number 422 on the box that affected me. Finally, we went to the cemetery to visit her parents' graves, laid side by side. As I stood there, I looked at the headstones that contained their respective photographs. I silently swore an oath as I stood there with Beth by their graveside that I would love and take care of their precious daughter. Then it was back to Lexington. It had been a long day.

The rest of the stay was spent with Beth showing me around the area, going to *The Stephen Foster Story* at Bardstown (at which I was given a CD of the show as one of the longest distance visitors), a tour of the horse farms, and basically anything specifically Kentucky.

I then visited with Beth's daughter, Sara, on a more personal level as the three of us met up for a coffee. She had a very bubbly character, which belied the interrogation I was about to undergo. She was asking questions about my family, myself, the sort of work I had been doing, my marriage, why it had broken down, why I had left, what my intentions with her mum were, and how I intended to support us in the future. I was very open and honest with my answers. There was no point in doing anything else. I had no intention of building a relationship on lies, no matter how hurtful the truth was. We seemed to get on well, for beneath the inquisitor's mask, she was genuinely concerned for her mother. I appreciated how she was looking out for her with a complete stranger.

Soon, it was time for the family reunion at her brother's farm. It would cover the Fourth of July, so I was advised to wear something red to represent the redcoats! This had been preplanned by Beth prior to my traveling over. I was quite nervous as we traveled to the farm. I would be the stranger amongst what I expected to be a close-knit family. I wondered how I would be viewed and treated, especially being British. My fears were soon laid to rest.

As we arrived and I got out of the car, Beth's brother, Ret, and his wife, Valerie (June was his first wife), were waiting on the back porch of the cabin to greet us. As I began walking toward them, I was greeted by Beth's brother with "Fee fi fo fum! I smell the blood of an Englishman!" He smiled a broad grin and gave me a very welcoming handshake. Laughter was an icebreaker, and I knew right away I was in for a fun family get-together. Unfortunately, it rained the whole time we were there, but I was shown around the farm in an ATV driven by Beth's brother's grandson, Bobby.

Beth's son and family arrived the next day, and I received nothing more than a polite greeting from Sawyer. I expected nothing more. He was polite all the time we were together, but I could sense he was very wary of me. Beth had been badly hurt by men in her life, and he did not want her to get hurt again. He was very protective of her. He did not know me, my family, or my background. In this area, they have a saying, "Who's your daddy?" Meaning whose family are you from? That gave away everything they ever needed to know about a person. I was a rank outsider they knew nothing about. Even though Sara had phoned Sawyer a few times to give him her opinion of me, he needed to evaluate me himself. At the end of the weekend, I was sorry to leave the farm and Beth's family.

## THE QUESTION

Far too soon, it was time for me to return to the UK. There was something I had planned to do for the whole time I was there. That was to propose to Beth. The timing had to be right, and romantic. I would think about the best time. After much thought, I decided upon proposing at the airport, before I left. It was a romantic thought, probably brought on by seeing a lot of movies where the man did this before going away. It sounded perfect.

It was a dreary day in more ways than one. The skies were heavy with clouds and rain. We sat in the cafeteria as I waited to go through security to catch my flight. I stood up from my seat and turned to Beth, then got down on one knee, looked her straight in the eye, and asked her if she would marry me. Her eyes gleamed as her mouth formed a beautiful broad smile. She nodded and answered, "Yes! Of course, I will." I got up from the floor, and we hugged and kissed before it was time for me to sadly break the interlock. I looked into her eyes again and said to her, "The ring will need to come later." Beth smiled, then laughed. Then I needed to head towards the security check and climb the stairs towards my gate. The walk up the stairs towards the gate was a long, hard walk. I kept looking around and seeing Beth waving at me. I waved back until I couldn't see her anymore. I then made my way to my gate and plane. I knew I would be returning as soon as I could.

# Chapter Fifty-Two
## B.B.

### TRUST

Our time together passed far too quickly. By the end of Jim's seventeen days, we had had some deep conversations about our future together. As his retirement gift, he invited me to go back to England with him the next time he came to visit, and he would give me a similar sampling of life in the United Kingdom. I was totally amazed that he was willing to go to that kind of expense for me. Unless I retired, I would not be able to get the time off. At this point, I had had enough work drama for a lifetime.

On July 7, 2015, I drove Jim to the airport for his eight-hour return flight to England. We sat in the airport snack bar in the early afternoon, awaiting his departure at 4:10 p.m. I wanted so much to stretch out every remaining second we had together. I didn't even want to look at a clock. We ordered coffees and sat there, taking occasional sips while talking to each other.

In exactly three days, I would submit my notice of retirement. Taking this step required a huge leap of faith because I had no safety net apart from the promise of a future with Jim. Sometimes, you have to release what you're already clenching tightly in your hands in order to receive something far more valuable. I had no more time off available to make the journey back to England with Jim unless I followed through and submitted my retirement notice the following week.

An annual follow-up appointment with my orthopedic doctor in NYC was an opportunity to take Jim to a destination he had always dreamed of visiting. After that trip, I would be free to return to England with him at the end of August. A lot of things would be set in motion for both of us, but initially, it was up to me to spike the ball. We would work out major details on chat or video conferencing from across the ocean.

Soon, he would need to head through the security checkpoint and head toward his boarding gate. My coffee was now cold, but I didn't care. I was far too busy directing my attention to his beautiful smile, ocean-blue eyes, and dimpled cheeks. I studied and memorized every feature of his face. My ears recorded the sound and quality of his rich, deep voice. I was deeply in love with this man, and he had been worth every moment of the wait. I would treasure every thought of the warmth and love in his embrace. I would remember the tenderness of his touch and the softness of his lips. In the days and weeks ahead, while waiting for his return, I would visualize the loving moments of my head lying on his right shoulder, my right arm around his waist, and his right arm around my shoulder drawing me close. I would remember the winks and the boyish playfulness. Once, we were just a fifteen-year-old girl and a sixteen-year-old boy who were separated by unfortunate circumstances. Time had only enhanced our appreciation for each other. I would visualize moments when we were cheek to cheek, gazing into each other's eyes and needing no words to express our love. We would be separated, but our memories would comfort us until we were reunited.

Jim had asked me to marry him even before he made the journey to America. I had told him. "You've got to come over here and ask me in person." Seventeen whirlwind days had passed. Each was packed with laughter and in-depth conversations about our future together. Yet now, in the final few moments of his visit he still hadn't asked that important question.

Two other couples had been seated at a small, round table in the airport cafe when we arrived but had responded to earlier boarding calls and were now gone. It was early afternoon, and we were finally alone, except for one cashier at the counter who was occupied in a far corner restocking snack items. Passengers were steadily passing by the open entrance, carry-on luggage in tow, headed toward the security checkpoint around the corner. They were caught up in a rush, oblivious to us while we were caught up in one very special moment. Jim glanced at his wristwatch, then stood up.

"No!" I thought anxiously. "It can't be time to go yet."

Without saying a word, Jim stepped away from the table until he stood by my side. He slowly dropped down on one knee, reaching forward to take my hands in his. I was caught off guard by his timing and hadn't had so much as a hint of what was coming. Of course, I was the same person who hadn't recognized all his subtle attempts over the past year to let me know I had become far more important to him than simply a friend.

His voice softened as he asked, "My precious darling, will you be my wife? The ring will have to come later when we've had time to pick it out together."

I was nervous, giddy with excitement, and overwhelmed with joy. I had never been treated like such a valuable treasure. I had only seen scenes like this in movies, never dreaming that someday a man worth the wait would consider me to be his "precious darling."

"Yes! Of course, I will! I'd be honored to be your wife!" came my reply. "I love you with all my heart. I can't wait until the day when we can be together permanently."

We sealed the proposal with a kiss, and moments later, it was time for Jim to head for his departure gate for the return flight to England. If anyone noticed us, we certainly didn't notice them. We were oblivious to time during these incredible final moments together. This was an unlikely place for a marriage proposal, almost as unlikely as on a video call. Nothing about our relationship had been ordinary to this point, and the fun was just beginning.

There was much to be done. An application for a K-1 fiancé visa would be a major next step. It would be a complex journey, navigating an unfamiliar process. We would approach it as a joint effort, determined to go through the entire process without incurring the expense of an immigration attorney.

I took mental snapshots of Jim from a distance as he departed through the security checkpoint. I would remember that departing image: Jim's broad, straight shoulders and silver hair. I would remember the fluid, confident glide in his steps. Most of all, I would remember the love and respect he had shown me and how he had treated me like a treasure. I could not bring myself to take photos of him actually leaving. Once cleared by TSA security, he turned back for a last look, waved at me, and headed up the steps toward his gate. An overhang in the ceiling gradually blocked him from view as he ascended, and I watched until he became completely hidden from view. The bond of our friendship had transitioned to love along a journey of over forty years. Now that we had been united on common soil, that bond was stronger than ever. Watching him walk away from me, even temporarily, was incredibly hard. Part of me went with him.

Once he was out of sight, I turned and walked slowly out of the concourse toward the parking garage to my car. The heavens had opened up, and the rain was pouring down as Jim's plane taxied down the runway.

Emptiness suddenly engulfed me like the clouds overhead. Tears were flowing down my cheeks. I breathed a deep sigh, feeling suddenly alone. Once inside my car, I sat there for several moments, in silence, praying for Jim's safe journey back across the Atlantic and beyond. As I pulled away from the parking garage, his flight had just cleared the runway for takeoff. I couldn't bring myself to watch his plane ascend and disappear. It would be a long flight, and I had to keep reminding myself that soon his home would be here, with me. There was much to be done and many details to work out together.

Finally, the missing piece of my life had been identified, rediscovered, and connected. There had not been a single awkward moment between us during his entire visit. Apart from the playful booty-pinching episode upon his initial arrival at the Lexington airport, Jim had been a complete gentleman in every way. Until his return, I would treasure the memory of the evenings when I laid my head on his right shoulder, our cheeks touching. I would remember putting my right arm across his waist while his right arm was around my right shoulder. After too long a time separated by distance, the embrace of human touch is a priceless gift.

Being with Jim was as natural as breathing. It was as though we had always been together. Perhaps it's because we should have been. The lost years were now being bridged to the future. We had both been on quite a journey separately, but a much bigger journey was about to begin for each of us. It had taken me years to heal from my past, just as Jim had been wounded by his. The love of my life had been in a holding pattern, but finally, he had found his way home. My mind preserved the image of his face when he looked at me. All I could see was the love, the twinkle in his eyes, and the boyish mischief that had not diminished with years. This was the kind of joy I had never felt, until now.

# Chapter Fifty-Three
## J.D.

As I boarded my flight and took my aisle seat, I could think of nothing else but Beth and my next flight back. Turning my head, I could see through the window that the rain was getting heavy. We pulled away from the air bridge and began our taxi to the end of the runway. As we reached the runway, I could see the terminal building. I asked the passenger in the window seat if she could be so kind as to lean back a bit so I could look for and wave to Beth. I explained why, and she lovingly smiled and agreed. We rolled and accelerated along the runway, and I said to myself, "Bye-bye Beth, my love. I'll be back again soon. I love you."

Then we were up in the air, and I settled in my seat and closed my eyes as I headed towards Atlanta, then Manchester. When I closed my eyes, I could still visualize Beth's smiling face and feel the love in her eyes.

*Epilogue*

*B.B. & J.D.*

## THE LONG FLIGHT HOME

On July 10, 2015, three days after Jim's return to England, Beth submitted official notice of her retirement. By July 13, Jim had already booked his flight to return to the US on August 13. Jim had always wanted to visit New York City. On August 16, Beth and Jim flew to NYC for a whirlwind three-day tour and a Broadway show.

On August 29, the official date of Beth's retirement, they boarded a flight headed to England, Jim's retirement gift to Beth. They traveled to Jim's hometown of Fleetwood, visiting childhood landmarks and sharing "proper" fish and chips with mushy peas on the seafront. They traveled by ferry to the Isle of Man, sharing the emotion of passing near the site where Radio Avaline was once anchored when they first connected as pen pals. They visited Scotland and Wales, then traveled by ferry to Ireland. Jim introduced Beth to British culture, especially the proper way to drink a cup of tea.

Beth spent a great deal of time people watching, amazed at the variety of unusual hairstyles and ombre hair colors. Beth quickly decided she must have been working too many twelve-hour shifts to keep up with all the fashion changes that had taken place. She was stunned by the number of couples she saw on the sidewalks on mobility scooters, many enclosed with canopies due to the rainy UK weather. This observation led to long conversations about the differences between the National Health Service, American healthcare, and socialized medicine.

Beth met Jim's family, taking walks with them into town and along the seafront in the evenings. Sometimes, they even had fish and chips with mushy peas for breakfast. They stopped during one walk to observe the sport of crown green bowling being played at the bowling club in Thornton-Cleveleys. They were graciously invited and joined several club members in a game. They visited local markets, where Beth marveled at the variety of foods and vegetables she had never seen. She couldn't quite come to terms with the practice of not refrigerating eggs, being required to pay to use a public toilet, and the fact that there were no electrical outlets in bathrooms.

Beth was introduced to several British pubs. One was an iconic pub known as Deduns, the local fishermen's first "port of call" when they returned from weeks at sea. Later, Beth watched her first rugby match on the big screen at The Royal Arms. She was impressed by the intensity of uninterrupted play, the lack of padding and protective gear, and the cardio strength required to play the game.

In September, they celebrated Beth's birthday by touring The Alpine Cottage, a stunning old thatched-roof hunting lodge just outside Dublin, Ireland. Later that evening, they met Jim's artist friend Bridget for a birthday dinner in Clonmel.

In early October, they celebrated Jim's birthday at The Blenheim with two of his remaining family members. Jim arranged a couple of evenings with his old college friend Colin and his fiancée at a pub called Leatherspoon's in Cleveleys and also at a pub while they were in Wales.

They returned to the US together on October 10 and were met by a very emotional Sara at the airport, who, despite almost daily live video chats with Beth from the UK, had been convinced she was going to need to enlist the US embassy for her mother's safe return.

Jim didn't return to England again until November 3, 2015. By this time, he had further gained the trust and respect of Sara, based on his honesty in answering her brutally direct questions and the way he looked after and continued to show love for her mother. He had been "interrogated" by many of Beth's former coworkers, who had told him his kneecaps would not be safe if he hurt their friend. He had passed the "friends background check" with flying colors. Sawyer was beginning to warm up to Jim, but it wasn't until Jim asked Sawyer if they could have a private man-to-man talk that their relationship finally turned the corner.

During this time, Jim and Beth did considerable research into the immigration process and began gathering the documents that would be required for Beth to sponsor him and obtain a K-1 fiancé visa. They went on riverboat rides and on horse farm tours and watched thoroughbred horse racing. Jim got an in-depth look at American and Kentucky culture.

Jim returned to the US in November, and was later notified in an email from his Solicitor that his Divorce Absolute had been finalized in England. This was his first American Thanksgiving with Beth's family.

On December 6, at a special holiday dinner at a local bourbon distillery attended by Sara, her husband, and two of their friends, Jim officially proposed a third time. This time he presented Beth with an engagement ring they had selected together, making their engagement official.

In December 2015, Beth submitted a petition to the US Citizenship and Immigration Services (USCIS) as Jim's sponsor for a K-1 fiancé visa. It was ninety-two pages long with the required supporting documentation.

Before Jim returned to the UK in January 2016, the two of them selected a venue for their upcoming wedding. Ironically, in order for the fiancé visa to be approved, they had to prove they intended to marry within ninety days of being admitted to the US as a K-1 non-immigrant. Considering Jim's love of all things nautical, they settled on the next closest thing they could get in Kentucky, a riverboat on the Ohio River known as "The Queen."

Jim returned to be with Beth again in February, 2016, then returned to the UK in April, 2016. He received notice while in the US that his application had been approved and he was required to come to London, England, for a complete medical exam.

Jim made five trips to the USA within eleven months, totalling over 36,000 miles to be with Beth. His fiancé visa was approved at the US embassy in London in April, 2016, and he returned to the US on a one-way ticket, just ten days before their wedding in May, 2016.

Jim forfeited most of his material possessions when he came to America. Before his flight, he consolidated the things most valuable to him into 6 large cardboard boxes and dropped them off at a shipping company. These boxes contained the art Jim had personally created in acrylics and pastels, along with art supplies. Jim said these were only material things, and he was gaining far more. He had the loving family he had always wanted. To him that was priceless.

Jim and Beth planned every detail of their wedding without a wedding planner. The music they chose told their story through songs from the era when they first communicated as pen pals, including "The Letter" by The Box Tops and "Ain't No Mountain High Enough" by Diana Ross. Sawyer walked Beth down the "aisle" on the riverboat Queen the day they were married. British and American flags adorned the side rails, and a pirate flag, in honor of Radio Avaline, was flown on top. Although they had a plan, not a single rehearsal was done before the actual wedding.

Both Sawyer and Sara affectionately "roasted" Jim at the reception. Sawyer had recognized there was a missing piece in his mother's life and had seen her loneliness. He had actually prayed for his mother to have just the right man come along who would love and cherish her.

Jim's best man, Denver, was a friend of Beth's who she worked with at the prison. As soon as the minister pronounced Jim and Beth man and wife, Denver stepped up with a pair of handcuffs and cuffed their wrists together. Everyone in attendance was laughing, including the bride and groom. They danced away, swinging their cuffed right and left hands to the recessional tune of "Signed, Sealed, Delivered (I'm Yours)" by Stevie Wonder.

Safely tucked away in the pocket of his suit on their wedding day, Jim was carrying the bookmark Beth had given him. That token of friendship and love had come full circle.

Jim, who never had children of his own, soon became affectionately called "Papa" by Sara and became like a surrogate dad to both Sara and Sawyer. He experienced the joys of being a "papaw" to Sawyer's daughter Allie and Sara's son Jacob.

In June 2020, Beth and Jim, at the height of a global pandemic, and with the encouragement of family and friends, began writing their story…because they were convinced this world needed a love story.

Jim officially became a US citizen in July 9, 2020.

The Long Flight Home spans the course of over 50 years. As we glanced back over our shoulders, fitting the pieces of those lost years together, we realized each obstacle had been a stepping stone. Neither knew the struggles of the other until we began to write our story, piecing those lost years together and sharing our journeys with each other. Those memories were not all happy ones, and some moments were difficult to relive, even after healing over decades. There were times when each of us felt defeated, like failures. It was when we were on our knees that we were strongest and gained the strength to get back up and persevere. Completion of this book marks the long-awaited and joyous merging of two paths.

Perhaps it is now clear why we no longer believe in coincidences. From the writing of the first letter, to the timing of a radio being turned on at a specific moment, the entry of personal contact information on a website, the timing of rediscovery of an old bookmark tucked away in a drawer, and a host of other such events, we believe God had a plan. Finally, we're together, as we believe we were always supposed to be. We share this story of hope and of love that finally found a way.

\*\*\*\*

Beth & Jim Aubrey

First sight

Running to meet

First contact

Traveling to new adventures together

For more information or to connect with the authors, please focus your mobile phone camera on the QR code below and follow the link. Otherwise, connect with us at: https://www.BBAUBREY.com

# Acknowledgements

Marcia Trahan, Editor
Mark Reid, Cover Designer
Lorna Reid, Interior Design/Formatting
Jeff & Heather Summers, Photography